M000201361

Read this book online today:

With SAP PRESS BooksOnline we offer you online access to knowledge from the leading SAP experts. Whether you use it as a beneficial supplement or as an alternative to the printed book, with SAP PRESS BooksOnline you can:

- Access your book anywhere, at any time. All you need is an Internet connection.
- Perform full text searches on your book and on the entire SAP PRESS library.
- Build your own personalized SAP library.

The SAP PRESS customer advantage:

Register this book today at *www.sap-press.com* and obtain exclusive free trial access to its online version. If you like it (and we think you will), you can choose to purchase permanent, unrestricted access to the online edition at a very special price!

Here's how to get started:

1. Visit *www.sap-press.com*.
2. Click on the link for SAP PRESS BooksOnline and login (or create an account).
3. Enter your free trial license key, shown below in the corner of the page.
4. Try out your online book with full, unrestricted access for a limited time!

Your personal free trial **license key**
for this online book is: **6zdb-h42u-97yv-3pq5**

SAP® BusinessObjects™ Planning and Consolidation

 PRESS

SAP PRESS is a joint initiative of SAP and Galileo Press. The know-how offered by SAP specialists combined with the expertise of the Galileo Press publishing house offers the reader expert books in the field. SAP PRESS features first-hand information and expert advice, and provides useful skills for professional decision-making.

SAP PRESS offers a variety of books on technical and business related topics for the SAP user. For further information, please visit our website: *www.sap-press.com*.

Dr. Marco Sisfontes-Monge
Implementing SAP BusinessObjects Planning and Consolidation
2012, app. 400 pp.
978-1-59229-375-9

William D. Newman
Understanding SAP BusinessObjects Enterprise Performance Management
2011, 282 pp.
978-1-59229-348-3

Naeem Arif, Sheikh Tauseef
Integrating SAP ERP Financials
2011, 399 pp.
978-1-59229-300-1

Sridhar Srinivasan and Kumar Srinivasan

SAP® BusinessObjects™ Planning and Consolidation

Galileo Press

Bonn • Boston

Galileo Press is named after the Italian physicist, mathematician and philosopher Galileo Galilei (1564–1642). He is known as one of the founders of modern science and an advocate of our contemporary, heliocentric worldview. His words *Eppur si muove* (And yet it moves) have become legendary. The Galileo Press logo depicts Jupiter orbited by the four Galilean moons, which were discovered by Galileo in 1610.

Editor Meg Dunkerley
Copyeditor Ruth Saavedra
Cover Design Graham Geary
Photo Credit iStockphoto.com/Filmwork
Layout Design Vera Brauner
Production Graham Geary
Typesetting Publishers' Design and Production Services, Inc.
Printed and bound in Canada

ISBN 978-1-59229-397-1

© 2011 by Galileo Press Inc., Boston (MA)

2nd edition 2011

Library of Congress Cataloging-in-Publication Data
Srinivasan, Sridhar.
SAP BusinessObjects planning and consolidation / Sridhar Srinivasan and
Kumar Srinivasan. — 2nd ed.
p. cm.
Includes index.
ISBN-13: 978-1-59229-397-1
ISBN-10: 1-59229-397-2
1. BusinessObjects. 2. Business planning. 3. Strategic planning.
I. Srinivasan, Kumar. II. Title.
HD30.28S65 2011
658.4'01028553—dc22
2011010479

Contents at a Glance

Dear Reader,

If you are using or need to get up to speed on SAP BusinessObjects Planning and Consolidation, this is your must-have resource. In this second edition of our best-selling book, Sridhar Srinivasan and Kumar Srinivasan will help you navigate these vast, sometimes overwhelming waters by offering a practical and straightforward guide to the ins and outs of BPC. The book provides the tools and tips you need to understand how the SAP BPC NetWeaver version can be implemented.

I welcomed the opportunity to work with Sri and Kumar—it was a pleasure to witness such dedication and expertise in SAP. I'm confident that you will find their most recent book with SAP PRESS up to the same standard as their previous books.

We appreciate your business, and welcome your feedback. Your comments and suggestions are the most useful tools to help us improve our books for you, the reader. We encourage you to visit our website at *www.sap-press.com* and share your feedback about this work.

Thank you for purchasing a book from SAP PRESS!

Meg Dunkerley
Editor, SAP PRESS

Galileo Press
Boston, MA

meg.dunkerley@galileo-press.com
www.sap-press.com

Contents

3   Modeling an Application with SAP BPC for NetWeaver 71

4   Loading, Scheduling, and Managing Data in SAP BPC for NetWeaver 129

Contents

Foreword

Solutions around Planning, Budgeting, Forecasting and Consolidation are not new to SAP. After all, the "P" in ERP stands for Planning, which is SAP's forte. A little more than 10 years ago SAP launched the Strategic Enterprise Management (SEM) suite of products. This included Business Planning and Simulation (BPS) and Business Consolidation (BCS) plus a number of other solutions under the SEM umbrella. These solutions were installed as an add-on to the Business Warehouse (BW), which is SAP's data warehouse offering. Fortune 500 companies and other large customers that had an SAP R/3 footprint were the typical consumers of SEM applications. SEM was primarily designed for an IT audience to own and maintain while Finance, as the end user, provided some support in the form of power users. BPS and BCS were separate products and customers were able to integrate the data, but this was not an out of-the-box process. Both products were also shipped about 6 months after a BW release, so customers who had an embedded solution were dependent on the availability of an SEM release in order to upgrade their BW system. Some customers installed standalone systems and moved data between them to provide more flexibility, but this came with a higher Total Cost of Ownership (TCO). They also had to support separate security models, reporting tools, metadata, and so on.

SAP worked closely with various user groups including the Americas SAP User Group (ASUG) to gather requirements and feedback for the future development of planning and consolidation solutions. Customers requested tighter integration with BW and the ability to leverage the same tools, which would reduce implementation time and effort to train end users. About 5 years ago, SAP decided to create a next-generation planning solution called Integrated Planning (BW-IP), which would be the successor to BPS. The solution combined the analytic (OLAP) and planning engines into one, and utilized the same queries, variables, security, etc., as BW. It was designed to be a planning platform upon which other product areas within SAP, as well as ISV's, partners, and customers could build their own planning applications. On the surface, BW-IP looked like it would be a strong solution, and there was strong demand from customers and partners to get their hands on the beta version (Ramp-Up). However impressive, the technical advantages of BW-IP only solved part of the equation; the reality was that many businesses were growing tired of IT departments having to own and maintain planning and consolidation solutions, and they demanded solutions that the business could own and maintain with IT support, not ownership.

In early 2007, SAP formed a new organization focused on the Business User. This was a big departure from the traditional transaction-oriented and task-worker based applications that SAP was traditionally known for. An Enterprise Performance Management (EPM) team was launched under this area to address the needs being expressed by the CFO suite. Strategy Management was the first application in the portfolio and was the result of SAP's acquisition of Pilot. It was a very simple and easy-to-use solution for the business to leverage in defining strategy, initiatives, and results monitoring. In parallel, the EPM development team created planning prototypes on top of the BW-IP platform. The challenges they found were centered mostly around the constraints of Business Explorer (BEx) for Planning and Reporting. Since its first release in 1997, the BEx had moved far from its roots as a power user tool to being more open to the needs of a casual user, but it had not come far enough to deliver a world-class user experience. Although the interfaces were Excel- and web-based, the desired ease-of-use was difficult to achieve at the level customers expected and SAP strived for. So the EPM team evaluated potential acquisitions that had the desired ease-of-use and simplicity, and discovered it with OutlookSoft. The user environment was native Excel, which Finance users live and die by, but it also had another huge advantage. The founders of OutlookSoft came from Hyperion and they had endeavored to build a product that integrated planning and consolidation into one. This was a first in the industry and provided one solution to the customer. While the concept seemed promising, would OutlookSoft solve the problems our customers were telling us were important in their planning and consolidation decision-making processes?

Meanwhile, feedback from one of our BW-IP early adopters indicated that although BW-IP was a big improvement over BPS, the customer decided to the purchase OutlookSoft product so the business could own the solution. This customer validation of the strength of the OutlookSoft solution was important, and prompted internal stakeholders at SAP to divine some proof that OutlookSoft was as strong as the business case stated, and that it could be implemented as easily as claimed. Members of OutlookSoft and SAP were summoned to SAP headquarters in Walldorf. A business scenario was created and two teams were formed. The first was from SAP, and this included experts from BW, ABAP developers, web application development, and finance. In the other corner was the OutlookSoft team made up of a couple finance users with no data warehousing or development skills. The two teams split up and started building their planning applications using the two different solutions, BW-IP and OutlookSoft. About 30 minutes later the OutlookSoft team came back with a completed application; it took the SAP team over 6 hours to build the same application using BW-IP. This sealed the deal within SAP and through the acquisition of OutlookSoft, SAP now has the best user experience in the industry, planning and consolidation in one product, and a solution that is much faster and easier to implement. This is welcome news to our customers, as you might imagine

Prior to the acquisition, there was only about a 15% overlap between OutlookSoft and SAP customers. The OutlookSoft product was a Microsoft-centric application that leveraged SQL Server, Analysis Services, Reporting Services, and other Microsoft technologies. In order to give customers a choice, part of the agreement to acquire OutlookSoft was to offer the solution in another flavor as part of SAP NetWeaver. There are over 15,000 BW customers and if this solution is to eventually become the strategic planning and consolidation solution at SAP then it needed to have the tight integration not only with BW but also ERP. The development timelines were aggressive; the first version BW-based version was due in one year. What is now known as SAP BusinessObjects Business Planning and Consolidation for SAP NetWeaver was completed in July 2008 as planned, and the first Beta customers started their implementations in August. The rest is history. The adoption of the product has been nothing short of impressive, and BPC is the second-most demonstrated product to customers. In addition, one of the most compelling features of BPC 7.5 is the integration with the SAP BusinessObjects Business Intelligence (BI) tools. This allows customers to leverage the world-class features of the top BI tools in the market with not only BPC but the entire EPM suite, and provides one comprehensive set of reporting, query, analysis, and information management tools. The second version (BPC 7.5 NW) entered ramp-up in December 2009, and prior to the start the customer pipeline was two times greater than our KPI. As of February 2010, we achieved our Key Performance Index (KPI), with many more customers in the pipeline, making this one of the most sought after products in SAP history. The product became generally available August 2010, and finished ramp-up with three times the number of customers we were expecting. This comes with another set of challenges: supporting a product that is in such high demand requires all resources, including development, solution management, and the Regional Implementation Group (RIG), to take an active role. This is a nice problem to have. The third version (BPC 10 NW) will enter ramp-up in the May 2011 timeframe, and will further extend the market leading capabilities by introducing a new state of the art EPM Office Add-in and Web Ux, and productized integration with BI 4.0 and GRC 10. It will also take advantage of SAP HANA for in-memory processing, and this is planned for late 2011 or early 2012.

The analyst community has also overwhelmingly validated SAP's vision and strategy. Gartner rated SAP as a leader in the CPM Suites Magic Quadrant for 2010/2011, with the strongest vision in the market for the third year in a row. The Forrester Business Performance Solutions Wave Report 2009 was published in November and not only did it list SAP as one of four leaders in the market, it awarded SAP with the highest score for current product offering out of all vendors. IDC's 2009 annual analysis of the software markets reported SAP as the market leader in performance management and analytic application with a 20.3 percent market share of that year. Balanced scorecard creators Kaplan and Norton recently announced a software certification program and subsequently announced SAP as the first (and currently only) vendor to be certified in the Kaplan-Norton Balanced Scorecard and the Strategy Management system of which it is a part.

The authors of this book have a strong SAP background and specifically with BW-IP and BW, and were among the early implementers of the BPC NW product. They're able to leverage their deep expertise in planning and consolidation as well as data warehousing to compare and contrast the SAP solutions, and provide in depth knowledge around the BPC NW product. This book should serve as an excellent reference, and an implementation and information source for customers and partners. Whether you are sitting in an airport terminal and have some time to catch up on reading, onsite at a customer and have a question and need to get a quick answer, I hope you enjoy this book and that it will be something that you can utilize over and over whether you are an executive or a member of a project team implementing BPC NW. Enjoy and we hope BPC NW is a huge success for you now or in the future!

Bryan Katis
Vice President and General Manager
Enterprise Performance Management Solutions
SAP Business Analytics

Acknowledgments

This book has been produced with the help of several people who have reviewed the materials and offered invaluable suggestions in the shaping of the book. Their contributions and advice have helped in the realization of this book.

We would like to offer our thanks and special appreciation to the following people for their contributions:

▶ The editor of this book, Meg Dunkerley, for guiding us through the book development process.

▶ The production manager of this book, Kelly O'Callaghan, and production editor, Graham Geary, for managing the production and successful release of the book.

▶ Peter Jones, platinum consultant at SAP, who reviewed the chapter related to consolidation and provided feedback.

▶ Carl Satterfield at MWV, who reviewed the initial chapters of the book and provided us with ideas for presentation of topics related to planning and consolidation.

▶ Lucky Pandit at Halliburton, who reviewed the initial chapters of the book and provided perspective to planning that has been incorporated in the book.

▶ Buntic Georgian at VIP Consulting, who reviewed the initial chapters of the book and offered several points to consider in the functional areas of planning.

▶ We would like to thank our families for providing us the motivation and enthusiasm and for their support and patience as we spent long hours writing the book.

Sridhar Srinivasan
Kumar Srinivasan

Additional Information

Additional information on the topics covered in this book can be found in the following places:

▶ SAP Help Portal: *http://help.sap.com*

▶ SAP Developer Network: *http://www.sdn.sap.com*

▶ SAP Service Marketplace: *http://www.service.sap.com*

Introduction

Planning and financial consolidation are two areas that every organization implements to ensure the smooth functioning of its business. The main objective of planning is thinking ahead and coming up with the activities a company will do in the future. Consolidation is a process that is used to accurately report the financial results of an organization either for legal or management reporting purposes.

Every organization, big or small, has to plan for it to be successful in meeting its objectives and to stay competitive in the market place. A good planning system can help the organization to think ahead and come up with the right set of activities to get ahead of its competition. It is not uncommon to see how an organization in a good business has failed due to a lack of or inadequate planning. On the other hand, we see how an organization with a good planning system has surpassed its competition and become immensely successful in its history.

Gone are the days where you could be in a good business and expect to stay successful forever. Now, competition is rampant and technology is changing rapidly. Although a business may not be directly related to technology, the effect of technology and innovation in any industry makes it necessary to have a clear plan to address these changes and development. Planning is of the utmost important for meeting these needs effectively.

Planning affects every area and sphere of a business. It is relevant for different activities, including production planning, profitability planning, human resource planning, or financial planning. In addition, there are different timelines to planning that correlate to the type of plan that needs to be adopted. Planning can be strategic planning for the long term or could be operational planning for the short term. In essence, a good planning system can even help an organization spot opportunities, trends, and new ideas in the industry where it is operating and come up with the right kind of plan to be successful in its activities.

On the other hand, organizations report consolidated financial results in a particular format based on the country/countries where it operates. It is important to have a sound system that can report the results of the organization as a whole in a truthful manner and at the same time employ the best practices of accounting.

The process of producing consolidated results involves the following distinct tasks:

▶ Gather financial data of all entities

▶ Translate data in local currency to one or more reporting currencies

▶ Run business rules to perform calculations/validation (e.g., cash-flow)

▶ Reconcile intercompany transactions

▶ Eliminate intercompany transactions

▶ Consolidation of investments

▶ Post top-side entries using journals

▶ Report the consolidated results

These steps require setting up of the entity structure of the organization, account structure, ownership tree, exchange rates, data model, and business rules to perform the tasks. An efficient system will reduce time to perform financial closing and make the process more reliable by providing accurate results.

Software Planning Tools

It is in the context of the needs of an organization to meet the requirements of planning and financial consolidation that the importance of software planning tools assumes importance.

Many organizations use Microsoft Excel spreadsheets to maintain data related to planning and to prepare the financial results. The Excel spreadsheet is an excellent end-user tool for planning and consolidation. However, they are not robust in terms of security and don't have the level of control and functionality required to manage and maintain sensitive data related to planning and consolidation.

SAP BusinessObjects Planning and Consolidation (SAP BPC) (NetWeaver version) is an add-on tool available in the SAP NetWeaver Business Warehouse system (SAP NetWeaver BW) that can address the requirements of planning and financial consolidation of a business. SAP BPC provides the familiar Microsoft Excel front-end interface for users to configure and perform planning and consolidation. At the same time, it addresses the limitation of using Microsoft Excel as the primary tools for these requirements by securing the data and by providing robust functionality to perform planning and consolidation tasks. The tools available in SAP BPC helps an organization to configure the application that is right for its business and at the same time provides the best practices for application development and maintenance. The application provides out-of-the box tools to perform planning and consolidation tasks. These tools can be further customized for an organization via business rules. Financial data extracted from one or more source systems into the SAP NetWeaver Business Warehouse system can be used as source data to feed into a planning or financial consolidation application in the SAP BPC system. With all these advantages, SAP BPC is a sophistical tool that reduces the Total Cost of Ownership (TCO) for an organization to develop and maintain applications.

Using the SAP BPC system will not only enable an organization to perform planning and consolidation, but will also enable the organization to monitor the whole process and ensure delivery in a timely manner. The business process flow functionality can be enabled in SAP BPC that would allow the organization to track the status of where an organization stands in the planning or consolidation process. The ability to integrate the actual data in the SAP NetWeaver BW system with data in SAP BPC makes it a compelling reason for companies to use this software as the application of choice.

How This Book Can Help

The objective of this book is to help technical developers, functional analysts, consultants, and managers who work in the area of planning and financial consolidation understand and make best use of the capabilities of the SAP BusinessObjects Planning and Consolidation for NetWeaver tool. This book is unique in that it explains the features of the software through extensive examples in simple and easy-to-understand manner.

Structure of the Book

This book contains 10 chapters. Let's take a glimpse of the contents of each chapter:

▶ **Chapter 1: Overview of Enterprise Performance Management**
This chapter provides an overview of enterprise performance management (EPM) and introduces you to concepts in planning, budgeting, forecasting, and consolidation.

▶ **Chapter 2: Overview of SAP BPC**
This chapter provides an overview of the SAP BusinessObjects Planning and Consolidation software. This chapter discusses architecture of SAP BPC on a NetWeaver platform and discusses objects created on the SAP NetWeaver Business Warehouse and SAP BPC systems.

▶ **Chapter 3: Modeling an Application with SAP BPC for NetWeaver**
The third chapter will introduce you to a case study of a model company that has decided to plan its gross margin by implementing the NetWeaver version of SAP BPC. This chapter will explain the steps involved in modeling objects in SAP NetWeaver BW and SAP BPC systems.

▶ **Chapter 4: Loading, Scheduling, and Managing Data in SAP BPC for NetWeaver**
In the fourth chapter, we will discuss how to load data in the SAP NetWeaver BW and SAP BPC environments.

▶ **Chapter 5: Reporting, Planning and Analysis in SAP BPC**
The fifth chapter will discuss how to report, enter data using input templates, and analyze data using the SAP BusinessObjects Planning and Consolidation software, describing the various reporting and analysis options available in the tool.

▶ **Chapter 6: Developing Business Logic in SAP BPC**
In the sixth chapter, we will discuss different options available in SAP BusinessObjects Planning and Consolidation for defining logic and automating the process of deriving data and enforcing business rules. We will discuss dimension formulas, script logic, high-level usage of business rules and usage of BAdI to define business logic. We will describe how currency conversion and allocation are handled in SAP BPC. We will also discuss business rules in-detail in chapter 9 when discussing tasks related to consolidation.

▶ **Chapter 7: Process Management and Collaboration**
The seventh chapter introduces you to the collaboration tools and features available in SAP BusinessObjects Planning and Consolidation that facilitate the sharing and exchange of data. The chapter discusses configuring work status that is used to monitor and restrict changes to data in an SAP BPC application, adding and

viewing comments, distribution of input schedules to offline users, interfacing with Microsoft PowerPoint and Word and creating menu based application.

▶ **Chapter 8: Essential Tools for Building Applications**
The eighth chapter covers a range of topics that are important to understand when implementing a planning or consolidation application using the SAP BPC software.

- ▶ **Transport**: The objects developed in the SAP BPC development environment have to be transported to the quality and production environments. This topic explains in detail the process of transporting objects.

- ▶ **Locking**: This topic involves describes the locking mechanism used in SAP BPC to prevent two users from updating the same data at the same time.

- ▶ **Application Set and Application Parameters**: Parameters are used to influence the behavior of applications. Two types of parameters can be configured in BPC—application set parameters and application parameters. The different parameters setting that are available and how those settings impact the application are discussed here.

- ▶ **Security**: This topic lists the different objects you can configure to limit user access to data and tasks inside a SAP BPC application. The steps of setting up users and teams are discussed.

- ▶ **Statistics**: SAP BPC provides the tools to measure statistics and to gather information about how the system is used. Using these statistics, you can identify bottlenecks and take timely action before they become major issues. This topic describes how to collect statistics for a SAP BPC application.

- ▶ **Audit**: When sensitive data resides in an application and when changes to that data are to be monitored, auditing assumes importance. This topic describes how to configure and use the audit functionality in SAP BPC.

▶ **Chapter 9: Consolidation with SAP BPC**
The ninth chapter discusses in detail the process of how to consolidate data in SAP BPC. The first part of the chapter will introduce you to the steps involved in the consolidation process. We will discuss topics related to prepare, collect, and consolidate steps and detail usage of different types of business rules that can be configured in SAP BusinessObjects Planning and Consolidation. Business rules allows users to set up standard business processes such as carry forward balances, account transformation, intercompany booking, intercompany elimination, validation etc. without having to develop code. We will discuss the need to

perform matching of intercompany transactions and steps to match intercompany transactions. We will describe scenarios to illustrate consolidation of investments using different consolidation methods. We will discuss intercompany elimination using US elimination and automatic adjustment business rules. Finally, we will discuss the use of journals to create top-side entries.

▶ **Chapter 10: SAP BPC for NetWeaver Version 7.5**
The final chapter highlights additional features that are available in SAP BPC for NetWeaver version 7.5.

Summary

The introduction and overview provided in this chapter explain the key components and use of this book. In Chapter 1, we will provide an overview of Enterprise Performance Management and discuss concepts related to in planning, budgeting, forecasting and financial consolidation.

*This chapter introduces you to different components of SAP Enterprise
Performance Management suite of products and outlines basic concepts for
understanding planning and consolidation applications.*

1　Overview of Enterprise Performance Management

This chapter provides you with an overview of enterprise performance management (EPM) and introduces you to concepts in planning, budgeting, forecasting, and consolidation.

In Section 1.1, we'll discuss the definition and importance of EPM and its relevance in different areas of business.

In Section 1.2, we'll discuss concepts in planning, budgeting, and forecasting, and introduce you to methods and best practices in these areas.

In Section 1.3, we'll discuss basic concepts in consolidation and introduce you to the processes involved in consolidation.

So, let's get started.

1.1　Enterprise Performance Management

The importance of EPM is growing in this era of rapid technology development, global competition, modernization, and ever-changing customer needs. The need to make accurate decisions and at the same time meet regulatory requirements is important to gain a competitive edge, ensure control of business operations, and provide precise business status information to statutory bodies, shareholders, and business partners.

EPM deals with bridging the gap between the strategies set by top management and the execution of the strategy by operational staff. It streamlines the execution of strategy and ensures accountability. Its objective is also to provide timely and compliant reporting and to help companies optimize costs and improve profitability.

EPM provides the framework for establishing processes that are needed to meet strategic objectives and for monitoring the execution of these processes.

SAP BusinessObjects EPM solutions provide the following software tools:

▶ **SAP BusinessObjects Strategy Management**
This application allows you to prioritize and communicate strategic initiatives and effectively monitor, measure, and collaborate on strategy.

▶ **SAP BusinessObjects Planning and Consolidation**
The SAP BusinessObjects Planning and Consolidation (BPC) application helps you to perform planning, budgeting, and forecasting tasks. It also allows you to perform financial consolidation and reporting. The objective of this book is to discuss the functionality available in this application in detail.

▶ **SAP BusinessObjects Financial Consolidation**
This application allows companies to perform financial consolidation and reporting.

▶ **SAP BusinessObjects XBRL Publishing**
The eXtensible Business Reporting Language (XBRL) is a new global standard for exchanging financial information and allows accounting jurisdictions such as banks, regulators, and agencies to download, codify, and analyze financial data. The XBRL Publishing application *by UBmatrix* allows you to create XBRL documents based on data available in SAP BPC, SAP BusinessObjects Financial Consolidation, and SAP Business Suite software.

▶ **SAP BusinessObjects Financial Information Management**
This application lets you access, map, and load data from different source systems to the SAP BusinessObjects Financial Consolidation and SAP BusinessObjects Profitability and Cost Management applications.

▶ **SAP BusinessObjects Intercompany**
This application lets you reconcile intercompany balances in real time via the Web, enabling your organization to close its books more quickly.

▶ **SAP BusinessObjects Profitability and Cost Management**
This application allows you to accurately and effectively measure product, customer, and channel profitability, and develop and dynamically test ways to improve profitability.

▶ **SAP BusinessObjects Spend Performance Management**
This application provides you with insight into savings opportunities and compliance by enabling access to aggregated and enriched spend data.

► **SAP BusinessObjects Supply Chain Performance Management**
This application helps you improve the effectiveness of supply chain operations such as lowering costs and improving return on working capital. It also provides an accurate measure of whether you are meeting your supply chain goals, warns you of potential bottlenecks, and alerts you to new opportunities.

SAP's solution in the area of EPM complements its existing software product offerings; SAP is a leader in the enterprise resource planning software arena, which helps reengineer business processes and execute them efficiently. SAP's offerings in other areas—such as business intelligence, supplier relationship management, supply chain management, customer relationship management, and industry-focused solutions—help accelerate innovation and improve return on investment (ROI). Continuing this trend, SAP's acquisition of BusinessObjects ensures its ongoing leadership and its ability to help you devise effective business strategies.

Figure 1.1 details how SAP software solutions integrate insight, strategy, and decisions across governance, risk, and compliance (GRC); EPM; and business intelligence platforms. It also shows how these solutions bridge into business applications that can run on any technology platform. This closed-loop business performance optimization allows companies to obtain a complete picture of their business performance.

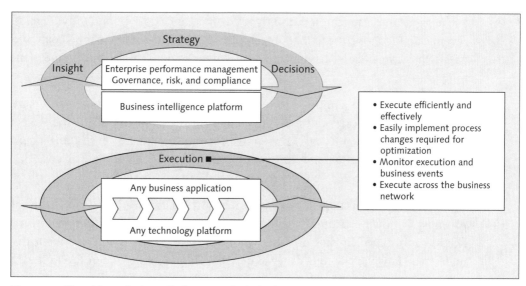

Figure 1.1 Closed-Loop Business Performance Optimization

In the next section, we'll review basic concepts used in planning, budgeting, and forecasting.

1.2   Planning, Budgeting, and Forecasting

In simple terms, *planning* involves thinking ahead and formulating a set of activities you'll execute in the future; in other words, it is the process of modeling or projecting future business activities. Companies strive for profitability and growth in complex business environments where they have to deal with global competition, rapid technology development, geopolitical situations, and ever-changing customer needs, and planning is a key management cycle component that allows companies to position themselves in these complex environments.

The process of planning identifies the individual tasks involved in reaching a goal, provides the time frame for executing the tasks, and determines the resources needed for successful completion of the tasks. It is an iterative activity where the actual performance is measured against set targets and refined accordingly. A business, as part of its existence, has to plan for multiple resources, and to ensure that these activities are undertaken in an optimal manner, a good system of planning should be in place. A good idea or a good product does not necessarily contribute to a company's success; the company must make decisions to sell the right product at the right time, and through the right channel, and more importantly increase revenue and reduce costs in that process. To best achieve the company's goals, the plan to achieve these goals must be clearly defined and refined during the planning process.

Although strategic planning objectives are set by top management, a company may formulate and carry out multiple plans at lower levels to achieve the targets set at the higher level. So it is imperative for the company to ensure that there is complete coordination and unity of objectives among the different plans. This should be taken into account when planning decisions are made.

A majority of organizations have used Microsoft Excel spreadsheets for financial planning, but their limitations are many: accessibility issues, lack of security, insufficient control mechanisms on who can modify data, and an inability to clearly understand how the planning data was derived. This is one area where SAP software can help, and a topic we will come back to in Chapter 2.

When discussing EPM, it is important to understand the differences between planning, budgeting, and forecasting.

As discussed above, *planning* is the process of modeling and projecting future business resources. Depending on the type of planning, the planning horizon can be short, medium, or long term.

Budgeting is the process of allocating resources once the company's management has approved and accepted the planning process. It is the start of the action phase following the planning process. The budgeting process is usually executed before the start of the budget year. In the budgeting process, requisite details are worked out for the implementation of the plan. This is also the period where financial allocations are made to various departments such as finance, sales, information technology, human resources, and so on.

Forecasting deals with the realization of the plan and is used as a monitoring mechanism to facilitate the success of planning. Business environments do not remain the same—what was planned for yesterday may not be the same today. Forecasting is done during the course of the current budget year with a key objective to provide visibility on the current state of the business in a timely manner so that corrective action can be taken when there is a significant difference between the current state of the future and what was planned for during the planning process.

In the subsections that follow, we'll discuss several aspects of the planning process: the planning horizon, planning types, planning areas, common scenarios for planning, and some of the important business elements you should take into account when planning.

1.2.1 Planning Horizon

The planning horizon determines the time frame for planning. Planning horizons are divided into three categories, which we'll discuss in more detail.

Short-Term Planning

The planning time frame in short-term planning is usually a year or less. You use this type of planning when the business has clear-cut short-term goals. Examples of short-term planning include cutting costs, increasing labor productivity by freezing new hires, and effectively training the workforce. Short-term planning is also suitable in situations where the industry in which the business is operating is constantly changing and where it is difficult to make reliable long-term projections.

Medium-Term Planning

Medium-term planning usually covers a period of one to three years and is applicable if the business can reasonably plan the outlook for this time period. You might develop a medium-term plan to increase market share in a particular segment of the business, for example.

Long-Term Planning

Planning is considered long term when the duration of the plan exceeds three years. This type of planning usually involves the investment of a large amount of capital to achieve company objectives. This is also applicable for businesses where projects have a long gestation period. In these types of industries, there is a long time gap between initial investment and final realization of sales and profits; this is true for companies in the utility, steel, and biotechnology industries, for example.

It is important to understand that the level of detail in short-term planning is high because it represents the immediate future. In medium-term planning, the level of detail is reduced. In long-term planning, the level of detail again is very high. Although you can use different time frames for planning, there is no single formula to decide on the option to be used; instead, the period selected depends on the business requirements.

In reality, you may use different terms for different areas of your business. For example, your business may come up with a short-term plan to reduce costs in the immediate future. But at the same time, you may also have a long-term plan in place to gain the highest market share in your industry.

In general, routine business operation plans that address the immediate future are good candidates for short-term planning. Programs and plans that involve large capital investment and that take more time to mature and yield results are categorized as long-term plans.

1.2.2 Planning Types

The planning type provides more clarity to the process by clearly differentiating the objective of the plan. It is based on the planning horizon and the granularity of the planning process. We'll discuss each of the planning types next.

Operative Planning

Operative planning is typically used for the short term and is generally conducted at a company's operational level. This type of planning usually has an immediate objective in mind, for example, to improve productivity by controlling variable costs. With this type of plan, employees at the bottom level of the hierarchy may be part of the planning process to make it successful. The planning method used during the operative planning process is bottom-up planning, where the planners involved in executing the plan are also involved in the creation of the plan. Upon completion of the plan, planners send the plan to their supervisors, and after approval by the supervisors, plan implementation begins.

Using bottom-up planning is very helpful for getting employee commitment to the planning process. Because employees are involved in the planning process, the probability that the plan will be successful is increased.

Tactical Planning

Tactical planning is associated with planning for the medium term and is generally conducted at a company's division level. It is suitable for projects that can be completed in less than three years. For example, you might start an initiative to improve the quality of a product, which may take two years to realize. Although the tactical plan may be in consonance with the long-term plan, it may be developed at the middle management level.

Strategic Planning

Strategic planning is associated with planning for the long term and is generally conducted at a company's organizational level. Company management usually plays a major role in this type of planning. An example of strategic planning is when a company decides to finance research and development to develop a new line of products. The products may take more than three years to develop, and the company may want to develop a plan to finance the new program.

This type of planning usually begins at the company's top level and trickles down to lower levels. The company's top management agrees to the planning objective and process, which may be split into subplans during the implementation process.

In Figure 1.2, you can see how the different types of planning are categorized based on the granularity of the plan (high level versus detailed level) and the *gestation period* (time) to achieve the plan objectives. Strategic planning has the longest gestation period and the lowest level of granularity. Operational planning has the shortest gestation period and the highest level of granularity.

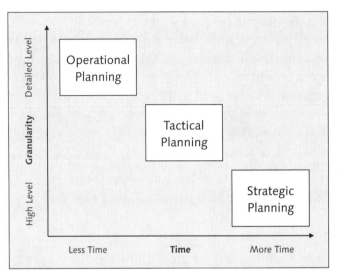

Figure 1.2 Planning Types

1.2.3 Planning Areas

Planning is a generic function applicable to all areas of business. The planning area is the subarea of the business for which you develop a plan. Next, we'll discuss how to understand the relevance of financial planning in several subareas of business.

Finance

The finance department is the control room of any business; it is responsible for planning, implementing, and directing the financial aspects of the business. Examples of financial planning include investing in a new venture, maintaining an optimal cash position (liquidity), reducing costs, and increasing profits. The focus of this book is to illustrate the development of a financial planning application for a company that has an objective to increase its gross profit margin.

In this context, it may help to discuss certain areas of financial planning:

▸ **Liquidity planning**
Liquidity planning focuses on planning for maintaining optimal cash flow to be able to run the business. It involves taking the company's current cash position

into account, estimating the inflow of cash from customers and the outflow of cash to vendors and employees, and planning the liquidity over the next few months.

▶ **Cost center planning**
Cost center planning is done for costs the company will incur at various cost center levels. This includes planning for operational costs, nonoperational costs, and capital expenditures that the company will incur.

▶ **Asset planning**
Asset planning is concerned with planning for the purchase of new assets and the disposal and maintenance of existing assets, based on the company's objective to deliver products to its customers.

▶ **Profitability planning**
Profitability planning determines profitability by identifying sales revenue and costs that will be incurred in the future.

Production

You should plan how much to produce and when and where to produce it, with the goal of producing products in the most optimal manner while satisfying customer requirements and maintaining sufficient capacity to fulfill demand. You should take into account variables such as seasonal behavior, geographical demand, and user behavior when planning for this area. The financial implication of your production plan should be consistent with the company's overall financial plan, and the inventory costs and overhead costs incurred as a result of the production plan should be kept at optimal levels.

Human Resources

Every business should have the workforce required to run the business, and workforce requirements should be planned based on your company's overall growth objectives. When there is a shortage of employees in the industry, you will have to make decisions about whether to hire new employees, train existing employees on new technologies, or bring people in from the outside as consultants to meet requirements. This area of planning is especially important in industries that require large numbers of employees and where specialized skills are required for realizing the objectives of the business. Costs associated with meeting labor requirements have a direct impact on the financial plan.

Marketing

The marketing department provides the necessary information to plan the products that can be sold and the price at which they can be sold. You should also take into account the distribution of products and services to customers. The sales plan can be formulated based on actual sales in past years, revaluation based on future trends in the industry, the geopolitical environment in which your company has sales operations, and the company's strategic vision.

Maintenance

The maintenance department will typically develop a strategy for plant maintenance according to the equipment strategy and breakdown of the maintenance work into categories. These categories include in-program work, functional failures, and discretionary work. Based on the overall maintenance strategy, the maintenance plan can be developed to cover different types of maintenance activities within the plant such as turnarounds, preventive maintenance, breakdown maintenance, and so on.

Proper maintenance of plant equipment can significantly reduce the overall operational costs and boost the overall productivity of the plant. Costs associated with the maintenance costs have a direct impact on the financial plan.

The above-mentioned areas are critical for the survival of the business and have a direct or indirect effect on the company's financial plan. Planning for these areas is important to ensure the smooth functioning of business.

1.2.4 Common Scenarios for Planning in Business

You should plan for different scenarios depending on individual requirements at different times. This subsection delves into some of the common scenarios companies use for planning. These planning scenarios are based on the company's targeted objectives.

Gross Profit Margin Planning

The revenue obtained through the sale of a company's products, along with the costs that are incurred to produce or buy the product, is planned under this scenario. This usually starts with gathering external information on product demand. Often, prior-year revenue results can indicate a trend for future sales planning. This information, along with management's strategic vision and demand estimates provided by the sales force, helps the company plan its products' quantity and prices.

You can arrive at expected manufacturing costs using standard costing procedures. This process should take into account any expected increase to material, labor, and overhead costs in the future. You use expected revenue and manufacturing costs to determine the expected gross profit margin.

Profit and Loss and Balance Sheet Planning

This type of planning is related to the financial area of business. It is the process in which you prepare a profit and loss sheet, along with a balance sheet, to see whether it meets the returns expected by the business. This can also provide clues as to which areas may need corrective action. For example, it may become obvious from the projections that overhead costs are increasing every year; based on this, management may need to take corrective action.

Investment Planning

Investment planning is also associated with the financial aspect of business. It focuses on new investments the company is planning in the future. The expected ROI for the investment is a key metric in this planning.

Labor Planning

Labor planning is the process of planning workforce requirements for your company. It should take both new projects and expected expansion into consideration, which may require additions to the workforce. The plan should take into account expected attrition from the workforce, both from retirement and labor turnover. Human capital is crucial to the business, and labor planning is vital to ensure that the company has the right people with the right skills to operate the business.

Sales Planning

With sales planning, you develop a plan to sell the company's products. The focus is on developing a marketing plan that will be most beneficial to the company and help sell the company's products at the optimal price. The marketing plan should reflect the company's overall strategic vision—for example, a company may decide to place a lot of emphasis on two specific products. The sales plan will need to reflect this objective. The inputs for developing a sales plan are obtained based on market intelligence and opportunities data collected by sales managers.

Demand Planning

Demand planning presupposes that the process of sales planning is complete. Depending on the sales forecast, production planning is geared to fulfill the expected demand. Assuming that production capacity exists, demand planning uses the existing sales forecast to plan for material, labor, and machinery to produce the products.

1.2.5 Considerations in Planning

You should perform the planning process in a manner that is in tune with your company's strategic objectives. Consider the following key points.

Importance

Planning is an important component of every business that contributes to the company's success. There are many examples where good planning and execution have paved the way to the success of a business, as well as many examples where inadequate planning or no planning resulted in a company's failure. So management needs to understand the importance of planning in helping the company be successful in its business operations.

Skills

Planning is an art—and one that requires a lot of foresight. The ability to take all of the factors (internal and external) into account is the key to developing a successful plan. It takes a lot of experience, maturity, and knowledge to develop a plan. The person(s) entrusted with this responsibility should posses these skills.

Internal

The person(s) involved in developing a new plan should understand how the new plan relates to other projects that are currently underway, as well as those the company is likely to undertake in the future. Also, you should take cross-functional aspects into account. For example, if you undertake a plan to improve production capacity, you should study the question of financing before getting started with the plan.

Data

The data that is used in planning should be reliable. For example, if market research and intelligence is used as the basis for planning, the data used for this purpose should come from a trustworthy source. You must also take into account the possibility of error in the data.

Governance

A good governance process should be established for planning. The levels of responsibility should be clearly defined so that there is no ambiguity, and the people involved in planning should clearly understand their role in the process.

Communication

Good communication among all company levels is of vital importance at all times during planning. This ensures that the various participants stay well informed of the plan's progress and take actions at the different plan implementation stages.

Monitoring

A sound review process should also be in place to monitor the execution of the planning process. The availability of such a system helps identify any deviations and aids in taking corrective action.

Planning Method

There are two types of planning methods: top-down and bottom-up. With the *top-down planning process*, upper-level management decides what is to be done, and the lower levels of the organization implement the process. This type of process is relevant for strategic decision-making, for example, when management decides on which areas of the business the company should focus over the next 10 years. The *bottom-up planning process* is used more for operational planning, where planning starts at the lower levels of the organization and is approved by upper levels.

Participation

The planning process is more likely to succeed if people who are responsible for the execution of the planning process are consulted when the planning goals are initially set. This helps in participative decision-making and promotes cooperation from everyone involved in implementing the plan. It also provides an opportunity for management to solicit employee feedback regarding the identified planning objectives.

Issue List

If issues come up during the planning process, they should be recorded so you can track progress toward their resolution. There should also be a good system in place for employees to address these issues.

IT Department

The planning process involves collecting information from different sources. This information may come from cross-functional areas in the company (finance, production, marketing, or human resources), or sometimes from external sources. The IT department facilitates integrating this information, with the goal to build a process for planning that can meet business demands in a reliable and timely manner. The success of this process requires an IT department that can handle this responsibility effectively.

Flexibility

The planning process should be flexible so that it can absorb any necessary changes that may occur along the way. This will make the process less rigid and more open.

You should now have an understanding of the basic concepts in planning. In the next section, we'll discuss basic concepts in consolidation.

1.3   Consolidation

Consolidation is a process that is used to accurately report the financial results of an organization either for legal or management reporting purposes. An organization may be composed of a number of entities and subsidiaries. The subsidiaries may or may not be fully owned. The financial statements that combine the financial results of all entities and subsidiaries are referred to as *consolidated financial statements*. The consolidated financial statements present the financial results of the operations (income statement), financial position (balance sheet), and cash flows (cash flow statement) of all entities and subsidiaries, as if the group(s) of companies is composed of a single entity. The consolidated financial statements can also be generated at different levels of the entity hierarchy. In other words, an organization may consist of several separate entities, but they operate as one centrally controlled economic entity. The consolidated financial statements provide more useful information to shareholders than do separate financial statements of each entity. Consolidation of revenues, expenses, assets, and liabilities provide a clear picture of the operation and financial status of the consolidated single entity.

The process of producing consolidated results involves the following distinct tasks:

1. Gather financial data of all entities
2. Translate data in local currency to one or more reporting currencies
3. Run business rules to perform calculations/validation (e.g., cash flow)
4. Reconcile intercompany transactions (matching)
5. Eliminate intercompany transactions
6. Consolidate investments
7. Post top-side entries using journals
8. Report the consolidated results

To understand consolidated financial statements, you need to understand the basic concepts discussed in the subsections that follow.

1.3.1 Elimination of Intercompany Transactions

The consolidation of financial statements involves summing up the amounts across all separate entities and providing a unified view of the operations of the economic entity. But in this consolidation process, it's important to eliminate double-counting resulting from intercompany transactions. For example, if an entity sells products to another entity within the organization, the consolidated financial statement should eliminate this sale because it is an intercompany transaction. The objective of consolidated financial statements is to report the consolidated entity's transactions to outsiders.

The following intercompany transactions must be eliminated.

Intercompany Sales and Cost of Goods Sold

Any intercompany transaction between entities within an organization should be eliminated. Consider a case where an entity sells a product to another entity within an organization, and the second entity then sells the product in the same or a different form to an external customer. A consolidated financial statement of the organization should show transactions of the organization that relate to external companies. The transactions such as sales and cost of goods sold (COGS) that result from the exchange of goods or services within the organization should not be counted, so they should also be eliminated from consolidated statements.

Intercompany Receivables/Payables

When an entity sells a product to another entity within the organization, the amount associated with the sale is recorded as accounts receivable in the books of the selling entity. Similarly, the transaction is recorded as accounts payable in the books of the buying entity. This transaction does not result in the consolidated company receiving or owing any amount to an external customer or supplier. So the intercompany accounts receivable and payable transactions should be eliminated from the consolidated statements.

1.3.2 Consolidation of Investments

A corporation may have a number of subsidiaries that may or may not be fully owned. The consolidation of investment deals with elimination of ownership and booking of minority interest of these investments. There are 3 methods that are commonly used in consolidation of investments:

▶ Purchase Method

▶ Equity Method

▶ Proportional Method

The purchase method is generally used when the percentage of ownership is greater than 50%. The equity method is generally used when the percentage of ownership is less than 50%. The proportional method is similar to the purchase method and is generally used in Europe. In the chapters ahead, we'll discuss different methods of ownership, and detail how the consolidation of investments is handled in each scenario.

In the purchase method, at the time of purchase, the consolidation of investment process reflects the elimination of ownership that is common between the parent and subsidiary, goodwill for the premium paid for the purchase and minority stakeholders claim to the asset. After this first consolidation, assuming that the ownership percentage does not change, subsequent consolidations would post the parent and minority share of the subsidiary's earnings.

In the equity method, reported financial data of the equity unit is not taken into consideration in the consolidated financial report. The financial data for the equity unit is not entered into the consolidation system. Only the changes to the owner's equity are taken into consideration. This affects the investment value and goodwill stated in the consolidated balance sheet.

The proportional method of consolidation collects the units of the balance sheet and income statement into the consolidated statements based on the investor unit's proportion of ownership in the investee's unit. In other words, the percentage that is not owned is eliminated.

Let's take an example of a parent company that acquires 70% ownership in a subsidiary using the purchase method of ownership. At the time of acquisition, the following transactions are performed:

▶ Consolidate balances of parent and subsidiary

▶ Eliminate ownership that is common between the parent and subsidiary — eliminate the investment account of the parent that pertains to the subsidiary and common stock of subsidiary

▶ Post any excess value paid that is above the book value of the acquired subsidiary to goodwill

▶ Post minority interest. The amount of minority interest appearing in the balance sheet is calculated by multiplying common shareholder equity of the subsidiary by the percentage of the minority interest. The percentage of minority interest in this case will be 30%.

After the first consolidation, assuming that the ownership percentage does not change, subsequent consolidations would post the parent and minority share of the subsidiary's earnings.

In the following chapters, we'll discuss how you can use the SAP BPC application to perform the discussed tasks.

1.4 Summary

In this chapter, we discussed the importance of EPM software and introduced key concepts in the area of financial planning and consolidation. In Chapter 2, we'll discuss an overview of the SAP BPC application and its use for planning and financial consolidation.

This chapter introduces you to the architecture of the SAP BPC software tool for NetWeaver and discusses concepts and terminologies used in the SAP NetWeaver Business Warehouse and SAP BPC for NetWeaver systems.

2   Overview of SAP BPC

In this chapter, you'll find an overview of the SAP BusinessObjects Planning and Consolidation (BPC) application, NetWeaver version 7.5, and an introduction to some of its key features. We'll discuss the flexibility, control, and ease this application offers in managing and analyzing data and explain how you can use the software to meet both the planning and consolidation needs of your organization. We'll also detail the multifaceted range of applications where you can use it and expound on how you can use it to support a reliable and effective decision-making process. Finally, we'll discuss the architecture of the NetWeaver version of SAP BPC and introduce you to objects created in the environment.

In Section 2.1, you'll learn about a key requirement most business users look for when using a software application—the ability to manage and analyze data with less dependence on an IT solutions team—and explain how SAP BPC satisfies this need.

In Section 2.2, we'll explain how you can use the application to meet planning and consolidation requirements, discuss its implementation in different areas of planning, and explain how you can derive competitive advantage by using it. We'll also cover how the application provides an environment for performing legal consolidation and management consolidation of an organization. This is especially important for multiple-entity organizations that are required to perform legal consolidation and release financial results of the entire company per statutory requirements.

In Section 2.3, we'll discuss the architecture of the NetWeaver version of SAP BPC and explain how it interfaces with the SAP NetWeaver Business Warehouse (SAP NetWeaver BW) system.

In Section 2.4, we'll introduce you to the SAP NetWeaver BW system and explain the process of extracting, transforming, and loading data from a source system to an SAP NetWeaver BW system. The section also highlights the usage of Business Content to expedite the development of data warehouse applications.

In Section 2.5, you'll learn about the objects configured in SAP BPC and the relationship between these objects and the objects created in SAP NetWeaver BW.

2.1   Business User Owned and Managed

The needs of a business are sometimes predictable, but at other times, they are not clearly defined or are even unpredictable. This element of unpredictability has a direct bearing on the IT applications that are developed for business users. The model of an application should be free-form and must be flexible enough to meet the needs of the business users. Users will not accept a model that is rigid and that cannot satisfy the needs of the business. In these cases, the application will not be used and will not meet the objectives for which it was developed.

The cost of retooling an application to support additional business requirements is something that should be considered when the application is initially designed. A clear process should be in place for how the data model fits the current scope and how it will support the business if the design requires changes during the life of the application. We have seen how organizations have spent increasing amounts of money to redesign their applications to meet user needs; some of this money could have been saved if good design principles had been followed in the first place.

In addition to the design element, the software that is used for building the application should be flexible enough to support changes. Because not every business change can be anticipated, a good software tool should be able to accommodate changes in a fashion that does not involve too much cost or time.

2.1.1   Software Usability and Flexibility to Support Change

The following are some software tool aspects that ensure usability and flexibility to support changes:

▶ **Reporting**
You must be able to design custom reports on your own to support any analyses that may not be supported by standard reports delivered by the IT solutions team.

► **Control of data**

Users own data, and it is only right that you have the ability to control how this data is loaded into the system. The software tool should let you load data into the application so it can be used for analysis later. This is particularly important for users of planning applications, where you have the discretion to decide what data to use, when to use it, and how to use it. This applies to consolidation applications as well, regarding how you want to use your data for statutory reporting. The options in the software tool, such as the ability to schedule the loading of data and to replace existing data, enable you to make more efficient use of the application.

► **Business rules**

Business rules are used when you want to transform data that is loaded into an application. They are used to perform certain tasks such as currency conversion, account transformation, carry forward balance, and so on in planning and consolidation applications. You should be able to configure these rules and execute the processes.

► **Out of the box functions**

Depending on the application, the software should provide you with all of the functions that are used to meet the principal requirement of the application. These functions should be made available as part of the software tool. This not only reduces the total cost of ownership (TCO) but also helps you make real use of the application without relying on other tools to perform these functions.

► **Custom settings**

The software should enable you to see report descriptions in your own language (e.g., if you are in France, you should be able to see the application user interface in French).

► **Customization**

You should be able to customize the application without having to rely on the help of your IT solutions team. Customizations may involve a change to the data load process or reporting logic, for example.

► **Collaboration**

Some applications require collaboration to ensure that all members of the business team are in sync and have the latest information. For these applications, it is essential that the software provides features that allow collaboration. Collaboration may assume different forms. For example, you may post a document to get input from another user, or you may post a document for others to read and use in their decision-making.

► **Distribution and collection**
As a corollary to collaboration, it may be necessary to disseminate data to other business users who may in turn modify the data and may want to retract the modified data back to the application. The software tool will need to allow you to distribute and modify information and retract modified information back to the application.

► **Programming interface**
You may need to develop scripts that allow you to perform specific functions within an application. The software tool should provide an easy-to-use programming interface that enables this.

2.1.2   SAP BPC (Microsoft and NetWeaver)

How does SAP BPC measure up against the need to support usability and flexibility to support change? The application provides an environment that satisfies all of these requirements, in a manner that grants you sufficient flexibility in using your applications. Next, we'll discuss some of the features of the application and some of the disadvantages of relying solely on Microsoft Excel for planning purposes.

Features of SAP BPC

SAP BPC lets you develop your own reports, enabling you to decide how you view your data. Although the data you can view is governed by your security access, you can customize your reports in a fashion that suits your decision-making requirements.

The application also allows you to load data yourself. This has two benefits: First, it removes your dependence on the IT solutions team, and second, it allows you to load data at any time, which in turn provides more control.

SAP BPC supports the creation of business rules that dictate how data is transformed in the application. For example, you can set up business rules for performing currency conversions.

The application also provides out of the box functions for performing planning and consolidation. These functions can be used as-is or in combination with additional business rules to support specific application requirements. The following are some of the out of the box functions:

▶ **Currency translation**

You can use this function if your organization has its place of business in more than one country and/or does business in different currencies. Currency translation is used in both planning and financial consolidation applications. The currency translation process allows business users to translate transactions to one or more reporting currencies.

▶ **Intercompany elimination**

This is applicable for an organization that has entities that do business with each other. A consolidated balance sheet of an organization shows transactions that relate to external companies. The transactions such as sales and COGS or receivables and payables that result from exchange of goods or services within the organization should not be counted. In these cases, it is essential to eliminate the intercompany transactions. The intercompany eliminations process creates entries that eliminate intercompany transactions.

▶ **Allocations**

Planning may take place at a high level, and you may later allocate the plan to lower levels. For example, you may need to allocate planned expenses incurred by the corporate office to each of its divisions based on some ratio, perhaps allocating corporate expenses to divisions based on the planned revenues of each division. The logic to perform this allocation is available in SAP BPC.

▶ **Account transformation**

There are some scenarios where accounts are consolidated or transformed into another account, an activity that is used extensively in cash flow applications. Account transformation business rules are used to aggregate values posted to specific combinations of source Account, Flow, Category, and Data Source and post them to aggregated destination Account, Flow, Category, and Data Source.

▶ **Validations**

The validation rules functionality in SAP BPC is a check mechanism that enables an organization to ensure accuracy of data. For example, using the validation rule table, an organization can set up business rules that would compare balances in assets and liabilities/owner's equity accounts for a given period and report variances, if any, for that period.

▶ **Carry forward opening balances**
The carry forward of balances is an essential step in the creation of a balance sheet for an organization; it is when the closing balance of accounts for a fiscal period is transferred as the opening balance of a subsequent fiscal period.

▶ **Automatic adjustments**
The automatic adjustments logic supports the process of generating a consolidated financial statement. The automatic adjustment business rules are used for elimination of intercompany transactions and for consolidation of investments.

SAP BPC allows you to view and store information in multiple languages. It also includes a feature to augment collaboration by enabling you to enter comments about your data. This provides context information to the data (making it more understandable) and aids in decision-making. For example, you can enter a comment to explain a reduction in overhead expenses from last year to the current year. This is clearly a better solution than storing this information in a different location that may or may not be accessible to the user making the decision.

Another feature of the application, Work Status, allows you to lock data so that it cannot be changed in the application. Using this feature, you can define the range of data that can be modified or locked. For example, if a sales representative creates a sales plan and sends it to his manager for approval, during the approval time frame, the data can be locked from being changed.

SAP BPC also enables the distribution and collection of financial data. The application allows you to send plan information to other people, even people who do not use the application. The recipient can then make modifications to the data, and the changes can be retracted back to the system. This facilitates the exchange of data and truly supports collaboration between and participation of all people involved in fulfilling the organization's planning objectives.

Another important feature of this application is its easy-to-use programming interface, which allows you to create and execute logic that may be used for planning and consolidation. For example, you can develop a script to perform revaluation of a plan by a certain percentage. The application lets you implement logic using a variety of methods to manage the data, and it lets you include logic than can be categorized into three broad areas. We'll discuss this at length in Chapter 6; for now, we'll only offer a brief description of each area.

▶ **Dimension logic**
You configure this via simple mathematic formulas. For example, you could set a formula in the application to subtract the cost of goods sold from the gross sales to obtain the gross profit.

▶ **Business rules**
You can develop rules to perform a certain function in planning or consolidation. For example, you can define custom business rules for currency translations, intercompany transactions elimination, account transformations, and so on to tailor the application to the needs of the business.

▶ **Script logic (or K2 script logic)**
You can develop scripts that perform certain functions. This feature is generally used to apply detailed business logic to achieve a specific function, especially when out of the box functionality cannot satisfy the business requirement. The script logic is a fully developed language for this application and can meet any special requirements not available in the standard application. For example, you may require script logic when you want to determine the depreciation of a certain group of assets based on some logic; if the logic is not readily available, you'll need to create it in SAP BPC.

The application frontend for planning, consolidation, and reporting runs on top of Microsoft Excel, which is widely used by planners and accountants all over the world. This lets you perform planning and consolidation functions in the familiar Excel environment and helps you avoid spending time learning new software. Creating graphical data in Excel provides an intuitive display of the data that can be easily understood, interpreted, and analyzed.

Microsoft Excel versus SAP BPC

Some organizations solely use Excel for planning, but there are many disadvantages to this approach:

▶ **Managing Excel spreadsheets**
In Excel, planning data is stored in spreadsheets, which can be an issue from a security perspective; the only option to control access is to keep the files on a shared network drive and provide access only to select users. This in turn creates additional work for the IT solutions team. SAP BPC alleviates this issue by storing the data in a database and enforcing security on the data.

▶ **Versions**
When a new version of data is required, SAP BPC can store the data in a separate version while maintaining the current data. In Excel, the data file has to be saved under a new name as the new version, which leaves room for user error when naming files.

▶ **Floating files**
In Excel, it's possible for different users to maintain the same file on their respective computers, which makes it difficult to track whose file is the latest and most reliable version. SAP BPC is a central repository for financial data and can be accessed by several users at the same time.

▶ **Collaboration**
Excel does not support true collaboration, whereas SAP BPC allows you to store comments that can inform other users of important information.

SAP BPC also lets you integrate data into Microsoft Word and Microsoft PowerPoint® for reporting purposes.

2.1.3 SAP BPC (for NetWeaver)

The NetWeaver version of SAP BPC provides additional advantages. Because it is integrated into the SAP NetWeaver Business Warehouse (BW) system, the data is stored in SAP NetWeaver BW InfoCubes and enjoys all of the advantages of this system. Some advantages specific to the NetWeaver version are as follows:

▶ **Star schema**
The technical architecture of an SAP NetWeaver BW InfoCube consists of a central fact table surrounded by several dimension tables, all grouped in the form of a star schema. The NetWeaver version of SAP BPC uses the extended star schema for storing data, which makes it a superior choice for reporting.

▶ **Database independent**
The NetWeaver version runs independently of the database and can run on major databases such as Oracle, DB2®, SQL Server®, and Informix®.

▶ **SAP NetWeaver BW Accelerator**
SAP NetWeaver BW Accelerator is an optional tool you can use in the NetWeaver version to improve reporting performance. SAP NetWeaver BW Accelerator provides enhanced reporting performance, even with a large data set. The investment in SAP NetWeaver BW Accelerator not only helps with providing an

enhanced reporting experience but also contributes to considerable cost savings by minimizing troubleshooting issues related to reporting performance.

▸ **ABAP language support**
The K2 script logic, which we mentioned earlier, is the programming language used for developing script logic. The NetWeaver version of SAP BPC also allows you to use ABAP to develop this logic. You can develop a business add-in (BAdI) interface in the backend SAP system using ABAP, which can then be called from the script logic that is developed in SAP BPC. You can use scripts coded using ABAP to handle complex business requirements and simultaneously leverage the experience and expertise of the IT solutions team. This feature helps reduce development time for organizations that have been using an SAP system for a long time, because developers will be familiar with the ABAP programming language and can use it to deliver customizations.

From the previous discussion, you now have an idea of the many features SAP BPC offers. Most of the features discussed require less assistance from the IT solutions team on an ongoing basis (although they will of course be involved in both the initial stages of the development of the applications and their ongoing support). The features that are built into this application allow you to automatically assume ownership of the application and then partner with the IT solutions team in fulfilling specific business needs.

In the next section, you'll see how to use the application for performing both planning and consolidation functions.

2.2   Unified Planning and Consolidation

SAP BPC provides a full-fledged environment for organizations to create flexible and powerful applications for different types of planning. It can also be used for consolidating and reporting financial data to satisfy your organization's legal requirements.

2.2.1   Planning in SAP BPC

In today's world of intense competition, it is necessary for organizations to plan and stay ahead. Planning is the life-blood of business, and the ability to spot opportunities and prepare for various courses of action has become imperative because the consumers' fast-changing needs require businesses to be vigilant and act with vision. To meet this objective, organizations are looking for software that can provide an enabling environment to handle planning needs.

As we have discussed, SAP BPC has many features that make it an ideal tool for planning, designed to maximize your ability to manage and take ownership of data. Its robust interface allows for customization and collaboration and makes it a compelling choice for planning. Unlike most software, this application reduces the dependence on the IT solutions team while providing more time for the team to handle the portions of application development and maintenance they best serve (i.e., system configuration and performance).

2.2.2 Consolidation in SAP BPC

The consolidation functionality of SAP BPC provides an environment to report the financial results of your entire organization. You can use it to determine the financial health of the company as a whole, after taking into account the currency translations, elimination of intercompany transactions, and other necessary adjustments. When the consolidation report is prepared, the application considers different types of investments among organizational units.

Consolidation provides the means for internal and external enterprise reporting of a company's financial data. When the reporting is external, it serves the objective of statutory compliance, also known as *legal consolidation*. This is classified as formal reporting and must satisfy the acceptable accounting practice that is applicable to the country where the consolidation is done.

Internal reporting is also called *management consolidation*. This provides more latitude and flexibility in defining the methods used for consolidating data. The objective of this type of consolidation is to provide you with the necessary tools for decision-making. You can consolidate based on customer-defined consolidation units, which can represent, for example, companies, plants, business areas, profit centers, or cost centers. You can also portray matrix organizations, for example, by using a combination of companies and profit centers.

The first step you perform in consolidation is to standardize the financial data reported by individual consolidation units to adhere to the group's accounting standards. You then translate the standardized financial data from the various local currencies into the group currencies (if the local and group currencies are different).

Finally, you eliminate the effects of intercompany transactions. So you calculate the consolidated financial statements as if the group were a single entity. You can use the reporting functions of SAP BPC to analyze and report on your consolidated financial statement data. You can use SAP BusinessObjects XBRL Publishing to create XBRL documents based on data in the SAP BPC application to exchange financial data with accounting jurisdictions such as banks, regulators, and agencies.

Next, we'll discuss the features and advantages of performing consolidation in SAP BPC.

Features

SAP BPC allows you to use different charts of accounts for consolidation, enabling you to generate several consolidated financial statements in parallel to accommodate different accounting principles.

You can collect data for consolidation in the NetWeaver version using the following methods:

- Online data entry
- Flexible upload from a data file
- Loading from an InfoProvider

The application allows you to execute the following tasks:

- Currency translation
- Account Transformation
- Allocation
- Balance carry forward
- Intercompany reconciliation (matching)
- Intercompany booking
- Intercompany eliminations
- Consolidation of Investments
- Validation

Advantages of Performing Consolidation in SAP BPC

Performing consolidation with SAP BPC has the following advantages:

▶ **Legal and management consolidation**
The application provides a systematic process to perform legal consolidation. You can also perform management consolidation using different sets of data to highlight different scenarios for management, as well as parallel consolidations with different categories of data and using different accounting principles.

▶ **Accuracy**
The design of the application's system for consolidation enables the consolidation process to run in a controlled manner, with the ability to perform checks and balances along the way. This mitigates any errors during the process and ensures the completeness and accuracy of the data.

▶ **Multiple source systems**
You can compile financial data from various source systems into a single system for the purpose of consolidation.

▶ **Reporting**
You can generate reports based on consolidated data, which you can then use as a tool for measuring the organization's performance. The reports allow you to view key metrics such as return on equity, ROI, and so on.

▶ **Validation of data**
You can analyze different sources of data used to generate the consolidated data to ensure that the data is valid and reliable. You can also reconcile the data in the application with the source system, facilitating reliability.

▶ **Collaboration**
The application supports the extensive collaboration needed to gather data from multiple sources. This helps with the consolidation of data from diverse sources.

You should now have an understanding of how organizations can use SAP BPC to meet both their planning and consolidation requirements. In the next section, we'll discuss the architecture of SAP BPC for NetWeaver and explain how it interfaces with the SAP NetWeaver BW system.

2.3   SAP BPC for NetWeaver Architecture

The architecture of SAP BPC for NetWeaver (Figure 2.1) is designed to leverage the capabilities of the planning and consolidation application and SAP NetWeaver BW. You can use the planning application frontend tool to configure planning and consolidation features. The data that is entered or loaded through this frontend application is then stored in the SAP NetWeaver BW system, which is based on the extended star schema and is designed to provide high-performance reporting.

Figure 2.1 shows the architecture of the system for NetWeaver. The architecture consists of four tiers, discussed in more detail next.

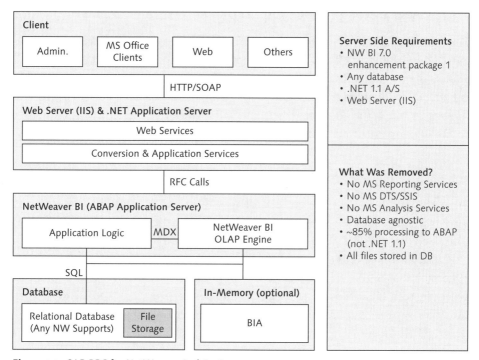

Figure 2.1 SAP BPC for NetWeaver Architecture

2.3.1 Client Interface

The client interface comprises the Microsoft Excel-based Admin Client, Microsoft Office Client, and a web-based tool for configuring and reporting. You can use the Excel Admin Client tool to configure the application; the tool includes a robust and intuitive interface for defining the configuration and managing the development process. All aspects of the development, including setting up security, are performed using this interface. In addition to using Excel, you can also use other Microsoft tools such as Word and PowerPoint to report data in SAP BPC.

You can use the Excel-based Office Client to plan and consolidate data in the application and to create and execute reports. The web interface is a zero footprint option available to create web-based reports, manage unstructured documents, monitor the status of a planning application, and set certain custom parameters for an application.

2.3.2 Web Server and .NET Application Server

The tools available as part of the client interface use web services to connect to the .NET Application Server tier. This server manages requests from the client interface and enables requests for service to be directed to the ABAP application server that is part of SAP NetWeaver BW. The main purpose of this layer is to convert data flowing between the client interface and the SAP NetWeaver Application Server so the two servers understand the data formats.

2.3.3 SAP NetWeaver Application Server

The SAP NetWeaver Application Server is also the ABAP Application Server. This is the tier where requests are processed. The request from the .NET application server is processed in the SAP NetWeaver Application Server as a remote function call (RFC). The requests may be to either report data or update information in the database. When the SAP NetWeaver Application Server receives a request, it processes it and sends the results back to the .NET Application Server. The .NET Application Server then receives the result and sends it back to the client interface.

2.3.4 Database Server

The database server is the tier where data is stored. The SAP NetWeaver BW system is the backend system where objects are created and the data is stored for SAP BPC. The NetWeaver version is database-agnostic and supports all popular databases including Oracle, Informix, SQL Server, and DB2.

The client interface interacts with the SAP NetWeaver BW system to manage objects and data. When you create, read, update, or delete objects or data using the client interface, the system performs these tasks on the SAP NetWeaver BW system.

Although a majority of the development tasks related to SAP BPC are accomplished using the client interface, a few tasks are performed directly in the SAP NetWeaver BW system. These include activities related to performing restore and backup

(Transaction UJBR), viewing files in the file system (Transaction UJFS), improving performance, setting validation rules (Transaction UJ_VALIDATION), and creating custom ABAP programs. Custom process chains, which may be used to schedule data loads, are also created directly in the SAP NetWeaver BW system.

You may sometimes extract master, text, hierarchy, and transaction data from a source system into the SAP NetWeaver BW system before loading the data to an SAP BPC system. In this case, the SAP NetWeaver BW system is used as a staging system for data before being loaded to the planning and consolidation application. The objects related to setting up the staging environment are created directly in the SAP NetWeaver BW system.

> **Note**
>
> We recommend that you *not* perform any manual configuration for SAP BPC directly in the SAP NetWeaver BW system, except for the few tasks mentioned. You should configure the application using the frontend tools (Admin Console, Office Client, and web interface).

As you can see, the integration of SAP BPC with NetWeaver provides many benefits to leverage the power of Excel and SAP NetWeaver BW systems.

In the next section, we'll introduce you to objects created in the SAP NetWeaver BW system.

2.4   Introduction to SAP NetWeaver BW

When you create an object using the SAP BPC frontend, the system creates equivalent objects in the SAP NetWeaver BW system. In addition, the SAP NetWeaver BW system may sometimes be used to stage data coming from various source systems before being loaded to the planning and consolidation application. In the subsections that follow, we'll discuss the objects in SAP NetWeaver BW, the data flow process the system utilizes, process chains, and Business Content.

2.4.1   Objects Used in SAP NetWeaver BW

In this section, we'll introduce you to the objects used in SAP NetWeaver BW.

InfoObject

An *InfoObject* is the basic object for building a data model in SAP NetWeaver BW. There are several different types of InfoObjects:

► **Characteristics**

  ► A characteristic InfoObject represents an entity of a business or an attribute related to an entity. Examples of business entities include customers, materials, and employees.

  ► An InfoObject that provides additional information about an entity is called an attribute. Attributes are InfoObjects but are used in conjunction with the parent InfoObject. Examples of attributes are customer address and phone number. (These InfoObjects are included as attributes in the Customer InfoObject.)

  ► You can configure an InfoObject to store master, text, and hierarchy data.

  ► When you define an InfoObject to store master data, it contains the master data table with the InfoObject and the attributes associated with it. For example, the customer number, along with city, state, zip code, and country, can be stored as master data.

  ► When you design an InfoObject to store text data, it contains the text values of the InfoObject. For example, the names of customers can be stored as text values.

  ► When there is an inherent parent-child relationship in data, you can define the InfoObject as a hierarchy InfoObject. This is useful for analysis where there is a relationship in data. For example, the reporting relationships between manager and employees can be defined as a hierarchy.

► **Time characteristics**

  ► The time characteristic InfoObject is used to set the value for the time-related characteristic of a transaction. Examples of time characteristics are calendar month, calendar year, fiscal year, and so on.

► **Unit characteristics**

  ► The unit characteristic InfoObject provides meaning to quantitative data. Currency and units of measure are examples of unit characteristics. For example, the sales amount for a transaction can be recorded as a currency. The quantity sold can be recorded as a unit (kilograms and pounds).

▶ **Key figures**

    ▶ The key figure InfoObject represents the quantitative measure associated with a transaction. Examples of key figures are the quantity and amount associated with a sales transaction.

InfoProvider

An InfoProvider is the object provided for storing data in SAP NetWeaver BW; it is comprised of a collection of InfoObjects. InfoProviders can contain characteristic, time characteristic, unit characteristic, and key figure InfoObjects.

There are two types of InfoProviders:

▶ **Physical InfoProviders**

    ▶ Physical InfoProviders are used to store data and can be InfoObjects, InfoCubes, and DataStore objects. They are also referred to as *data targets*, because they physically contain the data.

    ▶ An InfoCube is a collection of InfoObjects and represents the extended star schema architecture in SAP NetWeaver BW. It is made up of a fact table and a number of dimension tables. Related characteristics in an InfoCube are grouped together under dimensions. When you load data to an InfoCube, a dimension ID is created by the system for each unique combination of characteristics in a dimension. A record in a fact table is made up of the individual key figures and the dimension IDs associated with a transaction. The individual characteristics in a dimension, and the corresponding attributes of a characteristic, are related using surrogate IDs (SIDs). The InfoCube is the recommended approach for reporting in SAP NetWeaver BW, because it provides the full advantage of the star schema architecture.

    ▶ A DataStore object is a transparent table that usually serves as the first layer of extracting data from a source system. The data loaded in a DataStore is often used for detailed analysis, because it contains raw data extracted from the source system. The data extracted into the DataStore can be further loaded into another InfoProvider, depending on the particular requirements of analysis.

▶ **Logical InfoProviders**

    ▶ Logical InfoProviders do not physically contain data but are used for providing views of data. They are InfoSets, MultiProviders, and virtual InfoProviders.

▶ An InfoSet lets you join objects that store data. For example, two DataStore objects can be joined together to create an InfoSet. The joins created in an InfoSet are database joins. There is considerable flexibility when you define an InfoSet using inner and outer joins. Using an outer join, you can view all of the data defined in the left object of the InfoSet—for example, you can view the sales of all customers, including customers who did not have any sales reported in a particular period. InfoSets can also be used to combine data from an InfoCube and another InfoProvider.

▶ A MultiProvider provides a powerful feature to view data contained in more than one InfoProvider. For example, a MultiProvider can be used to view data from an InfoCube and a DataStore. The MultiProvider provides a union of data in the underlying InfoProviders. This helps to combine the data available in more than one InfoProvider.

▶ A virtual InfoProvider enables remote access of data from a source system connected to the SAP NetWeaver BW system.

2.4.2 Extracting, Transforming, and Loading Data in SAP NetWeaver BW

This section explains the process of extracting, transforming, and loading data into data targets in SAP NetWeaver BW.

DataSource

The DataSource is the source of data used for extracting data into SAP NetWeaver BW. DataSources can be configured to extract data from a variety of source systems:

▶ **SAP systems**
Data can be extracted from SAP systems (SAP R/3, SAP CRM, and other new dimension products offered by SAP) into SAP NetWeaver BW. There is a tight connection between SAP systems and the SAP NetWeaver BW system. The service application programming interface (API) provides the interface to extract data from these systems.

▶ **Flat files**
Data is extracted from a standard file into SAP NetWeaver BW (e.g., an Excel file). A DataSource is defined in the SAP NetWeaver BW system corresponding to the file layout for extracting data.

▶ **Web applications**
An XML interface can be used to extract data from a web application using the simple object access protocol (SOAP).

▶ **DB Connect**
A direct connection to a variety of external databases systems such as Oracle, Informix, and so on can be established using DB Connect.

▶ **Universal Data Connect**
This connection provides access to external relational databases and multidimensional databases via the Java 2 Platform, Enterprise Edition (J2EE) server.

▶ **Third-party systems**
A business application programming interface (BAPI) is used in conjunction with third-party tools to extract data into the SAP NetWeaver BW system. Some examples of third-party systems are Informatica® and Ascential.

DataSources can be configured for each of these source systems.

Flow of Data in SAP NetWeaver BW (Extracting, Transforming, and Loading)

The data transfer process in SAP NetWeaver BW provides a flexible and improved process of extracting data from a source system, transforming the extracted data, and loading the transformed data into a data target.

The following are the components of the data transfer process in SAP NetWeaver BW:

▶ **Persistent staging area (PSA)**

　▶ A PSA table is generated when a DataSource is activated in SAP NetWeaver BW. The PSA table is a transparent table and is the first layer for storing data.

　▶ When data is requested for a DataSource from a source system, the data is initially loaded into the corresponding PSA table of the DataSource.

▶ **Transformations**

　▶ A transformation process is defined between a source and target object in SAP NetWeaver BW. The objective of the transformation is to map data coming from a source to a target using specific rules. It also lets you apply changes to data coming from a DataSource.

► You can use the DataSource (PSA), InfoSource, DataStore object, InfoCube, InfoObject, and InfoSet as source objects in the transformation.

► You can use the InfoSource, DataStore object, InfoCube, and InfoObject as target objects in the transformation.

► The transformation rule allows you to map fields and InfoObjects to a target InfoObject, set a constant value to a target InfoObject, develop a routine in ABAP to perform the mapping, create a formula, look up master data attributes to determine the value of a target InfoObject, and perform time determinations.

► An InfoSource acts as an additional layer of transformation before data reaches a data target. You can use it as an optional process when two or more transformations are required before data is transferred from a DataSource to a data target.

► **Data transfer process**

► The data transfer process (DTP) facilitates the flow of data in SAP NetWeaver BW from one persistent object to another; for example, after data is transferred from a source system into the PSA, the DTP is used to load from the PSA to a data target.

► PSA, InfoObject, InfoCube, and DataStore objects are examples of persistent objects in the SAP NetWeaver BW system.

► The data transfer process may encompass one or many transformations. A transformation process is defined to provide the rules to map data between a source object and a target object. Transformation rules provide the ability to apply changes to the data coming from a source to a target. The data transfer process moves data from the source to the target using the rules specified in the transformation.

► **InfoPackage**

► An InfoPackage is the object used to request data for a DataSource from the source system. After the InfoPackage requests data, the data for a DataSource is transferred from the source system to the PSA table.

In Figure 2.2, you can see the flow of data in SAP NetWeaver BW. Transformation rules are created between the source and target objects, and a data transfer process is used to load data from one persistent object to another.

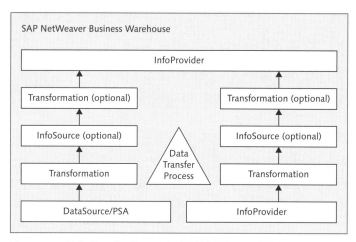

Figure 2.2 Data Transfer Process in SAP NetWeaver BW

2.4.3 Process Chains

A *process chain* provides different types of processes to manage data within the SAP NetWeaver BW system. You use process chains to automate the process of extracting, transforming, and loading data, as well as to more effectively administer data. For example, the InfoPackage that is executed to request data from the source system, and the DTP process that is used for moving data within SAP NetWeaver BW, can be automatically scheduled in a process chain.

2.4.4 Business Content

In the previous section, we mentioned that you can use SAP NetWeaver BW as a staging environment before loading data into SAP BPC. Business Content is what allows you to build this staging environment; it consists of preconfigured objects that help accelerate the process of development of an SAP NetWeaver BW application. Business Content is available in the following areas:

▶ **DataSources**
   SAP supplies DataSources to bring data from R/3 to SAP NetWeaver BW systems. The logic for extracting the data is supplied with the DataSource. This greatly reduces the time and effort involved in extracting the data. Some of the DataSources have delta capabilities for extracting data. A DataSource that is

delta-enabled brings over only the data that was created or modified since the last extraction from the source system.

- **InfoObjects**
  SAP supplies standard InfoObjects used in business applications, for example, Customer, Plant, Material, and Material Group InfoObjects.

- **InfoProviders**
  Standard business content InfoProviders are available for a wide area of applications. These include InfoCubes, DataStores, and MultiProviders.

In addition, Business Content is available for objects that are used to load data, for example InfoSources, transformations, and data transfer processes. SAP also delivers the processes to control data loading using InfoPackages and process chains.

You can see that the process of setting up the SAP NetWeaver BW system is greatly facilitated by Business Content. Although Business Content may not be able to provide a solution for all of the analysis requirements of a business, it can be used as the starting point to prototype a solution. Business Content can subsequently be enhanced to meet the analysis requirements of specific users.

In the next section, we'll introduce objects created in the SAP BPC system.

2.5 Terminology and Objects in SAP BPC

In this section, we'll discuss some of the terminology used and some of the objects created in SAP BPC for NetWeaver. We'll also explain how a request to create an object in the planning and consolidation application translates into creating an equivalent object in the SAP NetWeaver BW system.

2.5.1 Terminology

We'll discuss objects that are configured in the SAP BPC system that would lay the foundation to carryout planning and consolidation functions.

Application Set

An *application set* is the starting point for creating any application in SAP BPC. It can be described as a functional area designed to include the applications associated with a segment of the business. For example, you can create an application set for sales applications and another application set for head-count planning.

Although the general objective of creating application sets is to support a business requirement (such as sales planning, production planning, head-count planning, etc.), there are no rules about what applications can be contained in an application set. It is left for you to decide how you want to model applications within an application set.

You create the application set via the Admin Console in the planning and consolidation application. You can only create a new application set using another application set as the basis. When the system is initially installed, an application set with the technical name AppShell is available. This serves as a reference for creating other application sets in the system. We recommend that you do *not* make any changes to AppShell; instead, use it to create a new application set and customize that application set for the application. You should have system administrator access to create an application set.

Dimensions

Dimensions represent the entities of a business (e.g., accounts, company codes, and categories); they represent the master, text, and hierarchy data for each of the business entities. Dimensions belong to the application set in which they are configured. It is very important to note that dimensions cannot be used or shared across application sets.

Secured Dimension

A dimension can be marked as secure for an application. When a dimension is marked as secure, specific read and write access has to be granted to users who use the application so they can access the data.

Properties

A dimension is designed to include *properties*, which provide additional meaning to the dimension. For example, an account dimension can include an *account type property* to indicate the type of account (whether it is an income account or an expense account). You can use property values can be used as a selection criterion for reporting.

Dimension Members

The data points associated with a dimension are referred to as *dimension members*. Each dimension member record represents master, text, and hierarchy data associated with the key of a dimension. A dimension member can store hierarchical relationships with another dimension member in the same dimension, which is very useful for reporting hierarchical relationships between data. There is no restriction on the number of hierarchies you can create.

Application

An application is a repository that consists of several dimensions and is used to meet your planning, consolidation, and reporting needs. The application is configured based on the specific needs of the business. It is where you interface to plan, consolidate, and report data.

Data Manager Package

SAP BPC provides standard out of the box functionality to execute common tasks required for planning and consolidation such as currency translation, intercompany elimination, and so on. These tasks are executed via a data manager package.

User

A user is an individual who can use the applications in an application set.

Team

A team is a group of users and is created based on the users' roles. For example, all of the developers can be grouped together and identified as a team.

Tasks

A number of activities that you can perform in SAP BPC are known as *tasks*. Examples of tasks are creating an application set, running a report, configuring security, and so on. Users are granted access to specific tasks based on their role in the organization.

Task Profile

Several tasks can be grouped together and included in a task profile. Task profiles can be assigned to a user or to a group of users in a team.

Member Access Profile

The member access profile identifies data-level access to an application and is relevant only for dimensions that were identified as secured dimensions in the application. For each application that includes dimensions marked as secured dimensions, the member access profile is configured to identify the read and write access available to users for each of the secured dimensions.

Business Rules

SAP BPC includes a rule-based table for defining certain common requirements for planning and consolidation. A company that has business operations in different countries may need to translate their data to one or more reporting currencies for financial reporting. The rules-based table provides a method for defining how local currencies should be translated to reporting currencies.

You can set up business rules for account transformations, carry forward balances, validating data, eliminating intercompany transactions, and setting up methods and rules for consolidation of investments.

Script Logic

Script logic is designed to provide greater flexibility in managing data for an application and includes SQL- and MDX-based programming structures for custom programming. You should attempt to leverage business rules before writing script logic to meet a requirement. Business rules provide a convenient table-based approach to define the rules for different conversions. But there may be business scenarios that cannot be satisfied using business rules; in these cases, script logic provides the means to achieve that objective.

Relationship Between Objects Created in SAP BPC and SAP NetWeaver BW

When objects are created in the SAP BPC system, the system creates equivalent objects in the SAP NetWeaver BW system. The corresponding objects created in the SAP NetWeaver BW system are shown in Table 2.1.

Object Created in SAP BusinessObjects Planning and Consolidation	Object Created in SAP NetWeaver BW
Application set	InfoArea An application set in SAP BPC is equivalent to an InfoArea in SAP NetWeaver BW. When a request for an application set is initiated in the SAP BPC frontend, an InfoArea is created in SAP NetWeaver BW with InfoObjects and InfoCubes under it. In SAP BPC, objects added under an application set are not shared across other application sets. In SAP NetWeaver BW, objects created under an InfoArea can be shared by objects in other InfoAreas.
Application	InfoCube An application in SAP BPC is created with respect to an application set and is used for storing transaction data. When a request for creating an application is initiated in SAP BPC, an InfoCube is created in SAP NetWeaver BW.
Dimension	InfoObject A dimension in SAP BPC is equivalent to an InfoObject in SAP NetWeaver BW. It is created under an application set and is used for storing master data. Examples include account, product, and customer dimensions.
Property	Attribute A property is equivalent to an attribute included in an InfoObject and is dependent on the dimension under which it is created. Example: A customer dimension may include a property called "customer group."
Dimension member	Master data record The dimension member is equivalent to master, text, and hierarchy data in SAP NetWeaver BW.

Table 2.1 Relationship Between Objects Created in SAP BPC and SAP NetWeaver BW

Object Created in SAP BusinessObjects Planning and Consolidation	Object Created in SAP NetWeaver BW
Master data to store text and hierarchy data	In SAP NetWeaver BW, an InfoObject should be enabled to store text and hierarchy data for an InfoObject.
	In SAP BPC, a property with the technical name DESCRIPTION is automatically created as a property when creating a dimension to store text data.
	In SAP BPC, you can create a hierarchy when entering data for a dimension in the Excel worksheet by including the column PARENT(Hn), where *n* is the number of hierarchies for the dimension.
Unsigned data	Key figure
	Only one type of object is used for recording quantitative values for transaction data in SAP BPC: unsigned data. This object is equivalent to a key figure in SAP NetWeaver BW.

Table 2.1 Relationship Between Objects Created in SAP BPC and SAP NetWeaver BW (Cont.)

2.6   Summary

In this chapter, we introduced the concepts and terminology used in SAP BPC, and you learned how organization can use the SAP BPC application to meet both their planning and consolidation requirements. You also studied the architecture of SAP BPC for NetWeaver and were introduced to some of the advantages of staging an SAP BPC application on an SAP NetWeaver platform. In addition, you learned about certain objects that are configured in the SAP BPC and SAP NetWeaver BW systems. In the next chapter, we'll discuss the details of configuring an application using SAP BPC.

This chapter shows you how to configure a financial planning application using SAP NetWeaver Business Warehouse and SAP BPC for NetWeaver systems. We introduce you to a case study that will serve as basis for creating this application.

3 Modeling an Application with SAP BPC for NetWeaver

In this chapter, we'll introduce you to a case study of a model company that has decided to plan its gross margin by implementing the NetWeaver version of SAP BusinessObjects Planning and Consolidation (BPC). The chapter explains the details of the company and how it wants to use the software for planning. The case study is also used as the basis for all planning and consolidation examples presented in subsequent chapters.

Section 3.1 will introduce you to a case study that we use to illustrate the key features of the NetWeaver version of SAP BPC. This case study explains the details of an organization, Rich Bloom, Inc., which uses the software for planning its gross margin.

Section 3.2 will explain the steps involved in modeling objects in SAP NetWeaver BW to meet the requirements of the case study. The objects created in SAP NetWeaver BW are used in this case as a staging environment to store data coming from a transactional source system, before being loaded into SAP BPC.

Section 3.3 will explain the steps involved in modeling objects in SAP BPC for NetWeaver to meet the requirements of the case study. This section serves as a solid foundation to understand the features of the tool.

3.1 Rich Bloom

Throughout this book, we'll use a sample company called Rich Bloom to explain the features of SAP BPC for NetWeaver. In this section, we'll discuss the case study to better understand the model company and the objectives the company is trying to meet using SAP BPC for NetWeaver.

3.1.1 Business

Rich Bloom is a clothing retailer headquartered in the United States with a presence in Germany and England. The company began its operations in 2000 and has seen its growth and profit increase rapidly due to its excellent management and operation of its business. It has been able to vary its mix of products and consistently exceed customer expectations.

In a recent survey, the company determined that the ongoing worldwide recession has caused a reduction in the amount people spend on clothing. This has energized the company to further strengthen its planning process so it can continue to grow and thrive under difficult business conditions.

3.1.2 Offices

The company's business is incorporated as follows:

▶ 20—Rich Bloom, Inc., San Diego, CA, USA

▶ 22—Rich Bloom Corporate, Inc., Philadelphia, PA, USA

▶ 23—Rich Bloom New Markets, Inc., Houston, TX, USA

▶ 25—Rich Bloom Ltd., London, UK

▶ 30—Rich Bloom AG, Frankfurt, Germany

3.1.3 Products

The company sells clothing for teenagers and preteens, including the following products:

▶ RB T-shirts

▶ RB shirts

▶ RB jackets

▶ RB designer jeans

▶ RB Apollo shirts

The company has partnerships with large wholesalers involved in the clothing business, through which it sells its products. Rich Bloom also has a few retail outlets in several key locations, through which it sells products directly to customers. It introduced the RB Apollo shirt in 2008, and this product has been very successful. It has found wide acceptance among teenagers and preteens, which has considerably increased profit forecasts.

The company is facing stiff competition to some of its products. Increased competition has stalled the sales growth of these products, and the company is looking to increase returns by improving the efficiency of its operations and by introducing product innovations to grow sales momentum.

3.1.4 Currency

The company operates in more than one country and has business transactions in multiple currencies. The currencies used for its operations are as follows:

- U.S. dollar
- British pound
- Euro

The company reports the financial transactions in one currency, U.S. dollars, because the company is headquartered in the United States.

3.1.5 Case Study

Rich Bloom has been using SAP ERP Central Component (ECC) for recording its business transactions. It has also been using SAP NetWeaver BW as its data warehousing system to analyze information and make decisions. Using these systems has helped the company manage its business quite efficiently.

However, Rich Bloom wants to streamline the planning function of the business. The company currently does not have a systematic planning process. The global recession and stiff competition have made management look into improving its efficiency of operations and creating a sound planning system. Management recognizes that having a good planning tool will help the company face competition and retain leadership in the market.

Rich Bloom wants to be able to compare plan data with actual data to see if it is able to meet what it set out to accomplish in the first place. The company has been using Excel spreadsheets to manage its planning process, but this has proved wanting in several respects. First, the Excel spreadsheet does not provide a unified tool for entering plans and monitoring the planning process, which has resulted in multiple versions of plans created on user desktops, making it difficult for the company to distinguish between the latest and older versions. Second, the process of consolidating plan data from different Excel spreadsheets takes considerable time, making the entire process inefficient. Third, Excel lacks security controls. All of this has prompted Rich Bloom to look at other tools for planning. Although users have become accustomed to planning using Excel, Rich Bloom is grappling with its limitations and with using it exclusively for planning.

Rich Bloom has decided it will use the recently introduced SAP BPC for NetWeaver for planning. First, this tool has an Excel-based frontend for planning, with which users are familiar. Second, Rich Bloom wants to leverage the SAP NetWeaver BW environment, which uses an enhanced star schema architecture to provide a superior user experience. Rich Bloom also believes that SAP BPC for NetWeaver is an advanced tool for planning that will provide a much needed edge in the difficult and competitive marketplace.

The company will use SAP BPC for NetWeaver to plan its gross margin for 2010, using the actual sales and cost data for 2009 as the basis to plan for 2010. It will maintain an InfoCube in SAP NetWeaver BW that contains actual sales and cost data, and the initial plan data for 2010 will be created by copying the actual sales and cost data for 2009 into the plan version for 2010. Subsequently, users will be able to manually change the sales and cost data to reflect current market conditions.

Management will consolidate, review, and approve the plan data. After the plan data is approved, no further changes will be allowed.

3.1.6 Decision to Use SAP BPC for NetWeaver

Rich Bloom has decided to use SAP BPC for NetWeaver for the following reasons:

▶ It wants to reduce the cycle time required to complete the planning process.

▶ It wants to overcome the limitations of Excel as a stand-alone tool for planning. With Excel, data cannot be stored in a database, and the tool does not provide a robust method of securing the data.

- Users are familiar with Excel for planning and analysis. The SAP BPC for NetWeaver frontend is based on Excel, so the company can tap this existing skill set to successfully manage its planning process.

- SAP BPC for NetWeaver provides users with role-based access to the data. This enables you to provide the appropriate level of access to users, based on their role in the planning process.

- Rich Bloom believes it can leverage existing actual sales and cost data currently available in SAP NetWeaver BW as the basis for planning. Actual data can be directly loaded into SAP BPC and can be used for planning.

- The company wants to leverage the already existing SAP NetWeaver BW environment to provide enhanced reporting to SAP BPC users.

You should now have an understanding of Rich Bloom's requirement to develop a planning application to project gross margin using SAP BPC for NetWeaver. In the next section, we'll develop objects in the SAP NetWeaver BW environment that will be used to stage actual sales and cost data coming from the SAP ERP system before being loaded into SAP BPC for NetWeaver.

3.2   Building the Data Model in SAP NetWeaver BW

As previously discussed, Rich Bloom wants to plan its gross margin for 2010 using actual sales and cost data from 2009. In this section, we'll discuss the development of the staging environment in SAP NetWeaver BW that will house the actual sales and cost data. This data will eventually be loaded into SAP BPC for NetWeaver to be used for planning.

Figure 3.1 displays the flow of data from SAP ERP to SAP NetWeaver BW and subsequently to SAP BPC for NetWeaver. An InfoCube called Sales that will be used as one of the sources of data for planning for the future will be created in SAP NetWeaver BW to store the actual sales and cost data for the last four years. Market research will also be used to forecast future demand, and the necessary adjustments will be made for future sales and costs. The data in the Sales InfoCube will be loaded with data from the SAP ERP system on a daily basis.

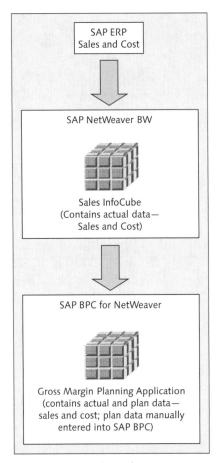

Figure 3.1 Flow of Data from SAP ECC to SAP BPC

We'll now build the objects necessary for storing the actual sales and cost data in SAP NetWeaver BW. The InfoObjects to be included in the Sales InfoCube are listed in the following tables and are SAP-delivered unless indicated by the words *custom InfoObject*.

▶ **Characteristics**
Table 3.1 lists the characteristics and their values.

▶ **Time characteristics**
Table 3.2 lists the time characteristics and their values.

Characteristics	Values
0COMP_CODE	20,22,23,25 AND 30
	20—Rich Bloom, Inc., San Diego, CA, USA
	22—Rich Bloom Corporate Inc., Philadelphia, PA, USA
	23—Rich Bloom New Markets Inc., Houston, TX, USA
	25—Rich Bloom Ltd., London, UK
	30—Rich Bloom AG, Frankfurt, Germany
0MATERIAL	CK2000,CK2001,CK2002, CY7000, RB_GN_PROD
	CK2000—T-shirts
	CK2001—Shirts
	CK2002—Jackets
	CK2003—Apollo Shirt
	CY7000—Jeans
	RB_GN_PROD—RB General Product
0CUSTOMER	C1-C4, C20-21, C30-31, RB_GN_CUS
	C1-C4—Customers in the U.S.
	C20-C21—Customers in the UK
	C30-C31—Customers in Germany
	RB_GN_CUS—RB General Customer
ZACCOUNT (Custom Characteristic)	Revenue, COGS, SGA and OVERHEADS
	REVENUE—Sales Revenue
	COGS—Cost of Goods Sold
	SGA—Sales, General and Administrative Expenses
	OVERHEADS—Corporate Expenses

Table 3.1 Characteristics and Values

Characteristics	Values
0CALMONTH	Calendar period for actual data
0CALYEAR	Calendar year for actual data

Table 3.2 Time Characteristics

▶ **Unit characteristics**

Table 3.3 lists the unit characteristics required.

Characteristics	Values
0CURRENCY	Used to store the currency associated with the amount value; used in key figure ZAMOUNT

Table 3.3 Unit Characteristics

▶ **Key figures**
Table 3.4 lists the key figures (quantitative measures) required for reporting.

Characteristics	Values
ZAMOUNT (Custom Key Figure)	Amount in local currency (key figure of type currency—associated with 0CURRENCY currency measure)

Table 3.4 Key Figures

3.2.1 Creating and Activating InfoObjects

Based on the requirements listed in the case study, we'll now start building the necessary objects. The InfoObjects listed in the previous tables are required for building the data model; most of them have a technical name that starts with 0. These are SAP-supplied InfoObjects. But before an InfoObject that is delivered by SAP can be used, it must be activated. We'll start by checking the status of InfoObjects and learn how to activate them if they are not yet active.

Checking the Status of an SAP-Supplied InfoObject

As illustrated in Figure 3.2, the following are the steps to check the status of an SAP-supplied InfoObject:

1. Open the EDIT INFOOBJECTS: START window using Transaction RSD1.

2. Under TYPE, select CHARACTERISTIC, and next to VERSION, select ACTIVE/REVISED (Figure 3.2, ❶ and ❷).

3. In the text field next to INFOOBJECT, enter the name of the InfoObject to check (Figure 3.2, ❸).

4. Click on the DISPLAY button (Figure 3.2, ❹).

If the InfoObject is not yet active, the following message is displayed in the status bar of the window: "Enter valid Characteristic ..."

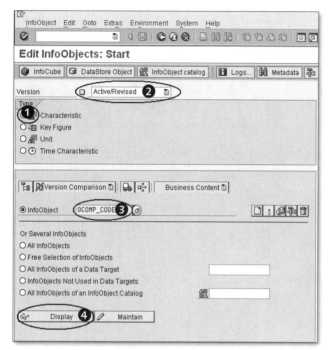

Figure 3.2   Checking the Status of an InfoObject

Activating an SAP-Supplied InfoObject

By default, none of the SAP-supplied InfoObjects are active, so we'll start by activating them. The process, illustrated in Figures 3.3, 3.4, and 3.5, is as follows:

1. Open the DATA WAREHOUSING WORKBENCH: BI CONTENT window using Transaction RSA1.

2. In the left pane, select OBJECT TYPES (Figure 3.3, ❶).

3. In the right pane, under GROUPING, select ONLY NECESSARY OBJECTS. For COLLECTION MODE, select COLLECT AUTOMATICALLY (Figure 3.3, ❷ and ❸).

4. Under INFOOBJECT, double-click on SELECT OBJECTS (Figure 3.3, ❹). This opens the INPUT HELP FOR METADATA dialog box.

5. In the INPUT HELP FOR METADATA dialog box, select all of the SAP-delivered InfoObjects that need to be activated for the case study, as outlined in Tables 3.1, 3.2, and 3.3.

6. When finished, click on TRANSFER SELECTIONS (Figure 3.4, ❺).

7. In the DATA WAREHOUSING WORKBENCH: BI CONTENT window, under INSTALL, select INSTALL to activate the InfoObject (Figure 3.5, ❻).

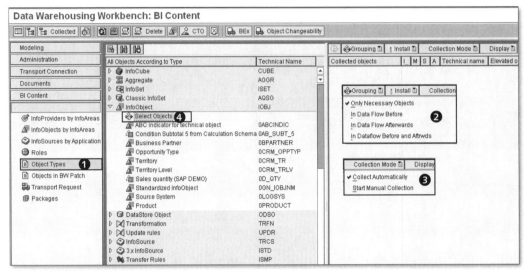

Figure 3.3 Settings to Activate an InfoObject

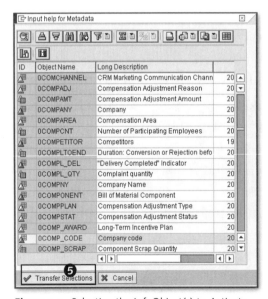

Figure 3.4 Selecting the InfoObject(s) to Activate

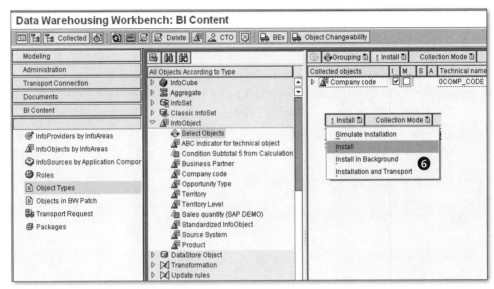

Figure 3.5 Activating an InfoObject

After you're done activating the SAP-supplied InfoObjects, you'll need to create and activate the custom InfoObjects needed for the case study, as outlined in Tables 3.1 and 3.4. Let's take a closer look at how to do this.

Creating and Activating a Custom Characteristic InfoObject

We'll start by creating the InfoObject ZACCOUNT (Account), as illustrated in Figures 3.5 and 3.6. This InfoObject should be a characteristic InfoObject.

1. Open the EDIT INFOOBJECTS: START window using Transaction RSD1.

2. Under TYPE, select CHARACTERISTIC (Figure 3.6, ❶).

3. In the text field next to the INFOOBJECT option, enter the technical name of the InfoObject ("Account") and click on the CREATE button (Figure 3.6, ❷ and ❸).

4. In the CREATE CHARACTERISTIC dialog box, in the LONG DESCRIPTION text field, enter a description ("Account"), and then click on the ENTER button (Figure 3.6, ❹ and ❺).

5. On the GENERAL tab of the CREATE CHARACTERISTIC <INFOOBJECT_NAME>: DETAILS window, specify the SHORT DESCRIPTION ("Account"), DATA TYPE ("CHAR"), and LENGTH ("13") (Figure 3.7, ❻, ❼, and ❽).

6. No attributes are required for this InfoObject, so you can click on ACTIVATE (Figure 3.7, ❾).

The ZACCOUNT InfoObject is now saved and activated.

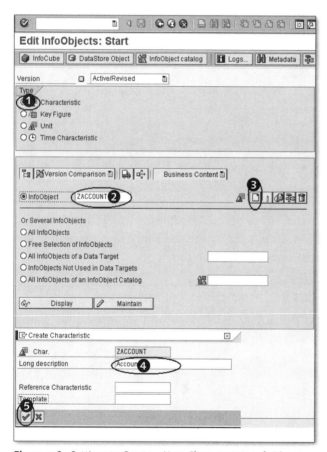

Figure 3.6 Settings to Create a New Characteristic InfoObject

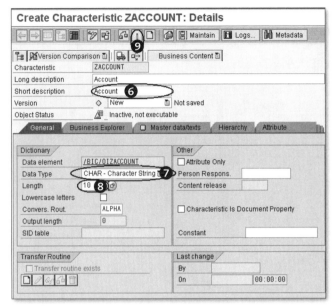

Figure 3.7 Activating a Custom InfoObject

Using a similar process, you'll now need to create and activate the remaining required custom InfoObjects, ZAMOUNT. Let's get started.

Creating a Custom Key Figure InfoObject

> **Note**
>
> You should activate the SAP-delivered unit currency InfoObject, 0CURRENCY, before creating the custom key figure.

We'll now create a custom key figure InfoObject, as illustrated in Figures 3.7 and 3.8. The technical name of the InfoObject is ZAMOUNT.

1. Open the EDIT INFOOBJECTS: START window using Transaction RSD1.

2. Under TYPE, select KEY FIGURE (Figure 3.8, ❶).

3. In the text field next to the INFOOBJECT option, enter the technical name of the InfoObject ("ZAMOUNT") and click on the CREATE button (Figure 3.8, ❷ and ❸).

4. In the CREATE KEYFIGURE dialog box, in the LONG DESCRIPTION text field, enter a description ("Amount") and then click on the ENTER button (Figure 3.8, ❹ and ❺).

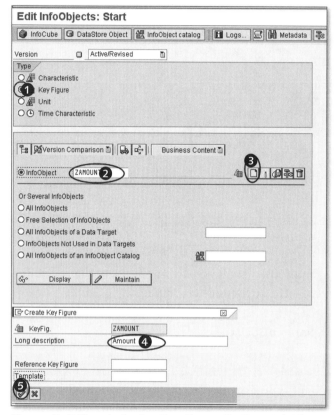

Figure 3.8 Settings to Create a New Custom KeyFigure InfoObject

5. In the CREATE KEY FIGURE <INFOOBJECT_NAME>: DETAILS window, enter a SHORT DESCRIPTION ("Amount") (Figure 3.9, ❻).

6. On the TYPE/UNIT tab, select AMOUNT and then select CURR—CURRENCY FIELD, STORED AS DEC (Figure 3.9, ❼ and ❽).

7. Per the requirements, the ZAMOUNT InfoObject should be attached to the 0CURRENCY InfoObject. So under CURRENCY/UNIT OF MEASURE, select 0CURRENCY (Figure 3.9, ❾).

8. Click on Activate (Figure 3.9, ❿). The ZAMOUNT InfoObject is now saved and activated.

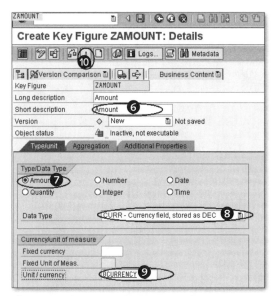

Figure 3.9 Settings to Create a New Custom KeyFigure InfoObject (ZAMOUNT)

Populating Master Data

The next step in the process is to load master data for InfoObjects with the values listed in the reference table for the characteristic values (Table 3.1). As we have mentioned before, master data can be populated from a variety of sources: an SAP R/3 system, a flat-file system, an Oracle Database system using DB Connect, and so on.

In this example, because there are only a few records in the master data table, we'll manually enter the values for the characteristics, but normally, the master data would be populated from a source system.

We now manually enter the data for the Company Code InfoObject (0COMP_CODE), as illustrated in Figures 3.10 and 3.11.

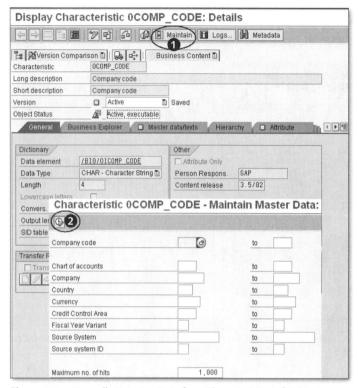

Figure 3.10 Manually Entering Data for a Characteristic InfoObject

1. Open the EDIT INFOOBJECTS: START window using Transaction RSD1.

2. Specify the InfoObject by entering its name ("0COMP_CODE") or selecting it from the dropdown list. Then click on the DISPLAY button.

3. In the DISPLAY CHARACTERISTIC <INFOOBJECT_NAME>: DETAILS window, click on MAINTAIN to create or modify data for this InfoObject (Figure 3.10, ❶).

4. In the CHARACTERISTIC <INFOOBJECT_NAME>—MAINTAIN MASTER DATA: LIST window, click on the EXECUTE button (Figure 3.10, ❷).

5. In the CHARACTERISTIC <INFOOBJECT_NAME>—MAINTAIN MASTER DATA: LIST window, click on CREATE to create a new record (Figure 3.11, ❸). Enter a value for the COMPANY CODE InfoObject ("20"), as listed in Table 3.1.

6. Click on the ENTER button (Figure 3.11, ❹), and then click on the SAVE button (Figure 3.11, ❺).

7. Follow steps 1 through 6 outlined here to insert master data for the other characteristics listed in Table 3.1.

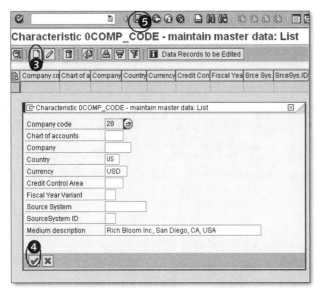

Figure 3.11 Manually Inserting a New Record for an InfoObject

Applying the Hierarchy/Attribute Change Process

When you create a new record in the master data table, no action is necessary for the changes to become effective. But any changes to an existing record require that you run the Apply Hierarchy/Attribute Change process, as follows and as illustrated in Figure 3.12.

1. Open the Data Warehousing Workbench using Transaction RSA1.

2. Select TOOLS • APPLY HIERARCHY/ATTRIBUTE CHANGE from the menu.

3. In the EXECUTE HIERARCHY/ATTRIBUTE CHANGES FOR REPORTING window, click on INFOOBJECT LIST to identify the characteristic InfoObjects that have undergone a change since the last change run (Figure 3.12, ❶).

4. Select the InfoObjects for which the changes to data should apply and click on SAVE (Figure 3.12, ❷ and ❸). InfoObjects that are displayed here but are not selected for the change run will not reflect the latest changes made to the data when reporting.

5. After you click on SAVE, the system automatically assigns a job name, and you're taken back to the EXECUTE HIERARCHY/ATTRIBUTE CHANGES FOR REPORTING window.

6. Click on the EXECUTE button (Figure 3.12, ❹).

7. Click on the REFRESH button to confirm that the changes have been activated. The CHANGE STATUS is displayed at the top of the table (Figure 3.12, ❺).

You can schedule the Apply Hierarchy/Attribute Change process from this location to run at selected times. You can also schedule it based on an event by clicking on the SELECTION button (Figure 3.12, ❻) in the EXECUTE HIERARCHY/ATTRIBUTE CHANGES FOR REPORTING window and then making the appropriate selections.

Subsequent events can be triggered following successful or unsuccessful completions of the change run.

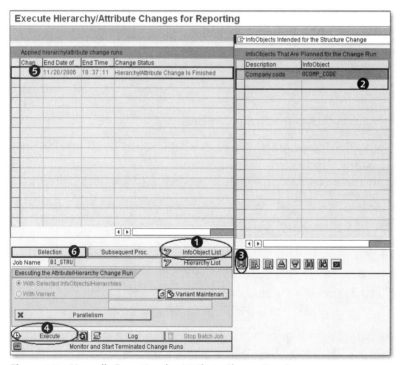

Figure 3.12 Manually Executing the Attribute Change Run Process

3.2.2 Creating an InfoArea

Now that you've created the InfoObjects, the next step is to create an InfoArea that will later contain InfoCubes. An InfoArea lets you group InfoProviders together.

The following are the steps to create an InfoArea, as illustrated in Figure 3.13:

1. Open the Data Warehousing Workbench using Transaction RSA1.

2. Select MODELING • INFOPROVIDER.

3. Right-click on INFOPROVIDER and select CREATE INFOAREA (Figure 3.13, ❶).

4. In the CREATE INFOAREA section, in the INFOAREA text field, enter the technical name for the InfoArea ("ZSALES"). In the LONG DESCRIPTION field, enter a description ("Sales Management") (Figure 3.13, ❷).

5. Click on ENTER (Figure 3.13, ❸).

Figure 3.13 Create an InfoArea

3.2.3 Creating a Sales InfoCube

Now that you've created an InfoArea, the next step is to create the Sales InfoCubes under it, as shown in Table 3.5.

InfoCube	Description
ZSLS_ACT	Sales Actual InfoCube

Table 3.5 InfoCube for Storing Actual Sales Data

This section explains how to create the Sales InfoCube based on the requirements listed earlier in Tables 3.1, 3.2, 3.3, and 3.4. Table 3.6 and Table 3.7 show the dimensions and key figures used in the Sales InfoCube.

Dimensions	Characteristics
Company	Company Code (0COMP_CODE)
Material	Material (0MATERIAL)
Customer	Customer (0CUSTOMER)
Account	Account (ZACCOUNT)
Time	Calendar Month (0CALMONTH)
	Calendar Year (0CALYEAR)
Unit	Currency (0CURRENCY)

Table 3.6 Dimensions for the Sales InfoCube

Key Figures	Description
ZAMOUNT	Amount in Local Currency

Table 3.7 Key Figures for the Sales InfoCube

The following are the steps and concepts you should follow to create the Sales InfoCube. The discussion includes creating dimensions and assigning characteristic InfoObjects to dimensions and assigning key figures to the key figure folder. This process is illustrated in Figures 3.14, 3.15, 3.16, 3.17, and 3.18. Let's get started.

1. Open the Data Warehousing Workbench using Transaction RSA1.

2. Select MODELING • INFOPROVIDER.

3. Right-click on the SALES MANAGEMENT InfoArea you created earlier and select CREATE INFOCUBE from the context menu (see Figure 3.14, ❶).

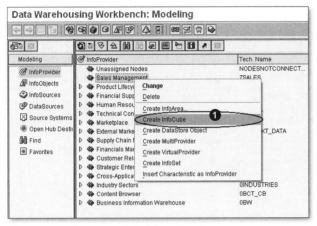

Figure 3.14 Creating an InfoCube—Part A

4. The EDIT INFOCUBE window appears (Figure 3.15). Enter the technical name of the InfoCube ("ZSLS_ACT"), and the long description ("Sales actual") into the text fields next to INFOCUBE. Make sure you've selected STANDARD INFOCUBE under INFOPROVIDER TYPE. Then click on ENTER (Figure 3.15, ❷, ❸, and ❹).

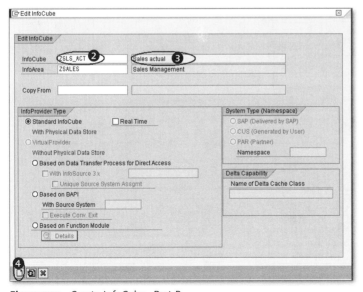

Figure 3.15 Create InfoCube—Part B

5. The EDIT INFOCUBE window appears (Figure 3.16). Notice that the system automatically creates the data package, time, and unit dimensions.

6. Create a new dimension by right-clicking on DIMENSIONS and selecting CRE-ATE NEW DIMENSIONS (Figure 3.16, **❺**). The technical ID of the dimension is automatically assigned and cannot be changed, but the description of the dimension *can* be changed.

7. In the CREATE DIMENSIONS window, enter a description for the dimension ("Account") (see Figure 3.16, **❻**).

8. Click on the CREATE button (Figure 3.16, **❼**). This creates the dimension and then opens the CREATE DIMENSIONS window again.

9. Enter the description for the next dimension ("Company").

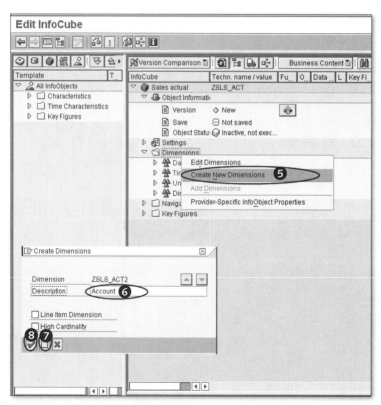

Figure 3.16 Create InfoCube—Part C

10. Repeat steps 8 and 9 to create the remaining dimensions for the Sales InfoCube that are specified in Table 3.6. They are:

   ▸ Material

   ▸ Customer

   ▸ Account

11. Click on ENTER when you're finished (Figure 3.16, ❽).

Note

You can create up to 13 user-defined dimensions in an InfoCube.

You've now created the dimensions needed for the Sales InfoCube. The next task is to assign characteristic InfoObjects to dimensions and key figure InfoObjects to the KEY FIGURES folder. Similar characteristics are grouped under one dimension. You can directly assign an InfoObject to a dimension or the KEY FIGURES folder (using the INFOOBJECT DIRECT INPUT option), as we'll show in the following steps:

1. Right-click on the DIMENSIONS or KEY FIGURES folder, and select INFOOBJECT DIRECT INPUT (Figure 3.17, ❾).

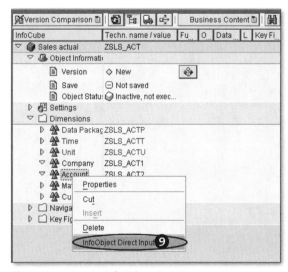

Figure 3.17 Create InfoCube—Part D

2. In the INSERT INFOOBJECTS window, select the InfoObjects you want to include in the dimension (Figure 3.18, ❿ and ⓫) or the key figures you want to include in the KEY FIGURES folder (not illustrated) and click on ENTER.

Assign the following InfoObjects to the dimensions:

▶ Dimension 1 (Company)—0COMP_CODE

▶ Dimension 2 (Account)—ZACCOUNT

▶ Dimension 3 (Material)—0MATERIAL

▶ Dimension 4 (Customer)—0CUSTOMER

▶ Time Dimension—0CALYEAR and 0CALMONTH

Assign the following key figure to the KEY FIGURES folder:

▶ ZAMOUNT

For key figures that are of the data types Quantity or Currency, the corresponding unit/currency measure associated with the key figure is automatically added to the unit dimension.

Figure 3.18   Create InfoCube—Part E

> **Note**
>
> An alternative way exists to include InfoObjects in a DIMENSIONS or KEY FIGURES folder. If the InfoObjects required for the InfoCube are in an InfoSource, DataStore, InfoCube, or InfoObject catalog, select the corresponding template in the left pane of the EDIT INFOCUBE window. Here, you can also select the INFOOBJECTS ALL template. This option lets you display all characteristic and key figure InfoObjects. Drag an InfoObject from the template to the preferred DIMENSIONS or KEY FIGURES folder.

The InfoCube is now ready to be saved and activated. Click on ACTIVATE to activate the InfoCube (Figure 3.19, ⓬).

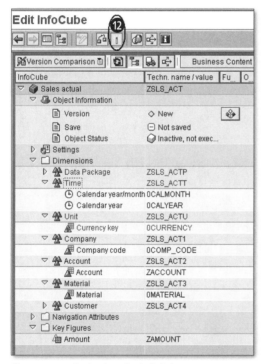

Figure 3.19 Activating the InfoCube

We have now created the InfoCube to store actual sales and cost data in the SAP NetWeaver BW system. We'll discuss how to load data into this InfoCube in Chapter 4. In the next section, we'll configure the objects required for this case study in the SAP BPC system.

3.3 Building Applications in SAP BPC

In this section, we'll teach you how to configure an application in SAP BPC. This application contains actual and plan data related to sales and costs. Rich Bloom requires the following pieces of data in the application to be able to plan effectively:

▶ Account

  ▶ Account ID

  ▶ Description

  ▶ Account type (income account, expense account, etc.)

  ▶ Rate type (average, year end, etc., to indicate the rate to use for currency translation)

▶ Entity

  ▶ Entity ID (the company ID)

  ▶ Description

  ▶ Currency (the currency the company uses)

▶ Category

  ▶ Category ID (denotes the nature of data—actual, budget, etc.)

  ▶ Description

  ▶ Year

▶ Time

  ▶ Time ID

  ▶ Description

▶ Currency

  ▶ Currency ID (the currency associated with the transaction)

  ▶ Description

  ▶ Reporting (indicator used for currency translation)

▶ Product

  ▶ Product ID

  ▶ Description

- ► Customer
  - ► Customer ID
  - ► Description
- ► Data source
- ► Quantitative measure (amount/quantity) — also called SIGNEDDATA

We must create dimensions for all of the characteristics listed. A *dimension* is a type of object that is used to build an application. It represents the master data associated with any characteristic. For example, the Entity dimension represents the different company codes and their descriptions. The key to any dimension is referred to as an ID, and each record that the ID identifies in a dimension is called a *dimension member*. In addition, *properties* can be described to provide meaning to the dimension member.

The SIGNEDDATA field is automatically available in all applications to store quantitative information. This field contains either quantity or amount information. An application has only this field to store quantitative data; the Account dimension qualifies the data in the SIGNEDDATA field. So you can see how SAP BPC uses the account-based data model, where there is only one key figure in an application that is qualified by the information in the Account dimension.

For this case study, we'll use two applications, one to store actual and plan data and the other to maintain currency exchange rates. Because Rich Bloom does business in more than one country and uses different currencies, we'll use a rate application that can be used to convert amounts from the local currency to the reporting currency.

We'll now review the steps of creating an application in SAP BPC.

3.3.1 Accessing the SAP BPC System

Recall the discussion from the last chapter about the architecture of SAP BPC for SAP NetWeaver. The SAP BPC client interface must be installed on every developer's computer. The Admin Console is the central interface for building applications in SAP BPC. Developers use this tool developers to configure and maintain applications.

Let's see how to access the SAP BPC system from the Admin Console. The following steps explain the process for logging in to the SAP BPC system from the Admin Console:

1. When the client interface for SAP BPC is installed on your computer, you can see the ADMIN CONSOLE icon. Double-click on it (Figure 3.20, ❶).

2. Click on CONNECTION WIZARD to connect to the SAP BPC application server (Figure 3.20, ❷).

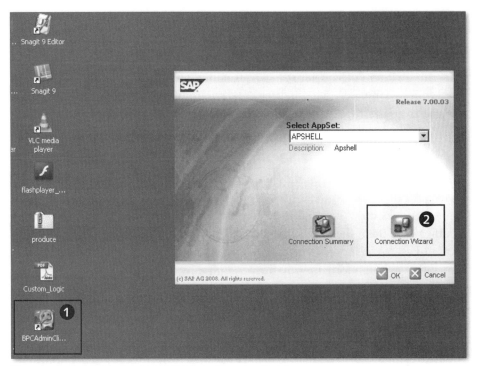

Figure 3.20 Accessing the SAP BPC Admin Console—Part A

3. Enter the name of the server to connect to under BPC SERVER NAME (Figure 3.21, ❸). Under CONNECTION OPTIONS, select the option that is applicable for your installation, and then click on NEXT (Figure 3.21, ❹ and ❺).

4. Select USE A DIFFERENT USER ID AND PASSWORD (Figure 3.22, ❻). Then enter your user ID, password, and domain name for the SAP BPC system to which you are connecting. Click on NEXT (Figure 3.22, ❼, ❽, ❾, and ❿).

5. The SAP BPC server, user name, password, and domain name are authenticated, and you are prompted to select an application set from the dropdown list. In Figure 3.23, ⓫, the APSHELL application set has been selected. Click on NEXT to access the selected application set (Figure 3.23, ⓬).

The application sets you see in the dropdown list are governed by your security access to the application set. If you do not see an application set, you do not have authorization to access it.

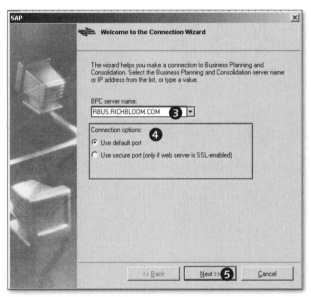

Figure 3.21 Accessing the SAP BPC Admin Console—Part B

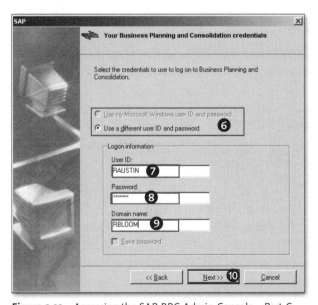

Figure 3.22 Accessing the SAP BPC Admin Console—Part C

Figure 3.23 Accessing the BPC Admin Console — Part D

You've now seen how to log into the SAP BPC system from the Admin Console and how to access an application set. Before we create new application sets, we'll discuss the key features of application sets and how to use them.

3.3.2 Application Set

The first step in building an application in SAP BPC is creating an application set (also known as an *appset*). An *application set* is designed to contain the applications for a given functional area; for example, one application set can be created exclusively for sales planning applications; another can be created for head-count planning applications. You cannot build a new application set from scratch; you always copy it from an existing application set. In this context, it is important to note that dimensions and dimensions members within an application set are not shared with other application sets.

One of the steps in the installation of an SAP BPC system is the installation of an application set with the technical name ApShell. This is the only application set that is available when the system is first created. This special application set comes with the standard dimensions and includes sample applications for planning and currency exchange translation. We do not recommend making any changes to the

ApShell application set; it should only be used as a reference or basis to create a new application set. The dimensions and applications included in ApShell are loaded with sample data, so it serves as a good reference point to understand how applications are built in SAP BPC.

When you create an application set, the application definitions are copied from the source application set to the new application set. When you copy one application set to another, a flag is available that provides the option to copy application data from the source application set to the new application set. If this flag is not selected, only the application definition is copied. If this flag is selected, the data from the source application set is copied to the new application set. Several options are available when you create a new application set; they are used to indicate the type of data you want to copy from the source application set to the new application set, and they are:

▶ Database records

▶ Content library

▶ Live reports

▶ Journals

> **Note**
>
> When an application set is created, the dimension members are automatically copied from the source application set.

Only a user with system administrator access can create and maintain application sets. When a request for the creation of a new application set is initiated in the SAP BPC system, a background job is scheduled in the SAP NetWeaver BW system. The background job creates all of the necessary objects, including InfoObjects and InfoCubes, based on the options selected in SAP BPC when initiating this request. You can also choose to have the data copied from the source application set to the new application set. Certain parameters can be set for an application set; we'll discuss these in Chapter 7 when we discuss the web interface for SAP BPC.

So far, you've seen how to access the Admin Console and log into the SAP BPC system to access an application set. We'll now discuss the process of creating a new application set.

Creating an Application Set

Our case study requires us to build an application for gross margin planning, which we do by using ApShell as the source. To create a new application set, proceed as follows:

1. Follow the steps listed in Section 3.3.1 to log into the SAP BPC system and to access the ApShell application set (Figure 3.24). The left pane lists the available options for maintaining and managing an application set. We'll discuss some of these options in this chapter and others in following chapters. The options displayed in the middle-right pane display context-sensitive menus based on the option selected in the left pane. For example, APSHELL is selected in the left pane (see Figure 3.24, ❶), so the action menu associated with an application set is displayed in the right pane. The lower-right pane (Figure 3.24), under AVAIL-ABLE INTERFACES, lists the additional tools used in SAP BPC for development and reporting. We'll discuss each of these tools later.

2. Click on the APSHELL application set, as shown in Figure 3.24, ❶).

3. The context-sensitive middle-right pane displays the various options for managing an application set. Click on ADD A NEW APPLICATION SET (see Figure 3.24, ❷).

Figure 3.24 Creating an Application Set—Part A

4. Enter the technical name ("ZRB_GM_PLAN") and description ("Gross Margin Planning") for the new application set (Figure 3.25, ❸ and ❹). Select the application set you want to use as the source for creating the new application set; in this case, select APSHELL from the dropdown list (Figure 3.25, ❺). Then click on GO TO NEXT STEP 2 OF 2 (Figure 3.25, ❻).

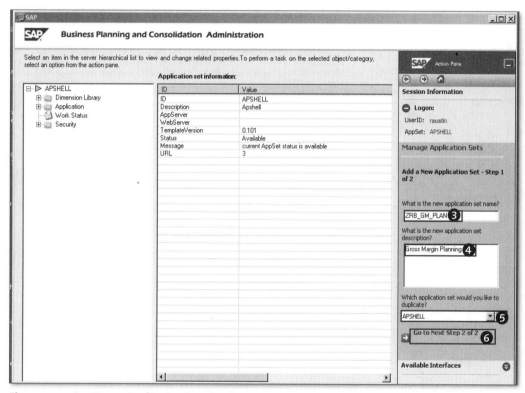

Figure 3.25 Creating an Application Set—Part B

5. Select the options you want to use for copying data from the source application set (Figure 3.26, ❼). When DATABASE RECORDS is selected, the application data is also copied to the new application set. For our case study, we'll deselect this option. Click on ADD A NEW APPLICATION SET (Figure 3.26, ❽). The SAP BPC system schedules a background job in the SAP NetWeaver BW system to create the objects and displays a status message to indicate that the new application set has been created successfully (Figure 3.26, ❾).

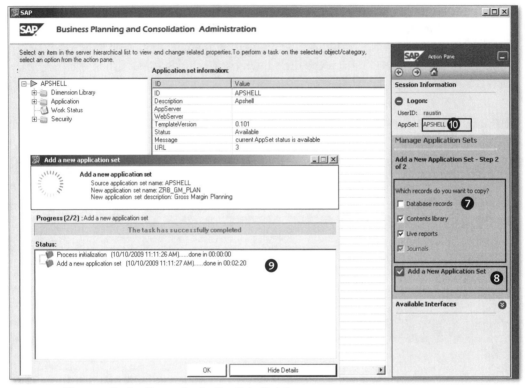

Figure 3.26 Creating an Application Set—Part C

Even though you've created a new application set, the session information continues to show the APSHELL application set, because you're signed on to this application set. To access the new application set, ZRB_GM_PLAN, click on APSHELL, as shown in Figure 3.26, ⑩. This takes you to the SAP BPC connection screen. But at this point, the new application set is still not available for you to select from the dropdown list; first, you must connect to the new application set using the Connection Wizard. After you've successfully connected to the new application set, it will be available in the dropdown box for subsequent logons. Refer to Figure 3.27, ⑪.

You should now understand how to create a new application set. We'll use the new application set we created for building the dimensions and applications for our case study.

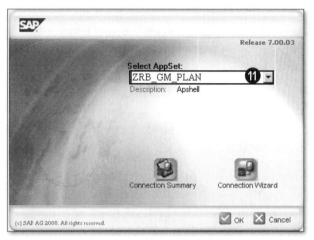

Figure 3.27 Creating an Application Set—Part D

Application Set Tasks

The following actions can be executed for a given application set:

▶ **Set availability of application set**
You can set an application set to NOT AVAILABLE by selecting the SET APPLICATION STATUS option in the action pane. A user who is not a system administrator in SAP BPC cannot access any application in the application set when the status of an application set is set to NOT AVAILABLE. An information message can be added to provide more information to users about this status, which is particularly useful when maintenance on the application set is in progress. The message can provide an estimate of when the application set will be back and when users can log back on.

▶ **Set template version**
SAP BPC lets you create and maintain standard templates specific to application sets for reporting. When changes are made to the standard templates, you can refresh them immediately. To do this, update the client cache and set a higher version by selecting SET TEMPLATE VERSION in the action pane.

▶ **Refresh client-side dimension files**
When you log into the application set, the dimension data is automatically updated and refreshed in the client cache. When dimension members or properties are updated, you can immediately refresh them by selecting REFRESH CLIENT SIDE DIMENSION FILES in the action pane.

▶ **Delete application set**

You can delete an application set by selecting DELETE AN APPLICATION SET in the action pane. When an application set is deleted, all of the objects under the application set are also deleted. Exercise caution when deleting an application set—it cannot be recovered.

▶ **Monitor user activity**

You can monitor the activity associated with an application set by selecting the USER ACTIVITY option in the action pane.

You should now have an understanding of how to create an application set and of the tasks associated with application sets. Next, we'll discuss how to use dimensions in SAP BPC.

3.3.3 Dimensions

Dimensions are the building blocks used in creating an SAP BPC application; they describe the elements of the business. Examples of dimensions are Account, Entity, Time, Customer, and Product. Note the following points related to dimensions:

▶ Dimensions are always created within an application set and can only be used in that application set. A dimension created in an application set cannot be shared or used in another application set.

▶ The name of a dimension can be a maximum of 16 characters.

▶ Dimensions can include properties. For example, the Account dimension can include a property called Account Type. Properties can be used as filter criteria for selections in reports. The length of a property can be set to any number. When the length of a property exceeds 60 characters, it is not available for selection when creating reports.

▶ The properties for a dimension can be classified under three distinct types:

  ▶ User-defined: These are properties the user defines for a dimension. For example, the Customer dimension can include a property called Country that indicates the customer's country.

  ▶ Reserved property: These are system-defined properties that are delivered with dimensions. The EvDescription property is automatically created for every dimension and stores the description for each of the IDs associated with a dimension. The scaling and format properties are system-supplied properties for the Account dimension.

▶ Hidden property: These are properties that are not visible but that the SAP BPC system uses internally.

▶ SAP BPC provides standard dimensions for planning and consolidation functions. Table 3.8 lists the types of dimensions available in SAP BPC.

Dimension Type	Examples
Category	Plan Version, Actual
Account	GL Account or Statistical Codes
Time	Calendar Months or Fiscal Periods
Entity	Company Code
Currency	Local or Reporting Currency
Data Source	Manual, Automatic
Inter Company	Trading Partner
Sub Tables	Flow Dimension—Opening Balance
User Defined	Customer, Product

Table 3.8 Dimension Types

▶ The Account, Category, Entity, and Time dimensions are required in all applications. A dimension type cannot be used more than once in an application; for example, an application cannot include more than one Entity dimension.

▶ When you create a new dimension, the dimension type is associated with it. The default properties of the dimension type are available in the new dimension. You can then add custom properties to the dimension.

▶ You can copy a new dimension from an existing dimension. When you copy a dimension, all of the dimension members from the source dimension, along with its properties, are also copied to the new dimension.

▶ You can modify a dimension to either include new properties or delete existing properties.

▶ You can delete a dimension, provided it is not included in any of the applications in the application set.

▶ In SAP BPC, when you create a dimension, the system creates an equivalent InfoObject with corresponding attributes.

▶ You can set security to restrict users' read and write access, based on specific values of a dimension. The security is set for each application. We'll explain how this is done when we discuss the security features in SAP BPC.

▶ Data in dimensions is referred to as *dimension members*. The key for the dimension is called the ID. The maximum length of the ID is 20 characters, and it is case-sensitive. You cannot rename the ID member value of a dimension once it is saved.

▶ You can add dimension data into a dimension via the Admin Console. A member sheet is available to enter data for a dimension.

▶ When you maintain dimension members, you must run the Process dimension to make the modified data available. When you request the Process dimension option, the SAP BPC system schedules an *attribute change run* for the corresponding InfoObject in the SAP NetWeaver BW system. This process activates the data and makes the modified data available in the SAP BPC application.

▶ A set of selected dimensions constitutes an application. You can select the dimensions required for an application when creating the application.

Reference Dimensions

The purpose of *reference dimensions* is to support the validation of member values that you can enter in the property of a dimension. Table 3.9 details the properties of dimensions belonging to a particular type that are validated based on values of members in the reference dimension.

Dimension Type	Property Name in Dimension	Reference Dimension	Reference Attribute Name
A—Account	Rate Type	A—ACCOUNT	ID
C—Category	Year	T—Time	Year
E—Entity	Currency	R—Currency	ID
I—Inter Company	Entity	E—Entity	ID

Table 3.9 Reference Dimension

Hierarchies in Dimensions

Certain applications require the use of a hierarchy. The data in dimensions such as Entity, Account and Time are structured in hierarchies. For example, you may want to setup separate legal and management trees for entities. You can do this using hierarchies, and SAP BPC lets you create any number of hierarchies for a dimension. You can create a hierarchy by adding a new column, called ParentH(n), where *n* represents the hierarchy in the Excel member sheet.

The rules for using hierarchies are as follows:

▶ The Excel member sheet is available for maintaining dimension member data. The system does not allow a hierarchy with ParentH3 to be created if ParentH1 and ParentH2 do not exist.

▶ The values in the hierarchy column should be valid dimension members as well.

▶ A parent in SAP BPC must have the same children if it is reused across multiple hierarchies.

Dimension Formulas

Dimension formulas automate the process of calculations in SAP BPC. A dimension can include a special property called a formula. This is used in particular in the Account dimension. Let's, for example, consider a scenario where you have entered the quantity and price for a product independently. You may want to calculate the revenue as *quantity × price*. This is possible using dimension formulas. To achieve this, you should include a property called Formula in the dimension.

When a formula is created, the calculation is automatically effected for all applications in the application set that contains the dimension. When this formula is used in reports, situations could occur with conflicts in the calculation of the formula. In this case, SOLVEORDER determines the sequence of how the formula should be calculated.

Displaying Dimension Properties and Member Data

We'll now explain how to review the properties of a dimension and display the members of a dimension. First, let's review the properties and members for the P_ACCT dimension.

1. Under DIMENSION LIBRARY in the left pane, click on the P_ACCT dimension (Figure 3.28, ❶). The middle-right pane lists the tasks associated with a dimension. Click on MAINTAIN DIMENSION PROPERTY (Figure 3.28, ❷) to view the properties. After reviewing the properties, click on the P_Acct dimension again to return to the previous screen.

2. The properties for the P_ACCT dimension are displayed (Figure 3.29, ❸). Click on the P_ACCT dimension to go back to the previous screen (Figure 3.29, ❹).

3. Click on MAINTAIN DIMENSION MEMBERS in the right pane (Figure 3.28, ❺ to display the DIMENSION MEMBERS (Figure 3.30). The member IDs and their descriptions are displayed (Figure 3.30, ❻ and ❼). Member IDs are case-sensitive. Hierarchies can be defined by using the convention ParentH(n) in the column headings, where n is the hierarchy number. The hierarchy for P_ACCT is displayed (Figure 3.30, ❽).

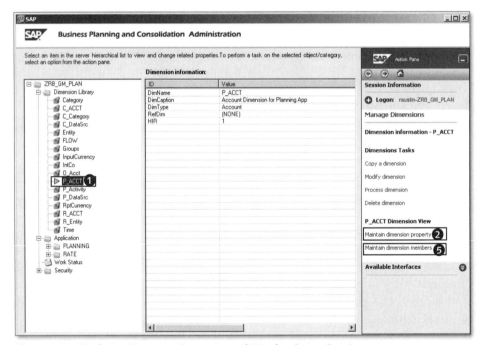

Figure 3.28 Displaying Dimension Properties and Member Data—Part A

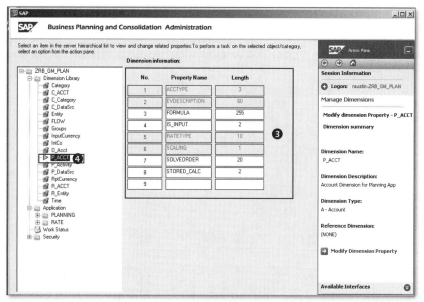

Figure 3.29 Displaying Dimension Properties and Member Data—Part B

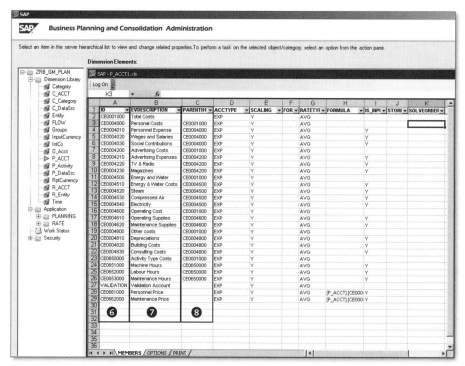

Figure 3.30 Displaying Dimension Properties and Member Data—Part C

Copying a Dimension

We'll now explain how to create a new dimension by copying from an existing dimension. Our case study requires us to maintain the following dimensions for the planning application:

▶ RB_ACCOUNT

▶ RB_CATEGORY

▶ RB_ENTITY

▶ RB_PRODUCT

▶ RB_CUTOMER

▶ RB_DATASRC

▶ RPTCURRENCY

▶ Time

We'll start by creating the RB_ACCOUNT dimension by copying it from the P_ACCT dimension. When you copy a dimension, the members of the source dimension are copied to the new target dimension.

1. To copy a dimension, click on DIMENSION LIBRARY in the left pane and then select COPY A DIMENSION (Figure 3.31, ❶ and ❷).

2. Select the dimension you want to use to copy to the new dimension. We'll select the P_ACCT dimension from the dropdown as the source dimension (Figure 3.32, ❸). Enter "RB_ACCT" as the technical name of the dimension (Figure 3.32, ❹). Enter "RB Accounts" as the description for the dimension (Figure 3.32, ❺). Click on SAVE AS DIMENSION (Figure 3.32, ❻).

3. A status message box indicates that the dimension was successfully created, and the newly created dimension is shown under DIMENSION LIBRARY in the left pane.

Similarly, create the RB_CATEGORY, RB_DATASRC, and RB_ENTITY dimensions by copying from the Category, P_DataSrc, and Entity dimensions. Because we're using the copy task, all of the dimension members from the source dimension are also copied to the new dimension. If you want to create a new dimension without copying from an existing dimension, you can use the ADD A DIMENSION task, which is available in the right pane.

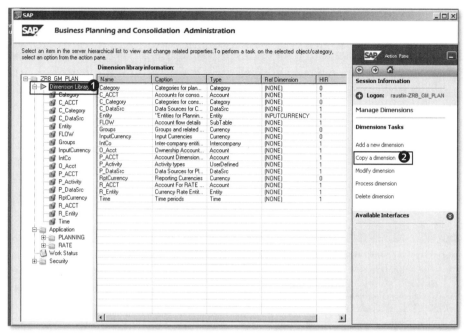

Figure 3.31 Copying a Dimension—Part A

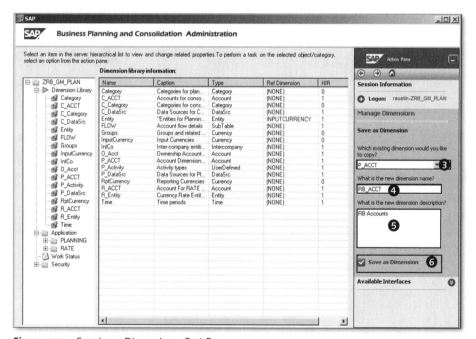

Figure 3.32 Copying a Dimension—Part B

Creating a Custom Dimension

Our sample company requires product and customer data for planning. These dimensions are not standard dimensions provided by SAP BPC; instead, we must create them as custom dimensions. We'll now create the product dimension as a custom dimension using the following steps:

1. Click on DIMENSION LIBRARY and select ADD A NEW DIMENSION from the right pane.

2. You're now prompted to enter the technical name and description of the dimension. Enter "RB_PRODUCT" for the technical name and "RB PRODUCTS" as the description (Figure 3.33, ❶ and ❷). Select GO TO STEP 2 OF 3 (Figure 3.33, ❸).

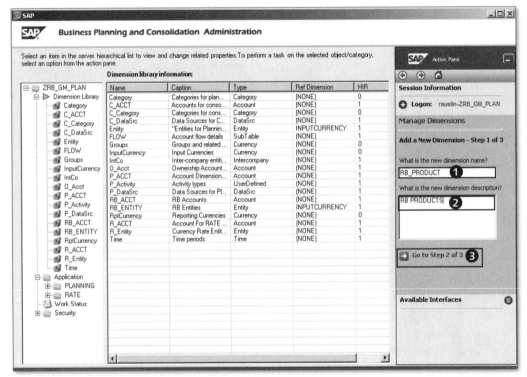

Figure 3.33 Creating a Custom Dimension—Part A

3. You're now prompted to select the dimension type from the dropdown list: U—USER DEFINED (Figure 3.34, ❹). Click on GO TO STEP 3 OF 3 (Figure 3.34, ❹, ❺).

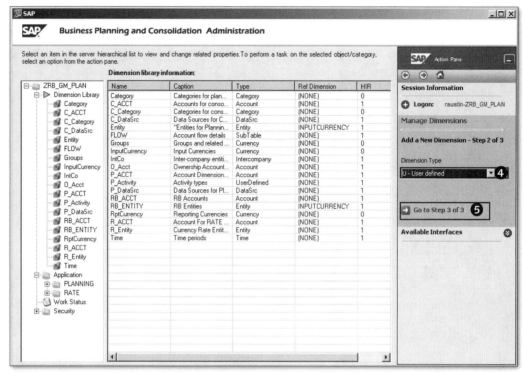

Figure 3.34 Creating a Custom Dimension—Part B

4. The standard properties are automatically added for the dimension type (Figure 3.35, ❻). You can now add new properties as needed, although we do not need to add any new properties to this dimension for our case study. Click on ADD A NEW DIMENSION (Figure 3.35, ❼). A status message indicates that the dimension has been created successfully (Figure 3.35, ❽).

Similarly, create another customer dimension with the technical name "RB_CUS-TOMER" and description "RB CUSTOMERS." Add the PARENTH1 property to this dimension to maintain hierarchy information for customers. Please note that we do not add the PARENTH1 hierarchy as a property directly to the dimension but while entering data for the dimension. We add it as a column to the Excel sheet that is used to maintain members for the dimension and title it PARENTH1. We'll discuss the process of manually entering data into a dimension in the next section.

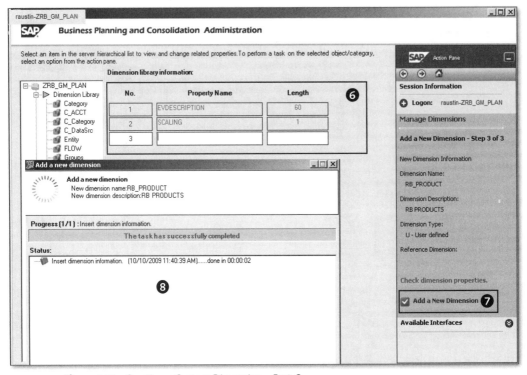

Figure 3.35 Creating a Custom Dimension—Part C

Manually Entering Data into a Dimension

Two options are available when entering data into a dimension in SAP BPC: You can load it from a flat file or enter it manually. We'll discuss the option of loading data from a file in Chapter 4, when we discuss the process of loading master and transaction data. You can use the option to enter data manually into a dimension when there are limited data records in the dimension.

Next, we'll explain how to manually enter data into the RB_ACCT dimension for our case study.

1. To add data manually, click on the RB_ACCT dimension in the left pane, under DIMENSION LIBRARY, and select MAINTAIN DIMENSION INFORMATION in the right pane. This displays the member, hierarchy, and·property data of the dimension. Delete the existing data in the dimension, because it was originally copied from the P_ACCT dimension, and enter the member data as shown in Figure 3.36. You

can delete a member ID only if it is not used in an application. If any application contains the member ID, you cannot delete it.

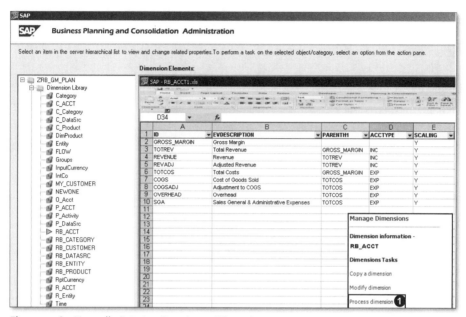

Figure 3.36 Manually Entering Data into a Dimension

2. The data entered into the dimension has to be processed in SAP BPC to take effect. Select PROCESS DIMENSION (Figure 3.36, ❶).

3. This opens the PROCESS DIMENSIONS dialog box (Figure 3.37). Processing a dimension causes a corresponding attribute change run for the InfoObject in SAP NetWeaver BW. Deselect TAKE SYSTEM OFFLINE. Select PROCESS MEMBERS FROM MEMBER SHEET. Confirm that RB_ACCT is selected in the dimensions. You can select more than one dimension. Click on OK to process the data for the dimension(s) selected.

You have now seen how to create dimensions and maintain them in SAP BPC. We displayed properties associated with dimensions and discussed how to use hierarchies in dimensions. We also created a dimension by copying from an existing dimension and created a custom dimension. We'll now discuss applications and how to create them.

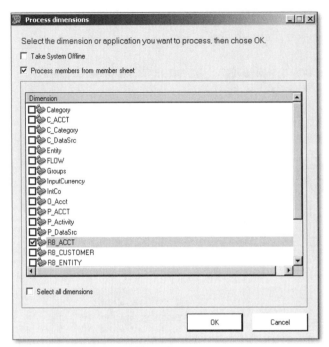

Figure 3.37 Processing a Dimension

3.3.4 Application

An application in SAP BPC meets a particular functional business requirement. It is used for storing transaction data and is available for reporting. Examples of applications are sales planning, gross profit planning, and head-count planning. The following are a few basic but important facts about applications:

▶ An application is created with respect to an application set and is a collection of dimensions. The dimensions for an application are modeled based on business requirements.

▶ An application can use any dimensions included in an application set.

▶ There are no restrictions on the number of dimensions included in an application, but we recommend that you limit the number to maintain good performance.

▶ Several objects and tables are created in the background, depending on the type of application created. Some of these include comment tables, journals, work status tables, audit tables, script logic files, file service folders, Web Admin parameters, and default packages to load and manage data for applications.

- Two options are available when you create an application:

  - ADD: Select this option when you need to create an application based on another application. When this option is selected, you can change the dimension assignments. For example, you can remove a dimension from what the template provided or add a new dimension to the application.

  - COPY: Select this option when you need to copy records from a source application to a target application.

There are two main types of applications:

- **Reporting**
  These applications are used for reporting; examples of reporting applications are sales planning and consolidation applications. The following subtypes are available under reporting applications:

  - Financial: This type of application is used primarily for planning.

  - Consolidation: This type of application is used for financial consolidation. Consolidation is the process of reporting financial results of an organization either for legal or management reporting purposes.

  - Generic: A reporting application that is neither a financial nor a consolidation application is categorized as a generic application.

- **Nonreporting**
  This type of application is used to support a reporting application. The following subtypes are available under nonreporting applications:

  - Rate: This application is used to store exchange rates and to enable currency translation for reporting applications. When a company does business in more than one currency, it may need to translate the business transactions into one or more reporting currencies. In these cases, the rate application is used to perform currency translations to one or more reporting currencies. In SAP BPC, we can report transactions in more than one reporting currency. The rate application (called RATE) is delivered as part of APSHELL. The exchange rate data in the RATE application needs to be maintained either manually using input templates or automatically loaded into the application.

  - Ownership: The ownership application is used for consolidating financial information. An organization may be composed of a group of companies with a different ownership mix; for example, it may hold a 50% stake in one company and have also made a significant investment in another company.

In such cases, it may be necessary for legal reporting to consolidate the financial data of all of the companies in the group as a whole. The ownership application stores the percentage ownership in different companies and helps perform legal consolidation.

▶ Generic: This type of application is used to support a reporting application. An application containing the price of products is an example of a nonreporting generic application.

All applications, whether reporting or nonreporting, must include the four basic dimensions: category, account, entity, and time.

When a request for creating an application is initiated in SAP BPC, a corresponding InfoCube and MultiProvider are created in the SAP NetWeaver BW system. A table, UJA_APPL, stores the technical name of the InfoCube and MultiProvider. The naming convention when creating the InfoCube and MultiProvider is as follows:

▶ **InfoCube**
/CPMB/<Application SetPrefix>I<ApplicationPrefix><1GeneratedChar>

▶ **MultiProvider**
/CPMB/<Application SetPrefix>M<ApplicationPrefix><1GeneratedChar>

It is easy to delete or add dimensions to an application in SAP BPC. When dimension data is deleted from an application, the SAP NetWeaver BW system creates a shadow InfoCube in the background and moves the data from the original InfoCube to the shadow InfoCube. After successfully loading the data to the shadow InfoCube, the system updates the database for the application to point to the shadow InfoCube and deletes the original InfoCube because it is no longer required.

> **Note**
>
> Do not change any application objects directly in the SAP NetWeaver BW system. Always use the SAP BPC frontend to make changes to an application.

Application Optimization

SAP BPC lets you optimize applications. Two options are available for this, as follows:

▶ **Lite Optimize**
When data is loaded into an application, an open request is created for the

InfoCube associated with the application in the SAP NetWeaver BW system. This request is open (shown with a yellow status) until a particular threshold of records is updated. When the threshold is reached, the request is closed (shown with a green status). When LITE OPTIMIZE is selected, all open requests are closed and set to green. The cube is compressed, and all of the indexes are built. The statistics for the InfoCube are also updated during this process.

▶ **Full Optimize**
FULL OPTIMIZE works the same as LITE OPTIMIZE, but it also reviews the data model for scope for additional optimization. If, during the course of the check, it is determined that the data model of the InfoCube requires changing, the necessary changes to the data model will be made. This process can take some time to complete, depending on the volume of data in the InfoCube.

Parameters for an Application

You can set several parameters for an application. One of these is YTDINPUT, which determines how quantitative data is stored in an application. By default, the value of this parameter is 0. This implies that the quantitative data for each record in the application is stored for the period for which it is entered. When the value of this parameter is set to 1, the quantitative data is year-to-date (YTD) and up to the period for which it is entered.

We'll use an example to illustrate the functionality of this parameter. Consider a situation where YTDINPUT is set to 1, with two records entered into an application. The first is for an amount of $200—entered for January 2009—and the second is for an amount of $500—entered for February 2009. In this case, the entries for these two months represent YTD values. So the periodic value for January 2009 is $200, and the periodic value for February 2009 is $300 ($500 – $200).

We'll discuss other application-specific parameters in Chapter 7.

Create Application

We'll now explain how to create an application for Rich Bloom to use for planning gross margins. The dimensions required for our planning application are as follows:

▶ RB_ACCT
▶ RB_CATEGORY

- ▶ RB_ENTITY

- ▶ RB_CUSTOMER

- ▶ RB_PRODUCT

- ▶ RB_DATASRC

- ▶ RPTCURRENCY

- ▶ Time

We'll create a new planning application that includes these dimensions. Proceed as follows:

1. Access the ZRB_GM_PLAN application set.

2. Click on the application option in the left pane and select ADD A NEW APPLICA-TION (Figure 3.38, ❶ and ❷).

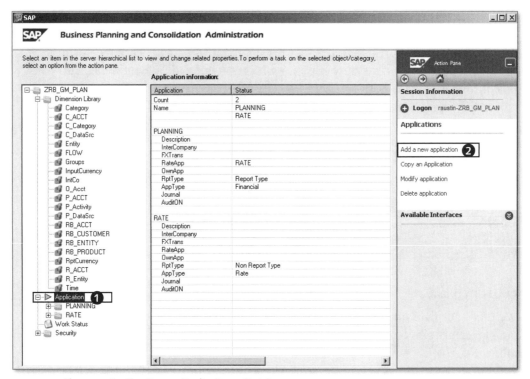

Figure 3.38 Creating an Application—Part A

3. You're now prompted to enter the new application name and description. Enter "ZRB_SALES_CMB" as the technical name and "Actual and Plan Sales Data" as the description for the application (Figure 3.39, ❸ and ❹). Select GO TO STEP 2 OF 4 (Figure 3.39, ❺).

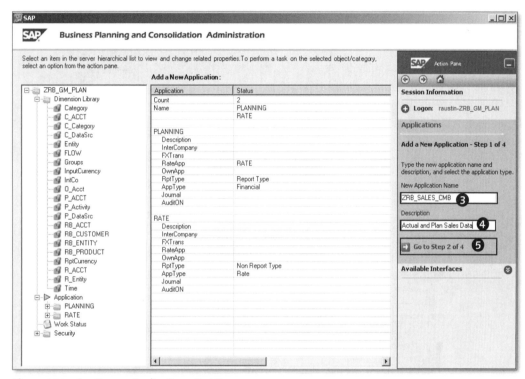

Figure 3.39 Creating an Application—Part B

4. You're prompted to select the application type. We want to create a financial application that can be reported. Under REPORTING TYPE, select FINANCIAL (Figure 3.40, ❻). Select GO TO STEP 3 OF 4 (Figure 3.40, ❼).

5. In this step, select the source application you want to use as the template for creating the new application. Select PLANNING, which is an application that is delivered as part of APSHELL and has been copied into the current application set (Figure 3.41, ❽).

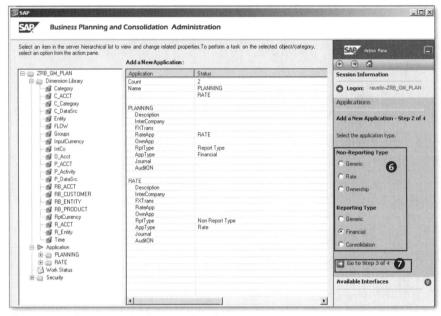

Figure 3.40 Creating an Application—Part C

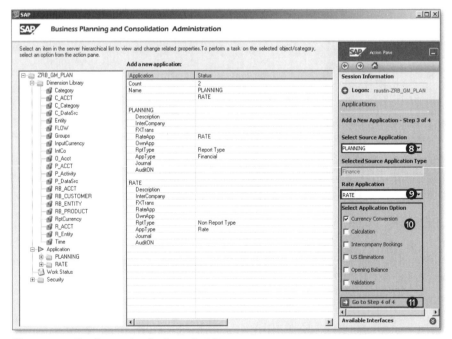

Figure 3.41 Creating an Application—Part D

6. Every finance application must be associated with a rate application; this is the application that is accessed for performing currency translations. An application called RATE is delivered as part of APSHELL and has been copied into the current application. Associate the RATE application with the current application (Figure 3.41, ❾).

7. Select the application options you want to use with this application (Figure 3.41, ❿). You can use these options for configuring currency conversions, intercompany bookings, and so on. For this application, select CURRENCY CONVERSION. Select GO TO STEP 4 OF 4 (Figure 3.41, ⓫).

8. In the next screen, deselect DIMENSIONS (Figure 3.42, ⓬). This enables you to change the dimensions that have been copied from the source application. Also deselect JOURNALS, because you will not be using it in our application (Figure 3.42, ⓭). Click on ADD A NEW APPLICATION (Figure 3.42, ⓮).

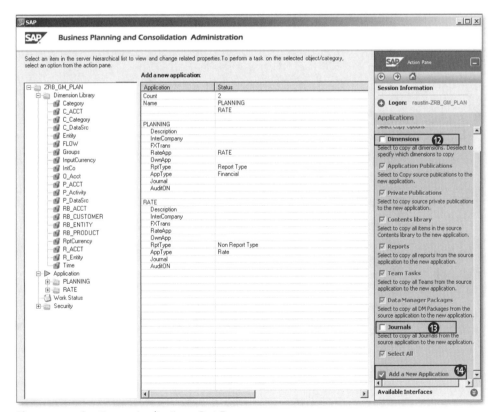

Figure 3.42 Creating an Application—Part E

9. In the next screen, use the arrows to remove and add dimensions to your application. Our application will not need the dimensions shown in Figure 3.43, ❶. Click on the arrow as shown in Figure 3.43, ❶, to remove them from the application.

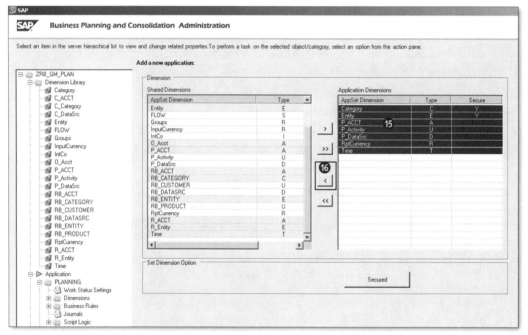

Figure 3.43 Creating an Application—Part F

10. Add the RB_ACCT, RB_CATEGORY, RB_CUSTOMER, RB_DATASRC, RB_ENTITY, RB_PRODUCT, RptCurrency, and Time dimensions (Figure 3.44, ❶) from the list of available dimensions in the left area to the new application in the right area using the right-facing arrow (Figure 3.44, ❶).

11. Mark RB_ENTITY as a secured dimension. Marking a dimension in this way assists with restricting data access for users based on values in that dimension. To do this, select the RB_ENTITY dimension (Figure 3.45, ❶) and click on SECURED (Figure 3.45, ❷).

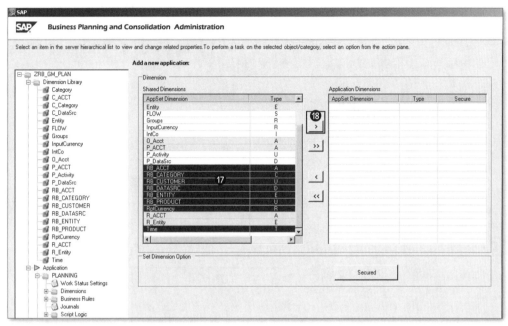

Figure 3.44 Creating an Application—Part G

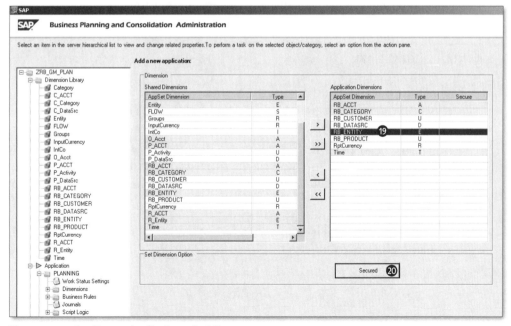

Figure 3.45 Creating an Application—Part H

12. Click on ADD A NEW APPLICATION in the right pane to add the new application. A status message indicates that the new application has been created. The Gross Margin Planning application is created and displayed under the APPLICATION folder in the left pane (see Figure 3.46).

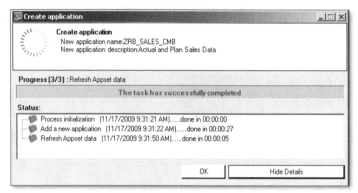

Figure 3.46 Creating an Application—Part I

We have now configured a planning application Rich Bloom will use for planning gross margins. We included all of the necessary dimensions in the application that will be used to develop a plan and compute the gross margin.

3.4   Summary

In this chapter, we introduced a case study of a sample company, Rich Bloom, which uses SAP BPC for gross margin planning. We developed the staging environment in the SAP NetWeaver BW system that will be used to store actual sales and cost data. We also discussed the building blocks of creating the planning application in SAP BPC. We discussed application sets, dimensions, and applications and saw how the objects created in SAP BPC translated to corresponding objects in the SAP NetWeaver BW system.

In the next chapter, you'll learn the steps for loading data into SAP NetWeaver BW and SAP BPC for SAP NetWeaver.

This chapter explains the extraction, transformation and loading (ETL) processes used in SAP Business Warehouse and SAP BPC systems. We will also demonstrate how to use the SAP BPC tool to create baseline plan based on actual data.

4 Loading, Scheduling, and Managing Data in SAP BPC for NetWeaver

In the last chapter, we discussed a case study for our model company, Rich Bloom. To meet the requirements of the case study, we built an InfoCube in SAP NetWeaver BW and an application in SAP BusinessObjects Planning and Consolidation (BPC) to store actual sales and cost data. In this chapter, we'll discuss how to load data in the SAP NetWeaver BW and SAP BPC environments.

Section 4.1 discusses the steps of loading data from a flat file to an InfoCube in SAP NetWeaver BW. If you're new to SAP NetWeaver BW, this section will help you understand the process of loading transaction data into an InfoCube.

Section 4.2 explains the options available to load master and transaction data into SAP BPC. You'll see how to use transformations and conversions when loading data to dimensions and applications. This section also explains the importance of data manager packages and discusses how to create and maintain them. Data manager packages enable you to perform tasks regarding loading and managing data in SAP BPC. In this section, we'll discuss the use of process chains in a data manager package and introduce the process types available for use in a process chain inside an SAP BPC application.

Section 4.3 discusses how to use 2009 actual sales and cost data to create baseline plan data for 2010. We'll copy actual sales and cost data for 2009 to a plan version for 2010.

4.1   Loading Data into an InfoCube in SAP NetWeaver BW

In this section, we'll discuss the steps of loading data from a flat file into an InfoCube in SAP NetWeaver BW.

4.1.1   Creating a DataSource

A *DataSource* is an object that provides data to load into an InfoProvider in SAP NetWeaver BW. The actual source of the sales and cost data for our sample company, Rich Bloom, is in an SAP ECC system. The daily sales and cost data created in the SAP ECC system is brought into the SAP NetWeaver BW system on a nightly basis. But for the purposes of our case study, we'll assume that the sales and cost data for 2009 exists in a flat file. We'll load the sales and cost data from this flat file into the Sales InfoCube in the SAP NetWeaver BW system.

Before you start creating the DataSource, you must create a flat file that contains the sales and cost data for 2009. We use a CSV (comma separated) format containing the following columns:

- Company Code
- Account
- Calendar Month
- Calendar Year
- Material
- Customer
- Amount in Local Currency
- Currency

Then enter the data as shown in Figure 4.1. Name the file "us_salesdata.csv" and save it to a directory called *C:\Planning*. (The us_salesdata.csv file is available for download at this book's website at *www.sap-press.com.*)

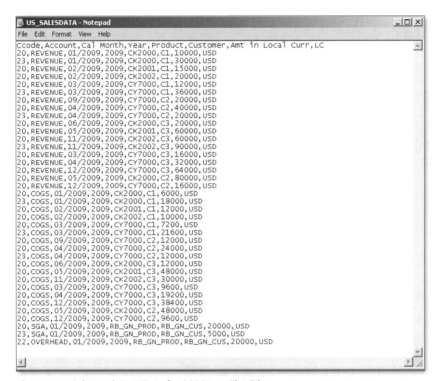

Figure 4.1 Sales and Cost Data for 2009 in a Flat File

Next, perform the following steps to create the DataSource, as illustrated in Figures 4.2, 4.3, and 4.4:

1. Open the Data Warehousing Workbench using Transaction RSA1.

2. Select MODELING • SOURCE SYSTEMS.

3. Select and double-click on a flat file source system for creating the DataSource. We used the PC FILE SYSTEM (Figure 4.2, ❶).

4. The DataSource for the <FILE SYSTEM> dialog box displays (in this case, PC_FILE PC FILE SYSTEM). Select any application component area (for example, NON-SAP_SOURCES), right-click, and select CREATE DATASOURCE from the context menu (Figure 4.2, ❷).

5. In the CREATE DATASOURCE window, enter the name of the DataSource ("ZSLS_ FILE") (Figure 4.2, ❸), and then select TRANSACTION DATA from the DATA TYPE DATASOURCE dropdown list (Figure 4.2, ❹).

6. Click on ENTER (Figure 4.2, ❺).

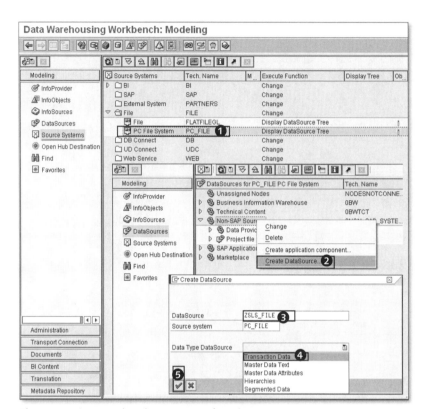

Figure 4.2   Create a Flat File DataSource for Sales Data—Part A

7. On the GENERAL INFO tab in the CHANGE DATASOURCE <FILE NAME> window, enter the short ("Sales actual file"), medium ("Sales actual file"), and long ("Sales actual file") descriptions for the DataSource. We'll be using this DataSource to load sales and cost data for 2009 from a flat file.

8. On the FIELDS tab, enter the list of fields for which data exists in the flat file. The sequence you use is the same as that used for the data in the flat file. Instead of entering a field name, you can enter the name of an InfoObject in the first row of the TEMPLATE INFOOBJECT column (Figure 4.3, ❻) that represents the field.

9. After you enter the first InfoObject (0COMP_CODE) and click on ENTER, the DEFAULT FROM INFOOBJECTS dialog box displays (Figure 4.3). Select DO NOT SHOW THIS QUESTION AGAIN IN THIS SESSION, and click on COPY (Figure 4.3, ❼ and ❽). This transfers all of the properties from the InfoObject to the corresponding field in the FIELD column (Figure 4.4, ❾).

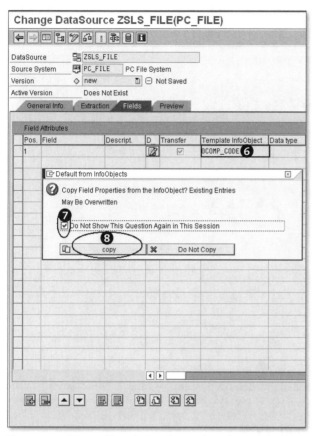

Figure 4.3 Create a Flat File DataSource for Sales Data—Part B

10. Continue to enter InfoObjects into the TEMPLATE INFOOBJECT column (Figure 4.4, ❿) by clicking on the INSERT button (Figure 4.4, ⓫), following the sequence of data coming from the flat file that contains the sales and cost data for 2009.

11. Click on the ACTIVATE button to save and activate the DataSource (Figure 4.4, ⓬).

When the DataSource is successfully activated, the system automatically creates an equivalent PSA table. The structure of the PSA table mirrors the structure of the file layout of the source data.

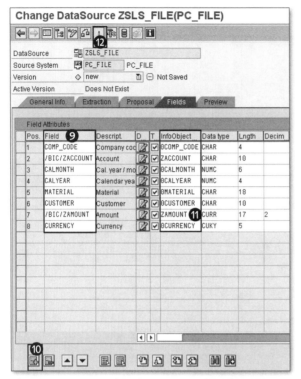

Figure 4.4 Create a Flat File DataSource for Sales Data—Part C

4.1.2 Creating Transformations

In SAP NetWeaver BW, the data coming from a source system is loaded into the DataSource or PSA in its original form as sent from the source system. The *transformation* process, however, lets you apply rules to modify the data coming from a DataSource before it is loaded into an InfoProvider.

At least one transformation process is required before data reaches the data target. For our case study, we will create a transformation process to transform the data from the PSA associated with the Sales DataSource to the Sales InfoCube.

Perform the following steps to create a transformation that loads data from the Sales DataSource created earlier into the Sales InfoCube, as illustrated in Figures 4.5, 4.6, 4.7, and 4.8:

1. Open the Data Warehousing Workbench using Transaction RSA1.

2. Select MODELING • INFOPROVIDER.

3. Under the SALES MANAGEMENT InfoArea, right-click on the SALES ACTUAL Info-
   Cube and select CREATE TRANSFORMATION from the context menu (Figure 4.5,
   ❶).

4. In the CREATE TRANSFORMATION window, select the source of the transformation.
   Select the OBJECT TYPE ("DataSource"), the DATASOURCE ("ZSLS_FILE"), and the
   SOURCE SYSTEM ("PC_FILE") (Figure 4.5, ❷, ❸, and ❹).

5. Click on ENTER (Figure 4.5, ❺).

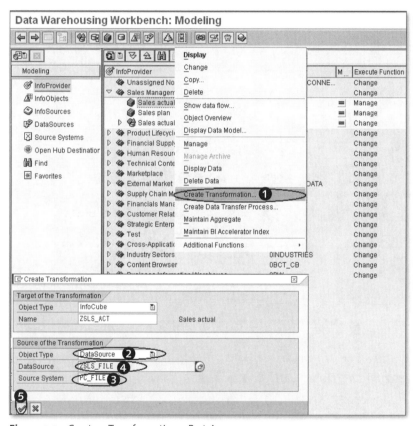

Figure 4.5 Create a Transformation—Part A

6. The TRANSFORMATION CREATE window appears (Figure 4.6). The system automatically proposes a mapping for the fields from the DataSource to the InfoObjects
   in the Sales Actual InfoCube. The proposal is based on the mapping of the
   InfoObjects in the TEMPLATE INFOOBJECTS column of the DataSource to the

same InfoObject that exists as a characteristic or key figure in the Sales Actual InfoCube.

You may at times notice that some of the InfoObjects are not mapped. This is because data for these InfoObjects is not available in the DataSource, so these values have to be directly set in the transformation. In these cases, select the appropriate InfoObject in the RULE GROUP: STANDARD GROUP table and double-click on it. There, you'll have additional options to map the value for those InfoObjects.

7. After you've assigned all of the mappings, click on the ACTIVATE button to save and activate the transformation object (Figure 4.6, ❻).

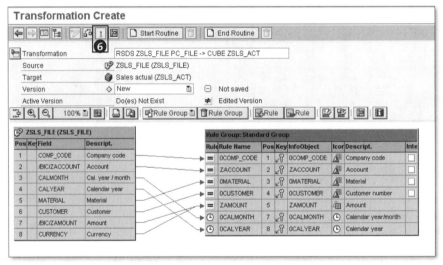

Figure 4.6 Create Transformation—Part B

4.1.3 Creating the Data Transfer Process

The data transfer process (DTP) provides the ability to extract and load data from one persistent object to another.

> **Note**
>
> It is important to understand that the transformation process we created earlier only provides the rules for the extraction and loading of data. The DTP then uses the transformation to actually load the data from one persistent area to another.

For our case study, we want to define a DTP that extracts data from the Sales Actual File DataSource, uses the transformation process we created earlier, and loads the data into the Sales Actual InfoCube.

We'll create a DTP by performing the following steps, as illustrated in Figures 4.7 and 4.8:

1. Open the Data Warehousing Workbench using Transaction RSA1.

2. Select MODELING • INFOPROVIDER.

3. Under the SALES MANAGEMENT InfoArea, right-click on the SALES ACTUAL Info-Cube and select CREATE DATA TRANSFER PROCESS from the context menu (Figure 4.7, ❶).

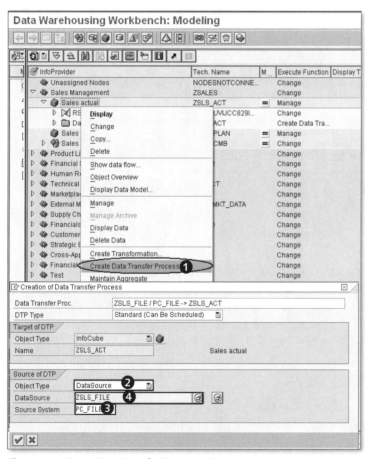

Figure 4.7 Create Data Transfer Process—Part A

4. We are creating a DTP that loads data from the Sales Actual File DataSource, which we created earlier, to the Sales InfoCube. In the CREATION OF DATA TRANSFER PROCESS window, select the source object for the DTP. Enter the OBJECT TYPE source ("DataSource"), the DATASOURCE we created earlier ("ZSLS_FILE"), and the SOURCE SYSTEM ("PC_FILE") (Figure 4.7, ❷, ❸, and ❹) and click on ENTER.

> **Note**
>
> A DTP can be created between a source and a target object only if a transformation process exists between the two objects.

5. In the CHANGE DATA TRANSFER PROCESS window (Figure 4.8), select the extraction mode. If you select FULL, all of the data from the source is loaded into the target. If you select DELTA, only the changes made since the last time the data was extracted from this source are extracted into the target. Because we have sales and cost data for 2009, use the FULL extraction mode.

6. Click on the ACTIVATE button to save and activate the DTP object (Figure 4.8, ❺).

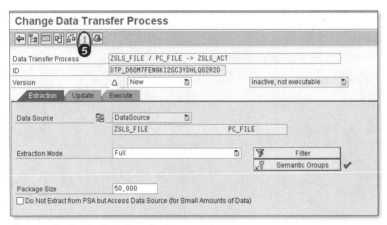

Figure 4.8 Create Data Transfer Process—Part B

4.1.4 Creating InfoPackages

In the previous steps, we configured objects such as the DataSource, transformation, and data transfer process that will be used to load sales actual data to the Sales

InfoCube. But the configuration of the objects by itself does not load the data; to do this, you must perform the following steps:

1. Schedule the loading of data from a DataSource to the PSA.

2. Schedule the load data from the PSA to a data target, which could be an InfoCube, DataStore, or InfoObject.

The InfoPackage is the object that is used to schedule the load of data from a Data-Source to a persistent staging area (PSA). Create an InfoPackage for loading the sales data using the following steps, as illustrated in Figures 4.9, 4.10, and 4.11:

1. Open the Data Warehousing Workbench using Transaction RSA1.

2. Select MODELING • INFOPROVIDER.

3. Right-click on the SALES ACTUAL FILE DataSource and select CREATE INFOPACKAGE from the context menu (Figure 4.9, ❶).

Figure 4.9 Create InfoPackage—Part A

4. In the CREATE INFOPACKAGE window, enter the name of the InfoPackage ("Load sales data") and click on ENTER (Figure 4.9, ❷ and ❸).

5. In the SCHEDULER (MAINTAIN INFOPACKAGE) window, select the EXTRACTION tab (Figure 4.10, ❹).

6. Choose the ADAPTER, which determines whether the file you want to load exists on a local workstation or an SAP application server. Because this file exists on your PC, select LOAD TEXT-TYPE FILE FROM LOCAL WORKSTATION from the dropdown list (Figure 4.10, ❺).

7. Enter the name of the file (*C:\Planning\US_SALESDATA.CSV*) that contains the sales and cost data for 2009 (Figure 4.10, ❻).

8. Specify the header rows to be ignored if you want the system to ignore header rows. (Refer back to Figure 4.1 for the layout of the file.) Because the first row of data contains the header, enter "1" in the HEADER ROWS TO BE IGNORED field (Figure 4.10, ❼).

9. Next to DATA FORMAT (Figure 4.10, ❽), select SEPARATED WITH SEPARATOR (FOR EXAMPLE, CSV) from the dropdown list, and, next to Data Separator, enter a comma (Figure 4.10, ❾).

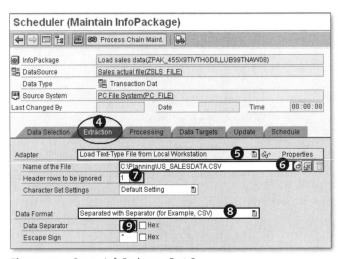

Figure 4.10 Create InfoPackage—Part B

10. Select the SCHEDULE tab (Figure 4.11, ❿). Ensure that START DATA LOAD IMMEDIATELY is selected (Figure 4.11, ⓫). Click on START (Figure 4.11, ⓬). The data

will now be extracted from the DataSource into the PSA. Click on the MONITOR button to check the status of the extraction process (Figure 4.11, ⓭).

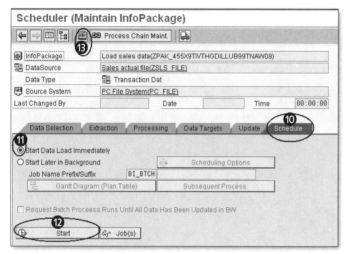

Figure 4.11 Execute InfoPackage

11. The MONITOR—ADMINISTRATOR WORKBENCH window in Figure 4.12 shows the status of the data extracted from the flat file DataSource into the PSA. If the data load is successful, the status of the load is displayed with a green traffic light.

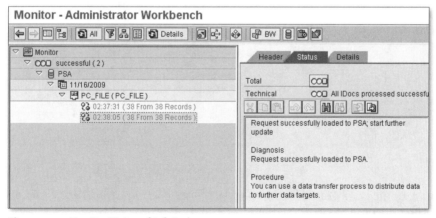

Figure 4.12 Monitor Status of InfoPackage

4.1.5 Load Data from the PSA to the Data Target

Now that we have loaded the data from the DataSource to the PSA, we're ready to schedule the load of data from the PSA to the Sales InfoCube using the data transfer process. The process applies the transformation when loading the data from the PSA to the data target.

1. Open the Data Warehousing Workbench using Transaction RSA1.

2. Select MODELING • INFOPROVIDER.

3. Locate the data transfer process created earlier under the Sales InfoCube, and double-click on it (Figure 4.13). The pane on the right displays the details of the DTP object.

4. Select the EXECUTE tab and then click on the EXECUTE button (Figure 4.13, ❶).

5. Click on the MONITOR button to check the status of the load (Figure 4.13, ❷).

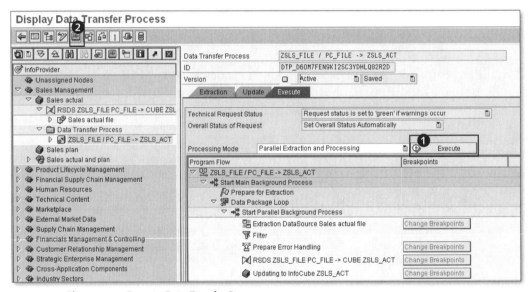

Figure 4.13 Execute Data Transfer Process

6. Return to the Data Warehousing Workbench by clicking on the BACK ARROW button. Select the MANAGE option of the Sales InfoCube.

7. In the INFOPROVIDER ADMINISTRATION window, select the REQUESTS tab to see the requests that were loaded into the InfoCube.

8. Figure 4.14 shows the request loaded into the Sales InfoCube.

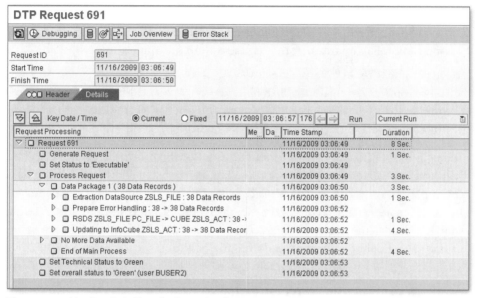

Figure 4.14 Monitor Data Transfer Execution Process

After reading this section, you should understand how to load data into an InfoCube using a flat file as the DataSource. Rich Bloom can now use the sales data for 2009 in this InfoCube as the basis for planning in 2010.

In the next section, we'll discuss the options for loading master and transaction data into SAP BPC. We'll demonstrate examples of how to load master and transaction data as it relates to our case study.

4.2 Loading Data into SAP BPC

Two types of data exist in SAP BPC: master data and transaction data. Master data is stored in a dimension, and transaction data is stored in an application. Although both master and transaction data can be manually entered into SAP BPC, it may not be feasible to adopt this approach for large volumes of data. To automate the process of loading master and transaction data, SAP BPC provides the following options:

▶ **Flat file**
When this option is selected, master or transaction data can be loaded into a dimension or an application from a flat file. The flat file is the most flexible method to load data into an SAP BPC application. In this case, the flat file is staged in the Application Folder area before it is loaded into the application.

▶ **InfoProvider in SAP NetWeaver BW**
In the NetWeaver version of SAP BPC, you can leverage the data in an InfoProvider in the SAP NetWeaver BW system. You can use an InfoCube or DataStore object as a DataSource to load data into an SAP BPC application.

To begin, we'll discuss the transformation and loading process in SAP BPC. When you load data, extended features are available to transform and convert the data coming from a source file. The transformation definition interprets the source of the data; it specifies the layout of the file, the columns in the file, and how the data should be loaded into the application. The conversion definitions are used when the source data should be interpreted differently before it is loaded into SAP BPC.

4.2.1 Transformation and Conversion

The transformation file specifies the definitions used to interpret data coming from an external source before loading it into an SAP BPC dimension or application. SAP BPC provides the interface to create and maintain transformations in an Excel file. The transformation file includes three sections:

▶ Options

▶ Mapping

▶ Conversion

Options

The Options section contains the options you want to use when interpreting the data from the external source. You can specify the options shown in Table 4.1 in the Options section.

Option	Default Value	Description
AmountDecimal Point=<value>	Period	This option specifies the character to represent a decimal point. The default value to represent a decimal point is a "." (period).
		This is useful in countries where a value other than a period is used to denote a decimal point.
ConvertAmount Dim=<dim_name>	Account	This option can specify a dimension for amount calculations. The default value for this option is the Account dimension.
		A formula should exist in the conversion file for the value specified here for the calculation to work.
CREDITPOSITIVE= YES|NO	YES	The default value for this option is YES.
		If this option is set to NO, all credit accounts (of type Owner's Equity and Income) will have a negative sign.
FORMAT=DELIMITED/ FIXED/ VARIANT		This is a required parameter.
		It specifies the format of the data in the input file.
DELIMITER	Comma	This option is applicable when the format option is set as DELIMITED. This option is relevant when loading data directly from a file.
		Specify a value that matches the format of the input file.
HEADER=YES/NO	YES	If the file includes a header row with column names, set the value of this option to YES.
		When a header is included, the column names in the header can be referred in the Mapping section of the transformation file to map the column names to the technical name of the target dimension of the application.

Table 4.1 Options

Option	Default Value	Description
MAXREJECTCOUNT	Empty string	This option is used for validating the data from the external source and indicates the number of rejected records that can be tolerated before the validation process ends.
		An empty string represents 500 records.
		A value of -1 indicates that processing should continue no matter how many rejected records are encountered.
		A positive value indicates the number of rejected records allowed before processing will end.
SUPPRESSCHARACTER	<TEXT>	This option will remove the value specified by <text> from the records.
		This is useful when certain pieces of text are not required when loading the data from an external source.
ROUNDAMOUNT = <INTEGER_VALUE>	Integer	This option rounds amount fields to the value specified in this option.
		The value for this option should be an integer number.
SKIP=<INTEGER_ VALUE>	Integer	This option skips the specified number of records from the top of the file.
		The value should be an integer number.
SKIPIF=<TEXT_ VALUE1>|<TEXT_ VALUE2>	Empty string	When text is specified for this option, a line will be skipped from the data file if it begins with the specified value.
		More than one text value can be specified when using this option, separated by the pipe delimiter.
SELECTION= <Dimension1_ techname>, <Dimension1_value>; <Dimension2_techname>, <Dimension2_value>	Empty	This option is relevant only when extracting data from an InfoProvider in SAP NetWeaver BW.
		The dimension name is the name of the InfoObject used in the cube.

Table 4.1 Options (Cont.)

Option	Default Value	Description
		The dimension value is the value for the InfoObject to be used when extracting the data.
		This option is useful when you need to selectively extract data from an InfoCube.
		Assuming a particular InfoCube includes two InfoObjects, Account and Material, the following selection will restrict the data into SAP BPC for the COGS account and the M1 material: SELECTION= 0ACCOUNT, COGS; 0MATERIAL, M1.
FORMULA=		A dimension can include a formula property to use in calculations.
		SAP BPC provides functions that can be used in formulas. They are referred to as K2 functions. When functions are used in dimension formulas, the library file that includes these functions is specified here.
CONVERT_ INTERNAL=YES|NO		A conversion sheet can be used for each dimension to convert values coming from an external DataSource.
		The conversion sheet can have an internal value and an external value for a dimension member. The external value is the data coming from the external system. The internal value is how it would be stored in SAP BPC. When this is set, the external value will be converted to the internal value when loading data.
		This option indicates whether the dimension member names should be compared with the internal names. This should be always set to No.

Table 4.1 Options (Cont.)

The following is an example of the Options section in the transformation file.

```
*OPTIONS
FORMAT=DELIMITED
HEADER=YES
DELIMITER=','
AMOUNTDECIMALPOINT=
SKIP=0
SKIPIF=
VALIDATERECORDS=YES
MAXREJECTCOUNT=
ROUNDAMOUNT=
```

Mapping

The Mapping section specifies how external data is mapped to an SAP BPC dimension or application. The mapping is defined by specifying a dimension to the left and assigning it to the name of a column or the column number from an external file to the right. The name of the InfoObject is specified when data is extracted from an InfoProvider like an InfoCube.

The example that follows specifies the format to use when mapping a dimension to a column value from an external file. In this case, Entity is the name of the dimension in the application, and Company_Code is the column name for the data coming from the flat file. For this to work, the Options section should have the value for header parameter set to YES, and the first record in the file should have a column named Company_Code.

```
Entity=Company_Code
```

The following is an example of a mapping when data is loaded from an InfoCube in SAP NetWeaver BW. In this case, Entity is the name of the dimension in the application, and 0COMP_CODE is the name of the InfoObject in the InfoCube.

```
Entity=0COMP_CODE
```

All dimensions in an SAP BPC application should be mapped in the Mapping section of the transformation. It is possible that the flat file or data coming from an InfoProvider does not contain the values for all dimensions in an application. These dimensions should be assigned with the *NEWCOL(<text_value>) parameter in the Mapping section, where <text_value> is the value for the dimensions. This ensures that a value is assigned to all of the dimensions during the load process.

Another example of a transformation that is often required when you're loading data from an external DataSource is to prefix the data coming from the source with a specific text string. For example, you may want to prefix all of the entity data coming from a flat file with the string "RB." This can be accomplished by specifying the following in the Mapping section:

```
Entity=*Str(RB) + Comp_Code
```

An example of a Mapping section is shown here:

```
*MAPPING
Account=Acct
DataSrc=New(FILELOAD)
Entity=*Str(RB) + Comp_Code
Category=Category
Time=Period
```

You've now seen a few examples of how to use the Mapping section. It supports more advanced features when you're assigning data. Table 4.2 describes the various mapping options.

Mapping Parameter	Description	Example
*COL(<NUMBER>)	This parameter can be set to assign the value of a dimension based on its position in the file. The <NUMBER> indicates the position of the column in the file.	Entity = *Col(4) This assigns the Entity dimension from the fourth column in the data file.
*COL(<NUMBER>, <POS1>: <POS2))	This parameter works the same way as the *COL(<NUMBER>) parameter and provides a feature to select only a subset of the column value. <POS1> and <POS2> indicate the start and end positions within the column.	Entity = *Col(4,1,3). This assigns the Entity dimension from the fourth column in the data file. Only the value from the first three characters of this column will be used in the assignment.

Table 4.2 Mapping

Mapping Parameter	Description	Example
*FCOL(A:B)	You can use this parameter when using fixed format data files to define starting and ending positions within a data row.	Entity = *FCOL(2:5) In this example, the values from character columns two to five in the data file will be assigned to the Entity dimension.
*MVAL	This parameter is especially useful in SAP BPC for NetWeaver 7.5 when you're loading data from an SAP BW InfoCube to an SAP BPC application. If a source record in the InfoCube has multiple key figures, you can use this parameter to map multiple key figures to different accounts.	ACCOUNT = *MVAL(0AMOUNT | *NEWCOL(AMOUNT) | |0QUANTITY | *NEWCOL(QUANTITY)) Let's say we're loading data from an SAP BW InfoCube to an SAP BPC application. In this example, the source record in an SAP BW InfoCube is translated to two records in the SAP BPC application. The data in 0AMOUNT is mapped to ACCOUNT=AMOUNT, and the data in 0QUANTITY is mapped to ACCOUNT=QUANTITY.
*NEWCOL(<TEXT_VALUE>)	In some cases, the data file may not contain the value for a dimension, and it may be necessary to set a constant value for the dimension.	DataSrc=NEWCOL(FILELOAD) The value for the DataSource dimension is set to the constant value FILELOAD in this assignment.
*str(<TEXT_VALUE>)	This parameter can be set when it is necessary to concatenate the data coming from a data file with other values. The text string can be used to prefix or suffix the column value.	Entity = *Str (BPC) + *Col(4) This assignment prefixes the string BPC to the data coming from the data file for the Entity dimension.

Table 4.2 Mapping (Cont.)

Mapping Parameter	Description	Example
*pad	This parameter has similar functionality as the *str parameter, but it can be used to prefix the data coming from a file. *pad(SAP)	Entity = *pad(SAP)
*if(condition1(is true) action1;condition2 (is true) action2; action3)	If condition1 is true, action1 is performed. If condition1 is false, condition2 is executed. If condition2 is true, action2 is performed. If both condition1 and condition2 are not satisfied, action3 is performed.	Imagine that you have two columns, Source and Product, in the data file. You want to apply the following rules when mapping the data: If you have the value SAP in the source field, you want to take the value of the product as it is coming from the file. If you have the value LEGACY, you want to add two zeros to the product field. If neither SAP nor LEGACY is assigned to the Source field, you want to assign the value Error to the product field. This would look as follows: Product=*IF (source=*Str(SAP) then product;source=*Str(LEGACY) then Str(00) + product;*str(ERROR))

Table 4.2 Mapping (Cont.)

Conversion File

A *conversion file* associates the external values of data to equivalent internal values of dimension members in SAP BPC. This is useful when data coming from a source does not match the data stored in SAP BPC for a dimension. For example, the data coming from a file or an InfoProvider may not match how a dimension member value is stored in the SAP BPC system, although they may mean the same. Using the conversion files, you can map the external values to the internal values.

When this conversion is required, you create a separate file or use a new spreadsheet for each dimension to define the conversions as necessary. The conversion sheet includes three columns: External, Internal, and Formula. The External column identifies how the data is coming from the external system. The Internal column defines how the data is stored in SAP BPC. The Formula column can be added if any calculations are required. It is not mandatory to have a conversion file and is required only when there are conversions between external and internal values. For example, the following conversions can be defined for the Time dimension data:

▸ 200801 can be defined as the External column.

▸ 2008.JAN can be defined as the corresponding Internal column.

When data is loaded into an application that includes this conversion, any data that includes 200801 for the Time dimension from an external data source will be interpreted as 2008.JAN in SAP BPC. You can also use the asterisk (*) and question mark (?) as wildcards in the External or Internal columns. An asterisk (*) refers to any string of characters, whereas a question mark (?) refers to a single character. You can skip a record containing an external value by setting the internal value as *SKIP. You can use the Formula column to represent any calculations. For example, you can have a formula to increase the revenue member of the Account dimension by 10%. This formula would read *value 1.10*. After the transformation and conversion files are created, the data can be loaded into the SAP BPC dimension or application.

The actual process of loading data into SAP BPC is performed using a data manager package. We'll discuss this next.

4.2.2 Data Manager Packages

Data manager packages in SAP BPC support a variety of tasks related to loading and maintaining data in a dimension or application. When a data manager package is executed, it in turn executes a corresponding process chain in SAP NetWeaver BW. A *process chain* automates the process of loading data in SAP NetWeaver BW. With the introduction of SAP BPC for NetWeaver, new process types have been introduced in process chains to enable loading and managing of the data for the SAP BPC environment. Each data manager package is associated with a process chain in the SAP NetWeaver BW system. Process chains automate the process of loading and managing data in the SAP NetWeaver BW system.

Four types of data manager packages are available to perform different tasks in SAP BPC.

▶ **Data manager packages**
This type of package is used for managing data—such as loading dimension and application data from flat files and InfoProviders in SAP NetWeaver BW, copying data, clearing data, and so on.

▶ **Financial process packages**
Financial process packages can be used for executing specific functions related to planning and consolidation applications. They can be used for executing tasks related to allocation, currency translation, intercompany elimination, and consolidation functions.

▶ **System administration packages**
These packages are related to performing system administrative tasks, such as running Light Optimize, Full Optimize, and so on.

▶ **Miscellaneous packages**
Miscellaneous packages serve more of a utility value for SAP BPC applications. The Import File and Send Mail data manager packages fall under this type and are useful for importing a file into SAP BPC and then sending an email to users. For this to work, email services should be configured in SAP BPC.

> **Note**
>
> Tables 4.3, 4.4, 4.5, and 4.6 list the common data manager packages that are used in SAP BPC. If you do not see a data manager package you want to use listed in one of these tables, you can easily create a new one in SAP BPC and associate it with a process chain that will perform a specific function.
>
> You can also create custom folders to store data manager packages.

The packages and process chains outlined in Tables 4.3, 4.4, 4.5, and 4.6 are delivered with the standard data manager packages.

Data Manager Package	Description	Process Chain
Import master data	This package is used for loading master data from flat files into an SAP BPC dimension.	/CPMB/ IMPORT_MASTER
Import master data description	This package is used to load text data into a dimension.	/CPMB/IMPORT_ DESCRIPT
Import transaction data	This package is used for loading transaction data using a flat file. The transaction file should be staged in the Application folder before it can be used in the data manager package. A transformation file is necessary to load transaction data in SAP BPC for NetWeaver. The transformation file's reference in the transformation file should be available in the respective folder before the package is executed.	/CPMB/IMPORT
Import transaction data from InfoProvider	This package is used to load data from SAP NetWeaver BW InfoProviders. The data can be extracted from different types of InfoProviders—InfoCubes, DataStore objects, and MultiProviders.	/CPMB/LOAD_ INFOPROVIDER
Import transaction data from InfoProvider (enhanced user interface)	This package is available as of SAP BPC 7.5 and is used to load data from SAP NetWeaver BW InfoProviders. It provides the option to select data from the InfoProvider.	/CPMB/LOAD_ INFOPROV_UI
Import InfoObject master data	This package is available as of SAP BPC 7.5 and is used to load master data from an SAP NetWeaver BW InfoObject to an SAP BPC dimension. This process chain eliminates the need to set up an open hub destination and custom process that was used in SAP BPC 7.0 for NetWeaver to transfer master data from SAP NetWeaver BW to SAP BPC.	/CPMB/IMPORT_ IOBJ_MASTER

Table 4.3 Data Manager Packages

Data Manager Package	Description	Process Chain
Import BW InfoObject master data hierarchy	This package is available as of SAP BPC 7.5 and is used to assign PARENTH% hierarchies in SAP BPC dimension member sheets.	/CPMB/IMPORT_ IOBJ_HIER
Move transaction data	This package enables you to move data within an application. A selection screen displays during the execution of the package. The following is the sequence of steps when this package is run: The data selected for the destination is removed from the corresponding InfoProvider. The data from the source is moved based on the selection. The data is deleted from the source for the selected data.	/CPMB/MOVE
Clear transaction data in InfoCube	This package enables you to clear or delete data in an SAP BPC application. A selection screen displays during the execution of the package. On the selection screen, you must select a value for at least one dimension.	/CPMB/CLEAR
Copy transaction data	This package is used when you must copy transaction data within an application. A selection screen displays during the execution of the package. This is very useful when you want to create a baseline of plan data for the next year. You can do this by copying the current year's actual data to next year's plan data. For example, the actual sales data for 2009 can be used as the baseline data for planning 2010 sales. You can achieved this using this package.	/CPMB/COPY

Table 4.3 Data Manager Packages (Cont.)

155

Data Manager Package	Description	Process Chain
Append transaction data	Executing this package does not affect the existing data. The data is appended to the existing application. This is available only when using a flat file as the data source.	/CPMB/APPEND
Trigger BW process chain	This package allows us to trigger the execution of an SAP NetWeaver BW process chain. When you run the data manager package, the system prompts you for the process chain that needs to be triggered.	/CPMB/ TRIGGER_BW_ CHAIN

Table 4.3 Data Manager Packages (Cont.)

Financial Process Package	Description	Process Chain
Allocation	Used for executing the allocation logic.	/CPMB/ ALLOCATION
FX restatement	Runs the currency translation logic.	/CPMB/ FX_RESTATMENT
IC elimination	Used to eliminate the intercompany transactions of the business.	/CPMB/ IC_ELIMINATION
IC data	Runs the ICDATA logic that creates entries for entities to reconcile intercompany transactions with their trading partners.	/CPMB/ICDATA
IC booking	Runs the IC booking logic that posts mismatches in intercompany transactions between entities and trading partners using the ICBOOKING business rule.	/CPMB/ICBOOKING
Opening balances	Runs the carry forward balance business rule.	/CPMB/OPENING_ BALANCES
Calculate ownership logic	Runs the calculate ownership logic. This is applicable for consolidation applications.	/CPMB/ OWNERSHIPCALC

Table 4.4 Financial Processes Packages

Financial Process Package	Description	Process Chain
Consolidation	Used for running the logic for performing financial consolidation.	/CPMB/LEGAL_CONSOLIDATION
Run CalcAccount	Runs the account transformation business rule.	/CPMB/RUNCALCACCOUNT
Clear journal table	Clears the journal table.	/CPMB/CLEAR_JOURNALS
Export journal table	Exports the journal table to an output file.	/CPMB/EXPORT_JOURNAL
Restore journal table	Restores the journal table from a file.	/CPMB/RESTORE_JOURNALS

Table 4.4 Financial Processes Packages (Cont.)

System Administrative Package	Description	Process Chain
Validate logic file	Validates a logic file for syntax.	/CPMB/ADMINTASK_VALIDATE
Validate transformation file	Validates a transformation file.	/CPMB/VALIDATE_TRANSFORM
Validation	Executes the validation rules as defined in the business rules for an application.	/CPMB/VALIDATIONS
Archive audit activity	When audit activity is enabled, a lot of data may be generated. This data has to be archived periodically. This package archives audit activity.	/CPMB/ARCHIVE_ACTIVITY
Archive audit data	Archives application data.	/CPMB/ARCHIVE_DAT0041
Clear comments	Clears comments from the comments table.	/CPMB/CLEARCOMMENTS

Table 4.5 System Administrative Packages

System Administrative Package	Description	Process Chain
Light optimize	Runs the light optimize process for an application. This process closes the open request, creates indexes, and updates database statistics. When the light optimize package is run from the Admin Console, it triggers a job to immediately execute this process chain.	/CPMB/ LIGHT_OPTIMIZE
Full optimize	This works like the light optimize process. In addition, the data model of the InfoCube is also optimized.	/CPMB/ FULL_OPTMIZE

Table 4.5 System Administrative Packages (Cont.)

Miscellaneous Package	Description	Process Chain
Import and send mail	Imports a file and emails the result to a list of users.	/CPMB/IMPORT_A_ SEND_EMAIL
Import using FTP	Imports a file into the current application.	/CPMB/ IMPORT_USING_FTP

Table 4.6 Miscellaneous Packages

4.2.3 Process Chains

You use *process chains* to automate the process of extracting, transforming, and loading data and to provide different process types for managing data within the SAP NetWeaver BW and SAP BPC systems. To enable common tasks to be executed in SAP BPC, SAP provides several standard process chains as out of the box functionality, ready to be used. The process chains provided by SAP have the prefix /CPMB and can also be enabled as Business Content. These process chains, created in SAP NetWeaver BW, are wrapped into a data manager package in SAP BPC.

You create and maintain the process chains using Transaction RSPC in the SAP NetWeaver BW system. Subsequently, data manager packages are created in SAP BPC and associated with the process chains created in SAP NetWeaver BW. Tables 4.3, 4.4, 4.5, and 4.6 list the process chains associated with data manager packages.

As mentioned, process chains used for SAP BPC applications are associated with the /CPMB namespace. You can also create custom process chains based on standard process chains and adapt them to your requirements. Several process types are specifically provided for use in SAP BPC applications.

Now that we've discussed transformation, conversion files, data manager packages, and process chains, we'll look into the process of loading data into a dimension using a flat file.

4.2.4 Loading Data from a Flat File into a Dimension

Rich Bloom stores customer data, including the customer hierarchy, in a flat file. This data must be loaded from the flat file into the customer dimension. Before you load transaction data into an application, you need to load master data into a dimension. If a master data record (dimension member) is not available in a dimension when you load transaction data to an application, the transaction data load will fail.

We'll now load the customer data for Rich Bloom from a flat file into the RB_CUS-TOMER dimension. The flat file we'll use is a comma-delimited file and contains the customer ID, description, and hierarchy node for each customer. Customer_Data. csv is available for download at this book's page at *www.sap-press.com.* Proceed as follows:

1. Log into the SAP BPC Office Client, select the application set ZRB_GM_PLAN, and select the application ZRB_SALES_CMB.

2. The first step in the process is uploading the flat file to the Data Files folder of the application set. From the EDATA menu option, select DATA UPLOAD (Figure 4.15, ❶ and ❷). This opens the DATA MANAGER—UPLOAD dialog box.

3. In the DATA MANAGER—UPLOAD dialog box, select the folder icon to locate the file (Figure 4.16, ❸ and ❹).

4. Select the folder under DESTINATION FILE to store the file in SAP BPC. This opens the SAVE dialog box. Select the destination file to store the file (Figure 4.16, ❺, ❻, and ❼). The destination file is in the Data Files folder under the application set of the SAP BPC server.

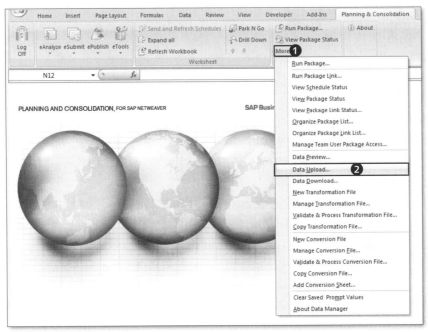

Figure 4.15 Loading Data from a Flat File into a Dimension—Part A

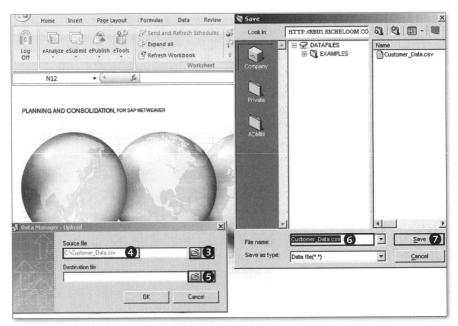

Figure 4.16 Loading Data from a Flat File into a Dimension—Part B

5. After selecting the destination file, click on OK (Figure 4.17, ❽).

Figure 4.17 Loading Data from a Flat File into a Dimension — Part C

6. You're now ready to create a transformation file to define the structure of the file you'll use to load data into the Customer dimension. From the EDATA menu option, select NEW TRANSFORMATION FILE (Figure 4.18, ❾).

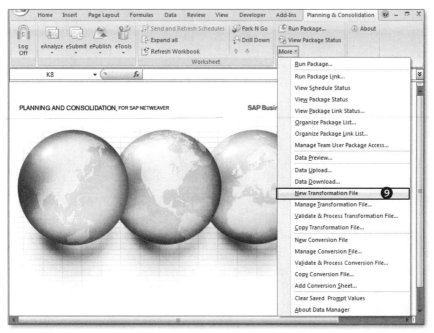

Figure 4.18 Loading Data from a Flat File into a Dimension — Part D

7. The flat file we're using is a comma-delimited file and contains the customer ID, description, and hierarchy for the customer data. The mapping is defined in the Mapping section. No data conversion is involved, so we won't use the Conversion section. The transformation file is defined as shown in Figure 4.19, ❿. From the EDATA menu option, select VALIDATE & PROCESS TRANSFORMATION FILE to validate and save the transformation file. This opens the VALIDATE & PROCESS TRANSFORMATION dialog box.

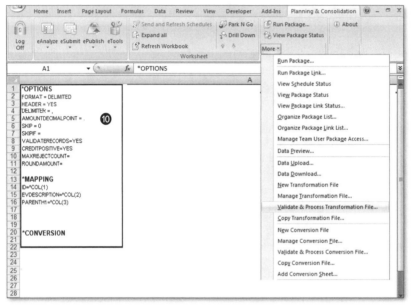

Figure 4.19   Loading Data from a Flat File into a Dimension—Part E

8. In the VALIDATE & PROCESS TRANSFORMATION dialog box, select the DATA TYPE for which this transformation file should be used (Figure 4.20, ⓫), the technical name of the dimension into which the data should be loaded (Figure 4.20, ⓬), and the DATA FILE that should be used as the source for this load (Figure 4.20, ⓭). Click on SAVE (Figure 4.20, ⓮).

9. The system validates the transformation file with the structure of the dimension and the data file. The system then outputs a log of the validation (Figure 4.21).

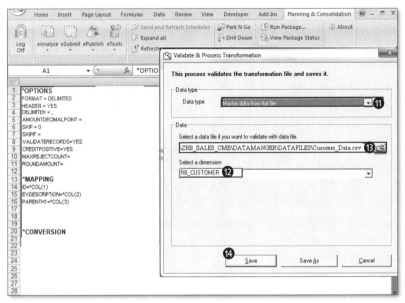

Figure 4.20 Loading Data from a Flat File into a Dimension—Part F

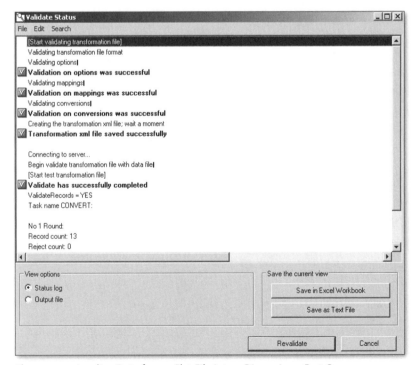

Figure 4.21 Loading Data from a Flat File into a Dimension—Part G

10. You're now ready to execute the data manager package to load the master data for customers. From the EDATA menu option, select RUN PACKAGE to run a data manager package. In the dialog box that lists the data manager packages, select the DATA MANAGEMENT group and execute the ImportMasterData data manager package (Figure 4.22, ⓯). This data manager package uses the /CPMB/IMPORT_MASTER process chain. Then click on RUN. This opens the DATA MANAGER RUN PACKAGE dialog box.

11. In the DATA MANAGER RUN PACKAGE dialog box, select the import file that should be loaded (Figure 4.23, ⓰). You can also preview the data file you'll load (Figure 4.23, ⓱). Then select the transformation file created in the earlier steps and enter the dimension name as RB_CUSTOMER for the Customer dimension (Figure 4.23, ⓲ and ⓳). Select RUN NOW, and click on FINISH (Figure 4.23, ⓴ and ㉑). Alternatively, if you want this to be loaded at a different time, you can select SCHEDULE option instead of running the package now.

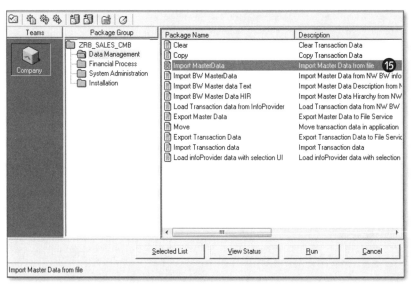

Figure 4.22 Loading Data from a Flat File into a Dimension — Part H

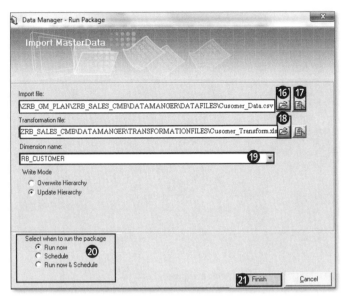

Figure 4.23 Loading Data from a Flat File into a Dimension—Part I

12. The job is scheduled as a background job, and the status of the job is refreshed every *n* seconds if the REFRESH STATUS EVERY checkbox is selected (Figure 4.24). The status is displayed as INPROGRESS, COMPLETED, or ERROR. You can display the log for the package by selecting the package and clicking on the DETAIL button (Figure 4.24, **❷**).

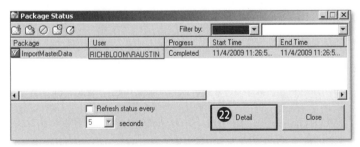

Figure 4.24 Loading Data from a Flat File into a Dimension—Part J

13. Figure 4.25 shows the detailed log of the package results.

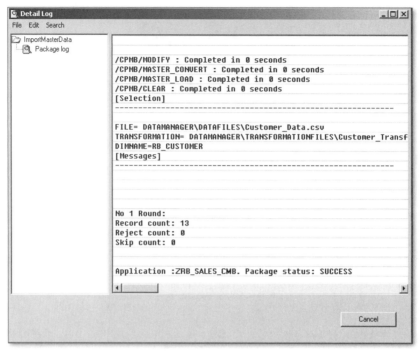

Figure 4.25 Loading Data from a Flat File into a Dimension—Part K

In this example, you've seen how to load master data from a flat file into a Customer dimension. In the next section, we'll load the actual sales and cost data that is in the ZSLS_ACT InfoCube in SAP NetWeaver BW into the planning application in SAP BPC.

4.2.5 Loading Data from an InfoCube into an SAP BPC Application

Rich Bloom stores its sales and cost data in the ZSLS_ACT InfoCube in SAP NetWeaver BW. This data needs to be loaded into the ZRB_SALES_CMB planning application in SAP BPC. Follow these steps:

1. Log into the Office Client, select the ZRB_GM_PLAN application set, and select the ZRB_SALES_CMB application.

2. Create a transformation to define the structure of the data coming from the InfoCube and to map the InfoObjects in the InfoCube to the dimensions in the application. Pull the actual sales and cost data from the ZSLS_ACT InfoCube.

3. This InfoCube contains sales and cost data for various time periods. We want to extract the data only for the calendar year 2009. This requires us to specify an option in the transformation file to restrict the data to only that of 2009. You can specify the criteria to select the data only for this period in the Options section. The SELECT option is available for this purpose and can be used only when extracting data from an InfoCube.

4. In the Mapping section, map the dimension names in the application to the corresponding technical names of the InfoObjects in the InfoCube. The data in the Sales InfoCube does not include the data for the Category dimension. All of the dimensions in an SAP BPC application must be mapped to an InfoObject or field from an external source when loading the data. When the external data source does not supply a value for a dimension, you can use the keyword *NEWCOL(<value>) to specify a value for the dimension. The <value> represents a member ID for the dimension. Map the Category dimension to the ACTUAL member ID value in the Mapping section. Similarly, set the Reporting Currency dimension to "LC" (local currency) for all of the data when loading data from the Sales InfoCube. Create a new transformation file with the definitions shown in Figure 4.26, ❶.

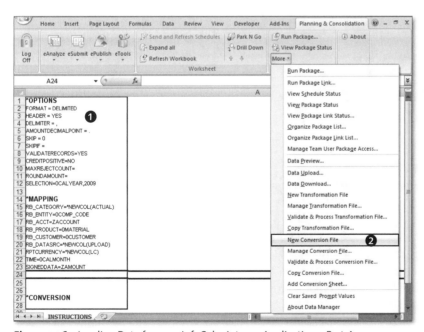

Figure 4.26 Loading Data from an InfoCube into an Application — Part A

5. The data for calendar month is in the YYYYMM format in SAP NetWeaver BW. You have to convert this into an equivalent SAP BPC format for the Time dimension, so you must define a mapping file for this conversion. From the EDATA menu option, select NEW CONVERSION FILE to create a new conversion file (Figure 4.26, ❷).

6. The conversion file contains three columns: EXTERNAL, INTERNAL, and FORMULA. In the EXTERNAL column, specify the value coming from the external source. In the INTERNAL column, specify the value as it is stored in SAP BPC. The formula can be used for any calculations on amount values. Use the conversion file for the Time dimension, as shown in Figure 4.27, ❸. From the EDATA menu option, select VALIDATE & PROCESS CONVERSION FILE to validate and save the conversion file (Figure 4.27, ❹).

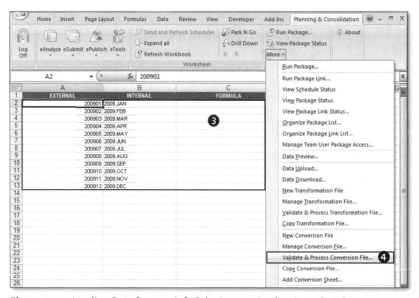

Figure 4.27 Loading Data from an InfoCube into an Application—Part B

7. The SAVE dialog box displays. Enter the file name as "RB_TIME" and click on SAVE (Figure 4.28, ❺ and ❻) for the conversion file. The conversion file is saved as an Excel file under the CONVERSIONFILES folder for the application set. The conversion file is validated with a message indicating that it was created successfully.

Figure 4.28 Loading Data from an InfoCube into an Application—Part C

8. In the Conversion section, map the Time dimension to the conversion file created in the previous step, as shown in Figure 4.29, ❼.

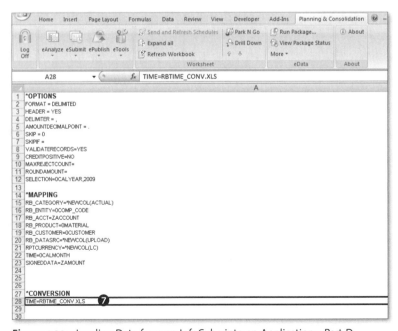

Figure 4.29 Loading Data from an InfoCube into an Application—Part D

9. Now, save the new transformation file you created in the previous step. You can optionally validate the transformation file for the options, mappings, and conversions specified in the transformation file during this process. You can see the log output of the validation in Figure 4.30.

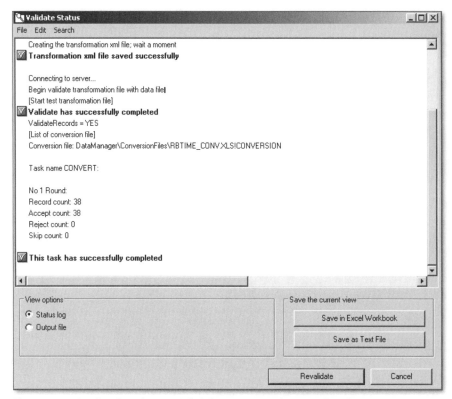

Figure 4.30   Loading Data from an InfoCube into an Application — Part E

10. You're now ready to execute the package to load the data from the ZSLS_ACT InfoCube into the SAP BPC application. Select the LOAD INFOPROVIDER DATA WITH SELECTION UI data manager package under the Data Management group, and click on RUN (Figure 4.31). This data manager package uses the /CPMB/ LOAD_INFOPROV_UI process chain. This will open the DATA MANAGER — RUN PACKAGE dialog box.

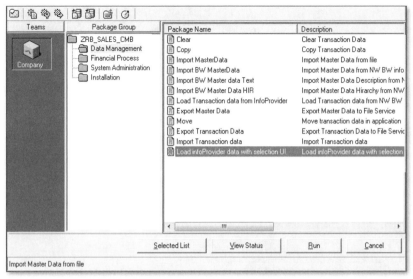

Figure 4.31 Loading Data from an InfoCube into an Application—Part F

11. In the DATA MANAGER—RUN PACKAGE dialog box, enter "ZSLS_ACT" as the InfoProvider from which to extract data (Figure 4.32, ❽). If you want to select data that is loaded from the ZSLS_ACT InfoProvider to the application, click on the SET SELECTION button (Figure 4.32, ❾) and enter selections. Select the transformation file created in the earlier step to use as the transformation file (Figure 4.32, ❿) when extracting data for this load.

12. Select the method of importing data from the database. Two options are available for this:

   ▶ Merge: This option does not delete any data in the application. When an InfoCube sends data and the corresponding record exists in the application, the record coming from the InfoCube updates the existing data in the SAP BPC application. If the record does not exist in the application, the record is added as a new record.

   ▶ Replace: When the REPLACE option is selected, the system deletes the records from the SAP BPC application based on the values of the Category, Entity, and Time dimensions in the incoming records. All incoming data from the source for these values will be first deleted from the application and then replaced with the values coming from the source.

For our example, select REPLACE & CLEAR DATAVALUES (Figure 4.32, ❶). Click on NEXT to proceed to the next step (Figure 4.32, ❷).

13. The default logic can be executed when a data manager package is run. We have not included any default logic for our application, and choosing YES or No should not matter (Figure 4.33, ❸).

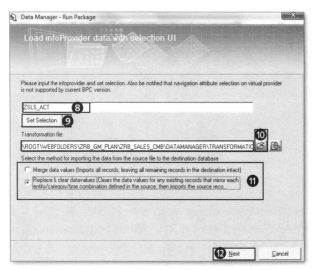

Figure 4.32 Loading Data from an InfoCube into an Application—Part G

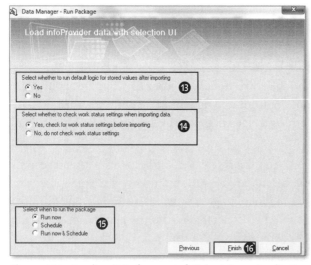

Figure 4.33 Loading Data from an InfoCube into an Application—Part H

> **Note**
>
> The name of the InfoCube you enter to use as the source data of the load is case-sensitive.

14. The work status lets you control updates to the data in an application. We'll discuss work status in detail in Chapter 9. For this example, select YES, CHECK FOR WORK STATUS SETTINGS BEFORE IMPORTING so you do not allow any updates if the work status for the updated data region does not allow for updates (Figure 4.33, ⓮). Select RUN NOW to immediately execute the package, and click on FINISH (Figure 4.33, ⓯ and ⓰).

15. The PACKAGE STATUS dialog box is displayed. After the package has run successfully, click on the DETAIL button to display the log for the package (see Figure 4.34).

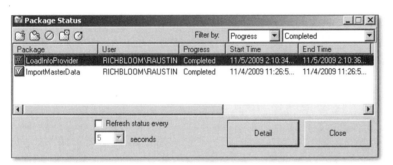

Figure 4.34 Loading Data from an InfoCube into an Application—Part I

16. The log displayed in Figure 4.35 displays the details of the package executed, along with the records processed.

In this example, you've seen how to load transaction data from an InfoProvider into an application in SAP BPC. We loaded the actual sales data for 2009 from the Actual Sales InfoCube in SAP NetWeaver BW into the planning application in SAP BPC. In the next section, we'll create baseline plan data for 2010 by copying the sales and cost data for 2009 as the plan data for 2010.

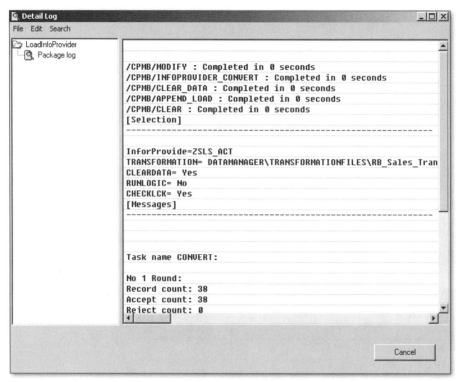

Figure 4.35 Loading Data from an InfoCube into an Application—Part J

4.3 Copying Data Inside an SAP BPC Application

To copy data inside an SAP BPC application, follow these steps:

1. Log into the Office Client, select the ZRB_GM_PLAN application set, and select the ZRB_SALES_CMB application.

2. You're now ready to copy the actual sales and cost data for 2009 as the plan data for 2010. From the EDATA menu option, select RUN PACKAGE. In the dialog box that lists the data manager packages, select the DATA MANAGEMENT group, select the Copy data manager package, and click on RUN (Figure 4.36, ❶ and ❷). The Copy data manager package uses the /CPMB/COPY process chain. This opens the DATA MANAGER—RUN PACKAGE dialog box.

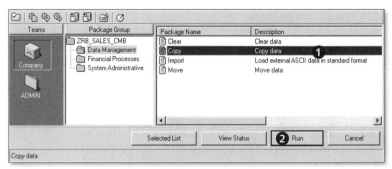

Figure 4.36 Copying Data Inside an Application—Part A

3. Next, select the options to replace and clear data values, run the default logic, and check the work status before data is imported (Figure 4.37). Then click on the NEXT button.

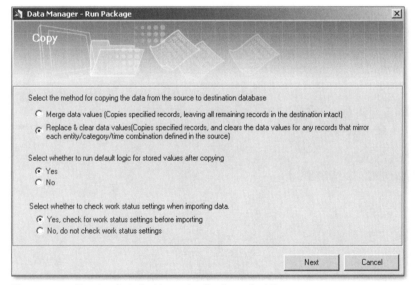

Figure 4.37 Copying Data Inside an Application—Part B

4. Our objective is to copy the data from the Actual category for 2009 to the Plan category for 2010. Under SOURCE dimensions, click on the folder icon for RB_CATEGORY to select a member value for the Category dimension (Figure 4.38, ❸). This opens a dialog box to select values.

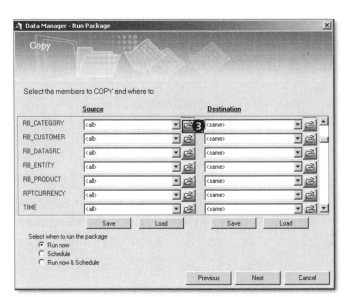

Figure 4.38 Copying Data Inside an Application—Part C

5. Select the ACTUAL member ID and click on COPY SELECTED (Figure 4.39, ❹ and ❺).

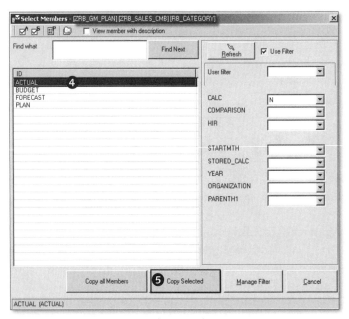

Figure 4.39 Copying Data Inside an Application—Part D

6. Under SOURCE dimensions, select the folder icon for TIME (refer back to Figure 4.38) to display a dialog box to select time periods. Select all of the 2009 time periods and click on COPY SELECTED (Figure 4.40, ❻ and ❼).

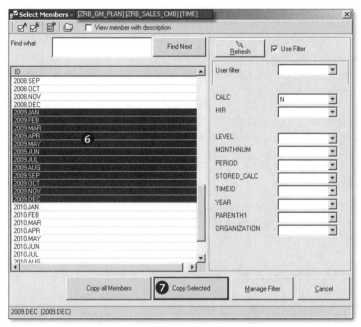

Figure 4.40 Copying Data Inside an Application — Part E

7. Now, under DESTINATION dimensions, select the PLAN member ID for the RB_CATEGORY dimension using the dropdown box (Figure 4.41). Also under DESTINATION dimensions, select all of the 2010 time periods for the TIME dimension, again using the dropdown box. After making the selections, select RUN NOW to immediately execute the package, and then click on NEXT (Figure 4.41, ❽ and ❾).

The next dialog box that displays (Figure 4.42) prompts you to confirm your selections. Select RUN NOW to immediately execute the package; then click on FINISH.

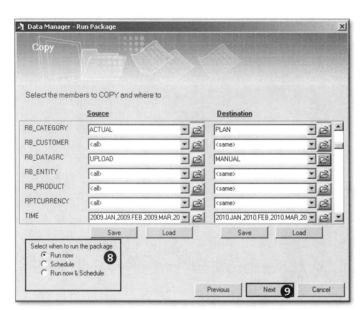

Figure 4.41 Copying Data Inside an Application—Part F

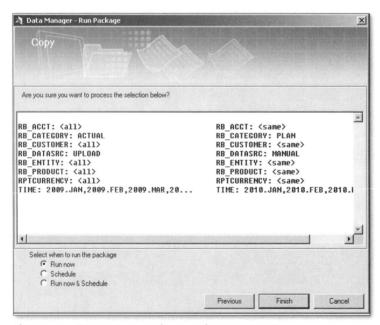

Figure 4.42 Copying Data Inside an Application—Part G

You should now understand how to copy data within an application. At this point, we have created the baseline plan data for Rich Bloom for 2010. This plan data can be revised as necessary to reflect market demand.

4.4 Summary

In this chapter, you learned how to load data from a flat file into an InfoCube in SAP NetWeaver BW. You also learned how to load data from a flat file to a dimension and how to load from an InfoProvider in SAP NetWeaver BW to an application in SAP BPC. In this process, you learned how transformation and conversion files are used when loading dimension and application data into SAP BPC. To satisfy the requirements of our model company Rich Bloom, we performed the following actions to bring data into our planning application:

▸ Loaded the customer master data from a flat file into the Customer dimension.

▸ Loaded the actual sales and cost data for 2009 from an InfoCube into the planning application in SAP BPC.

▸ Created baseline plan data for 2010 by copying the actual sales and cost data for 2009 to plan data for 2010.

In the next chapter, you'll learn how to report the data available in SAP BPC. You'll also learn how to manually modify the data using input schedules.

This chapter walks you through the development of user interface that would be used not only to report data but also to enter data into a SAP BPC application. We will discuss interfaces available for excel, word, power point and web.

5 Reporting, Planning, and Analysis in SAP BPC

In this chapter, we'll discuss how to report, plan, and analyze data using the SAP BusinessObjects Planning and Consolidation (BPC) application, describing the various reporting and analysis options available in SAP BPC. In the previous chapter, you learned how to load transaction data into an SAP BPC application; in this chapter, we'll describe the steps for setting up input schedules to enable users to manually create or modify data in an application.

Section 5.1 introduces the SAP BPC for Excel and the SAP BPC Web interface for creating reports in the application. We'll begin by explaining the usage of the Current View (CV) and Measure dimension in the context of reporting. We'll then discuss the steps for developing reports with different types of standard templates (also called *dynamic templates*). Subsequently, we'll explain how to build a custom report using Ev functions, which are standard functions used in reporting. In this context, we'll discuss some of the options available to filter, expand, and format data. We'll then present an overview of the web interface used for creating reports and conclude the section by providing tips for developing custom reports using structures and Visual Basic (VB) macros.

Section 5.2 discusses input schedules and explains how to manually modify the data in an SAP BPC application. When you set up an input schedule, you enable users to enter or modify data in an application; we'll explore the options available for this setup.

Section 5.3 summarizes what you've learned in this chapter and concludes that SAP BPC provides an intuitive and robust interface for entering plan data and for reporting and analyzing data.

5.1 Reporting and Analysis in SAP BPC

SAP BPC provides an easy-to-use and powerful interface for creating reports and maintaining data. The reporting options for SAP BPC can be classified under two broad categories:

▸ SAP BPC for Excel

▸ SAP BPC Web

An Excel interface is used to report data in SAP BPC, which can also be integrated with Word and PowerPoint documents. But SAP BPC for Excel is the primary tool used for planning, consolidation, and reporting.

The SAP BPC Web interface can be used as a complementary tool to create and enable reports on the Web.

The following are some of the key features of the reporting tool within SAP BPC:

▸ **Offers Excel tools with SAP data storage**
When you use the SAP BPC for Excel tool, you can use the functions and features available in Excel and, at the same time, store the data in an SAP BPC database. This enables users to use both Excel and a robust database for storing data, which is necessary for high-volume enterprise-wide applications.

▸ **Provides dynamic templates**
SAP BPC offers standard templates, also called *dynamic templates*, which support different types of analysis commonly requested by businesses. Standard templates can be used to develop different types of reports, including monthly comparison reports, yearly comparison reports, trend reports, and variance reports. The ability to use these templates with very little development effort reduces TCO.

▸ **Allows you to customize standard templates**
Standard templates are easy to customize to meet a particular business requirement. This easy-to-customize feature makes standard templates more appealing.

▸ **Offers flexible ways to display data**
The reporting interface is designed to provide maximum flexibility to display

data. There is no code involved in creating a report. Using selection criteria, the report displays the data that is required for analysis. The system-supplied Measures dimension lets you view the data in different ways, either by period, quarter to date (QTD), or year to date (YTD).

▶ **Provides Ev functions**
SAP BPC for Excel provides *Ev functions*, a table of functions used for reporting. This aids in creating and delivering sophisticated reports for efficient data analysis.

▶ **Allows offline analysis**
The data displayed in SAP BPC reports can also be used for offline analysis. Specific features allow users to take the data from a report offline, modify it, and retract it back into SAP BPC.

▶ **Enables data distribution**
The data in an application can be distributed to other users who may or may not have access to SAP BPC. This enables distributing data to users who may need access to it. These users can make changes to the data and send it back to SAP BPC based on their level of access.

▶ **Facilitates data maintenance**
In addition to reporting, SAP BPC can be used for entering and modifying data. We'll discuss this in detail when we talk about input schedules later in this chapter.

▶ **Provides features unique to planning and consolidation**
SAP BPC provides features that are used specifically in planning and consolidation applications. The ability to use spread, trend, and weight data makes it easy to allocate data and create projections for the future.

▶ **Offers standardized reports**
The reporting functionality includes out of the box system reports that can be displayed and executed on the Web, for example, journal reports, audit reports, and so on. They are tools to analyze metadata and to monitor changes to the objects in the SAP BPC system.

5.1.1   SAP BPC for Excel

The SAP BPC for Excel interface is used to create reports and to enter and modify data in an application. You can access this interface from the Admin Console by selecting it from the AVAILABLE INTERFACES panel on the right side of the action pane.

You can also launch the reporting tool by directly launching the BPC OfficeClient application from the desktop. When you launch this tool, you're prompted to authenticate as a valid user in the system. This authentication is similar to when you log in to the Admin Console. After the system authenticates you as a valid user, you see the Excel interface in the action pane to the right. The action pane and menu options allow you to navigate the interface.

When you log in, the logon information and the application set you are logged into are displayed (Figure 5.1, ❶). The current view (CV) list displays the application and dimension member selections (Figure 5.1, ❷). You can change the selections for the CV by clicking on the application or dimension members. To access a different application, click on the application; a new dialog box displays where you can select a different application in the application set. Similarly, when you want to make a different selection for a dimension, click on the current dimension member selection for that dimension; this displays a dialog box and enables you to select a new value to be selected.

In the lower half of the action pane, you can see a list of tasks from which you can select. The available tasks are as follows and shown in Figure 5.1, ❸.

▶ **Reporting & Analysis**
You can use this task to create reports and analyze data in SAP BPC.

▶ **Data Input**
This task enables you to create input schedules for manually modifying data. We'll will look at this in detail in the next section, about entering data into an application using input schedules.

▶ **Journals**
You use journals mainly in consolidation applications when you want to make adjustments to data. We'll talk about this in detail in Chapter 9.

▶ **Manage Data**
Use this task to perform activities related to the maintenance of data. We looked at the features of the Manage Data tasks when we discussed the process of loading data in the previous chapter.

▶ **Open SAP BPC System Reports**
You can view system-supplied reports that serve as tools to analyze metadata and monitor changes to objects by clicking on the OPEN BPC SYSTEM REPORTS task. We'll cover system reports in detail in Chapter 7.

In SAP BPC for Excel, you can also access the following interfaces from the AVAILABLE INTERFACES panel (Figure 5.1, ❹).

▶ Interface for the Web

▶ Interface for Word

▶ Interface for PowerPoint

▶ Administration

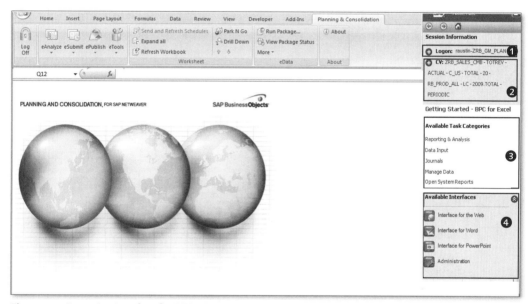

Figure 5.1 Reporting Interface for BPC—Part A

Clicking on the REPORTING & ANALYSIS task under AVAILABLE TASK CATEGORIES opens a set of tasks available for reporting data (Figure 5.2). You can build different types of reports using the Reporting & Analysis Options interface. The following options are available under the BUILD NEW heading:

▶ **Open a Blank Workbook**
Use this to create a new report.

► **Build a Report Using Drag & Drop**
This task is designed to create a report using a graphical interface by dragging and dropping dimensions into the report.

► **Build a Report Using a Dynamic Template**
You use this task to view a list of standard templates and to select a template that best fits your requirement for analysis (Figure 5.2, ➎).

Figure 5.2 Reporting Interface for BPC—Part B

The Reporting & Analysis Options interface also provides the following options under the OPEN EXISTING heading:

► **Open an Existing Report**
You can use this to open an existing report stored on the SAP BPC server.

► **Open an Existing Report from My Report Folder**
You can use this to open an existing report created by you and saved on your desktop.

Before we dive into the steps of creating a report in SAP BPC, we'll explain the terms *current view* and *Measures* dimension, which are used in the context of reporting.

5.1.2 Current View

Current view (CV) allows users to select data that needs to be displayed in a report such as applications and dimension member values. If you want to make selections for a dimension, click on a dimension member in the CV. Figure 5.5 lists the options available when using the select member lookup dialog box to select dimension member values.

1. Click on the Customer dimension member in the CV section (Figure 5.3, ❶).

2. The member values for the dimensions are displayed in a new dialog box (Figure 5.3, ❷).

3. This screen provides an option to display the member data as a hierarchy or in table format (Figure 5.3, ❸).

4. The option shown in Figure 5.3, ❹, works like a toggle to select or deselect sibling members of the highlighted member.

5. The option shown in Figure 5.3, ❺, works like a toggle to select or deselect children of the highlighted member.

6. The option shown in Figure 5.3, ❻, is used to copy the selected members to a clipboard. The selection members can then be pasted in the worksheet.

7. The option shown in Figure 5.3, ❼, is used to locate a member. Clicking on this option opens a dialog box where you can enter a search criterion to locate a member in the dimension.

8. The option shown in Figure 5.3, ❽, is used for specifying additional filters for dimension member values displayed in this dialog box. Clicking on this option opens a filter window where you can specify the property values for which you want to see member data (Figure 5.3, ⓫). After selecting the values, click on the REFRESH button (Figure 5.3, ⓬).

9. The option shown in Figure 5.3, ❾, is used for displaying the property member values of a member highlighted in the member list.

10. The option shown in Figure 5.3, ❿, is used to specify what happens when you double-click on a member. You can set the value to be transferred to the worksheet or use it as a toggle to expand or shrink the hierarchy when a member is double-clicked.

11. Click on OK to transfer the member value selected to the CV selection (Figure 5.3, ⓭).

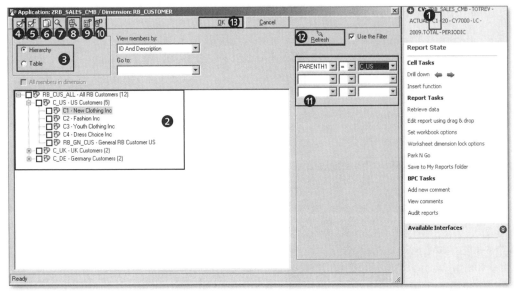

Figure 5.3 Current View Selections

5.1.3 Measures Dimension

It is important to discuss the importance of the Measures dimension in reports, because it impacts the way data is displayed in the report. The Measures dimension works in conjunction with the Time dimension and is available automatically in every SAP BPC application.

You use the Measures dimension to report quantitative information for a particular period of time, using a formula that distinguishes between balance sheet accounts and profit and loss accounts and reports information accordingly. The information for balance sheet accounts is as of the end of the period; the information for profit and loss accounts is cumulative. Three types of measures are supplied with the Measures dimension to be used in reports. They are as follows:

▶ **Periodic**
This measure displays the data for the period for which the data is selected. For example, if you select the Feb 2010 period in your report, selecting the periodic measure displays the data for that period. For profit and loss accounts, the total value for the period is reported, and for balance sheet accounts, the ending balance for the period is reported.

▶ **Quarter to date (QTD)**

This measure displays the quarter-to-date data up to the period selected. The system determines the quarter for the period displayed in the report and cumulates the data from the beginning of that quarter to the period displayed in the report. For profit and loss accounts: If you select Feb 2010 and select the QTD measure, the data from the beginning of that quarter, Jan 2010, through Feb 2010 is reported. For balance sheet accounts: The ending balance for Feb 2010 is reported.

▶ **Year to date (YTD)**

This measure displays the year-to-date data up to the period selected. For profit and loss accounts: If you select May 2010 and select the YTD measure, all of the data from the beginning of the year, Jan 2010, through May 2010 is reported. For balance sheet accounts: The ending balance for May 2010 is reported.

The data for an application can be stored as either periodic or YTD, and the storage type is dictated by the web admin parameter associated with the application. The default storage type for an application is periodic.

The formula for the Measures dimension is maintained at the application level. You can view the formula in the SAP NetWeaver BW system using Transaction UJA_MAINTAIN_MEASURE_FORMULA. Enter the application set ID, application, and user ID. When entering the user ID, do not forget to enter the domain name along with the user ID (RICHBLOOM\RAUSTIN in our example).

Listing 5.1 shows the YTD measure for an application when data is stored periodically. The YTD measure formula, based on the type of account (profit and loss or balance sheet), either sums up the values from the beginning of the year or provides the balance as of the end of a period.

```
MEMBER [MEASURES].[YTD] AS 'IIF([%P_ACCT%].CURRENTMEMBER.PROPERTIES("2/
CPMB/ACCTYPE")="INC",SUM(PERIODSTODATE([%TIME%].[LEVEL00], [%TIME%].
CURRENTMEMBER),-[MEASURES].[/CPMB/SDATA]),IIF([%P_ACCT%].CURRENTMEMBER.
PROPERTIES("2/CPMB/ACCTYPE")="EXP",SUM(PERIODSTODATE([%TIME%].
[LEVEL00], [%TIME%].CURRENTMEMBER),[MEASURES].[/CPMB/SDATA]),IIF([%P_
ACCT%].CURRENTMEMBER.PROPERTIES("2/CPMB/ACCTYPE")="AST",([MEASURES].
[/CPMB/SDATA], CLOSINGPERIOD([%TIME%].[LEVEL02])),IIF([%P_ACCT%].
CURRENTMEMBER.PROPERTIES("2/CPMB/ACCTYPE")="LEQ",-([MEASURES].[/
CPMB/SDATA], CLOSINGPERIOD([%TIME%].[LEVEL02])),-[MEASURES].[/CPMB/
SDATA]))))';SOLVE_ORDER=3
```

Listing 5.1 YTD Measure Formula for Periodic Data

If you're familiar with MDX formulas, you can create your own formulas by using Transaction UJA_MAINTAIN_MEASURE_FORMULA.

You've now seen how to use the Measures dimension in SAP BPC to report data for different periods. In the next section, we'll discuss the steps to develop reports using dynamic templates.

5.1.4 Develop Reports Using Dynamic Templates

A *dynamic template* provides a quick entry point to create a report. Predefined templates are available for different types of analysis, and you can select a template that best supports your reporting need. You can further customize the report based on a particular business requirement.

Dynamic templates let you create a report quickly and reduce development effort. The templates serve a variety of standard analyses and can be used as the basis for developing a new report. Table 5.1 shows a list of standard templates and their descriptions.

Template Name	Description
Trend	Displays the current trend of data based on the Time dimension. You can have any dimension in the row. The Time dimension is used in the column to indicate current trends.
	You can display the data in the row as a hierarchy and can customize the hierarchy levels.
Consolidating	Displays the entity data in the rows and the Time dimension in the column.
Variance	Displays the Category dimension in the column and any dimension in the rows. This report is used to calculate the variance between two different categories for a time period. The difference between the values (e.g., actual vs. budget) is displayed for the selected period.
Comparison with Prior Year	Provides a comparison of the current and prior years' periodic and YTD values for different categories (e.g., plan vs. actual).

Table 5.1 Standard Templates for Reporting

Template Name	Description
Comparison with 3 Year	Provides for year over year comparisons.
Drill in Place	Performs drill in place.
Sort on Values	Sorts by data value.
Sort on Member	Sorts by member descriptions.
Nested Rows	Allows more than one dimension to be nested in the rows, and allows one dimension in the column.
Drill Across Dimensions	Allows you to drill from one dimension to another in the rows.

Table 5.1 Standard Templates for Reporting (Cont.)

1. To create a report based on a standard template, click on BUILD A REPORT USING A DYNAMIC TEMPLATE (Figure 5.2, ❺).

2. A new REPORT WIZARD dialog box is displayed, showing the available templates (Figure 5.4). Clicking on a standard template displays a description of the template's purpose (Figure 5.4, ❻ and ❼).

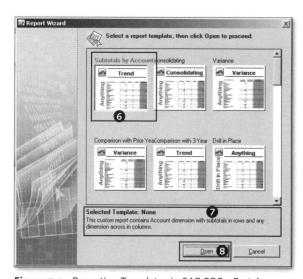

Figure 5.4 Reporting Templates in SAP BPC—Part A

3. For our example, select the SUBTOTALS BY ACCOUNTS (TREND) template, and click on OPEN (Figure 5.4, ❽).

4. A report is now automatically built with the subtotals based on the Account dimension (Figure 5.5). The selection for the report is based on member values selected in the CV.

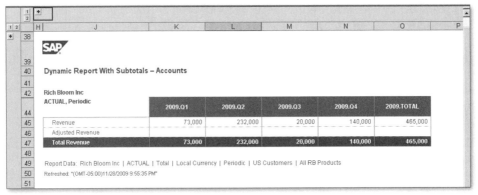

Figure 5.5 Reporting Templates in SAP BPC — Part B

You've now seen how to use dynamic templates to build a report in SAP BPC. Next, you'll see how to build a report using Ev functions.

5.1.5 Developing Reports Using Ev Functions

Several standard SAP BPC functions are available for reporting and updating data in SAP BPC. You can use them to perform tasks such as manage data, enter comments, and set the work status for an application.

SAP provides a variety of functions, called Ev functions, for reporting and managing data. The EvDRE function is one of the main functions available for creating and configuring a new report in SAP BPC. You enter this function in cell A1 of any blank workbook before configuring a report or input schedule. Table 5.2 shows a list of Ev functions. The descriptions explain the purpose of each function and its usage in reports.

Function Name	Description	Example
EvSND	Sends data to SAP BPC using a cell as reference. This function can be used only in input schedules.	The following function can be inserted in a cell to enter and send a value: EvSND(R12,"Finance","SalesPlan",CO GS,RB2, "Budget", "P1",2010.Jan") Any dimension in the application that is not specified in the send command is taken from the CV. The previous command sends the value in cell R12 of the worksheet. We are assuming the following application set and dimension members exist: Application set: Finance Application: Sales Plan Accounts: Cost of goods sold (COGS) Entity: RB2 Category: Budget Product: P1 Time: Jan, 2010
EvAST	Returns the ID or the technical name of the current application set.	EvAST()
EvASD	Returns the description of the current application set.	EvASD()
EvAPP	Returns the ID of the current application.	EvAPP()
EvAPD	Returns the description of the current application.	EvAPD()
EvUSR	Returns the user name of the user currently connected to an application.	EvUSR()

Table 5.2 List of Ev Functions

Function Name	Description	Example
EvSVR	Returns the name of the server to which the user is connected.	EvSVR()
EvDIM	Returns the name of the dimension when a dimension type is specified. The following dimension types can be used: A (Account), E (Entity), C (Category), T (Time), R (Currency), U(x) (User Defined, where x is the number of the user-defined dimension)	EvDIM("E") This function outputs the name of the entity dimension for the current application.
EvTIM	Specified time offsets.	EvTIM("SALESPLAN", 2010.Feb, 3) This function returns "2010.May" as the output. The first parameter, "SALESPLAN," denotes the application. The second parameter denotes the time member on which the offset should be performed. The last parameter denotes the offset. A positive or negative value can be specified.
EvCVW	Returns the dimension member values set in the current view for an application.	EvCVW(AppName,Dimension,Filter) This function returns the value of the dimension member of the dimension in the CV. In addition, if you double-click on a cell that contains this function, it returns the list of members in a dimension filtered based on condition specified in the filter.

Table 5.2 List of Ev Functions (Cont.)

Function Name	Description	Example
EvGTS	Retrieves the data from an application based on dimension member selections that are passed to this function. If selection criteria are not specified for a dimension, the selections are taken from the CV.	EvGTS(AppName, ScaleValue, Member1, Member2,.. Membern)
EvPRO	Returns the property value of a specified dimension member.	EvPRO(AppName, Member, Property)
EvBET	Performs a better or worse comparison of two values, based on the account type property of the account member.	EvBET(AppName, AccountMember, Value1, Value2,...) This is a useful function when you're comparing actual data and budgets. For example, you can use this function to compare the Revenue account to see how well you've performed with respect to the budget.
EvHOT	Links one report to another report. Clicking on a cell containing this function opens another report.	This is useful when it is necessary to jump from one report to another using the data in the original report as the context.
EvDRE	This is the main function used to configure new reports and input schedules. It is bi-directional and can be used to retrieve data and to enter or modify data. This function is optimized for large sets of data; we recommend using this function instead of EvSND or EvGET.	EvDRE(AppName, KeyRange, ExpandRange)

Table 5.2 List of Ev Functions (Cont.)

195

Function Name	Description	Example
EvCOM	This function is also bi-directional and can be used to retrieve and send comments. The range to which the comment should be retrieved or from which it should be sent is specified, along with the dimension members with which the comment is associated.	EvCOM(CommentRange, AppName, Member1, Member2,...)
EvEXP	Performs row or column expansions.	EvEXP(AppName, Member, KeyRange, DataRange, ExpandDown(TRUE or FALSE))
EvMBR	Allows you to select a member from the Member Selector dialog box.	This is useful when you want to provide a custom selection option to let users select a dimension member from the list.
EvMNU	Allows you to create menu tasks that can be used as links to perform several SAP BPC tasks. For example, a menu function can be created to open an input schedule when the link is clicked.	EvMNU(Macro Name, Display Name, Parameter)

Table 5.2 List of Ev Functions (Cont.)

1. To create a new report, select the OPEN A BLANK WORKBOOK task from the BUILD NEW list of tasks shown in Figure 5.2.

2. Enter "EvDRE()" in cell A1 in the new worksheet, and press Enter (Figure 5.6, ❶).

3. Click on REFRESH WORKBOOK to configure the settings for the new report (Figure 5.6, ❷).

4. This opens the BPC—EVDRE BUILDER dialog box. The available dimensions for the application are displayed (Figure 5.6, ❸). Drag the dimensions from this location to the columns and rows as required for your report.

5. In this example, we've pulled the RB_ACCT dimension to the rows and the Time dimension to the columns (Figure 5.6, ❹ and ❺).

6. Specify a dimension in the SPREAD ACROSS WORKSHEETS field if you want to create multiple EvDRE reports for each value selected for that dimension. For example, if want to create a profit and loss report for each entity in the organization as a separate worksheet, you can include the Entity dimension here.

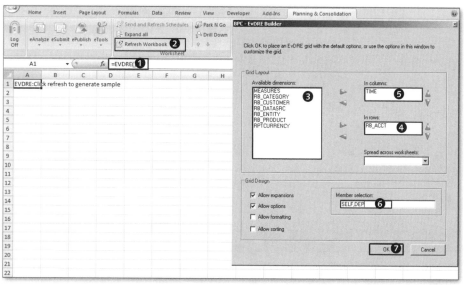

Figure 5.6 Creating an EvDRE Report—Part A

7. You can select the preferred options in the GRID DESIGN area to allow for expansions and for enabling formatting and sorting of data in the report. The ALLOW EXPANSIONS option is useful for allowing users to drill down to details.

8. The data is displayed based on the values selected in the CV. For the dimensions included in the rows and columns, specify how you want to select the dimension member values. In our example, we have specified the "SELF,DEP" member selection (Figure 5.6, ❻). This displays the member value selected in the CV, because we have included "SELF" in the selection. In addition, because we have specified "DEP," if the member value is a hierarchy node, then the dependent values are also displayed.

9. Click on the OK button when you have completed the selections (Figure 5.6, ❼).

10. This displays the report based on dimension member value selections in the CV (Figure 5.7). The data displays the actual sales for Rich Bloom for 2009 and lists the sales by quarters.

11. Click on the + sign that is available above column D to make further changes to the report format and selections (Figure 5.7, ❽). This will open the report's control panel.

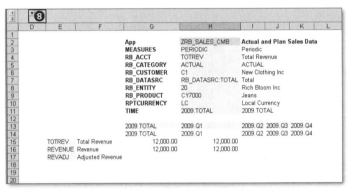

Figure 5.7 Creating an EvDRE Report — Part B

Note

If two different dimensions contain the same member ID, then we should reference the dimension member ID using that dimension. For example, in Figure 5.7, the member TOTAL in RB_DATASRC dimension is specified as RB_DATASRC:TOTAL. (TOTAL is the parent of all RB_DATASRC dimension members.)

---

12. Let's us assume that we want to see the sales totals by the individual months (January to December), not by quarters. The months are the base members for the Time dimension. Change the setting for the report to display only the base members for the Time dimension. Set the MEMBERSET parameter for the Time dimension to "BAS" (Figure 5.8, ❾).

13. We'll also display the Account Type property of the Account dimension member in the rows. To accomplish this, insert a new column using the Excel functionality between columns F and H (Figure 5.9, ❿). Under column G14, to the right of ACCOUNT DESCRIPTION, enter a formula to retrieve the Account Type property of the accounts to be displayed in the rows (Figure 5.9, ⓫). To do this, select BPC FUNCTIONS to see the list of functions, select the EvPRO function, and click on OK (Figure 5.9, ⓬, ⓭, and ⓮).

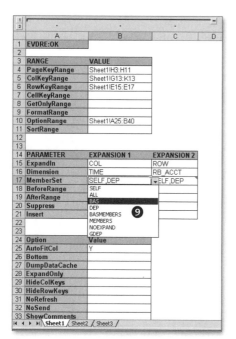

Figure 5.8 Creating an EvDRE Report—Part C

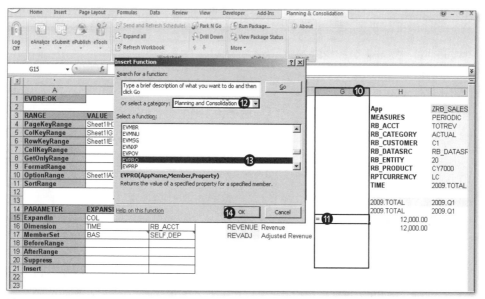

Figure 5.9 Creating an EvDRE Report—Part D

14. In the FUNCTION ARGUMENTS dialog box, enter "ZRB_SALES_CMB" as the name of the application, select the cell reference that corresponds to the first account member value displayed in the row for which you want to display the property, and specify "ACCTYPE" as the property name (Figure 5.10, ⓯). Click on the OK button to continue (Figure 5.10, ⓰). Then click on the EXPAND button (Figure 5.10, ⓱).

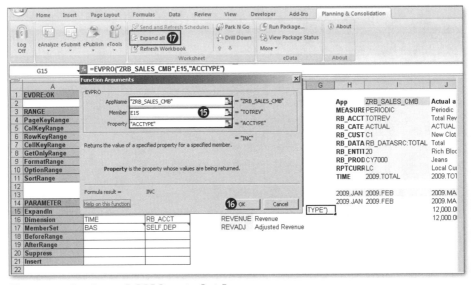

Figure 5.10 Creating an EvDRE Report—Part E

15. After you click on the EXPAND button, the report shown in Figure 5.11 is displayed. It displays the total revenue for 2009.

16. Next, we'll display details of the Gross_Margin account on the report. First, modify the Account dimension member selection in the CV to point to the GROSS_MARGIN account (Figure 5.12, ⓲).

17. For the MemberSet parameters for the Account dimension that is displayed in the rows, select BAS and click on the EXPAND button to refresh the data (Figure 5.12, ⓳ and ⓴). This displays all of the base members for the Gross_Margin account on the report.

18. Next, we'll build a filter for the Account dimension displayed in the rows by using the Build Filter feature in SAP BPC. Right-click on the red icon that is displayed to the right of the MEMBERSET parameter for the Account dimension (Figure 5.12, ㉑).

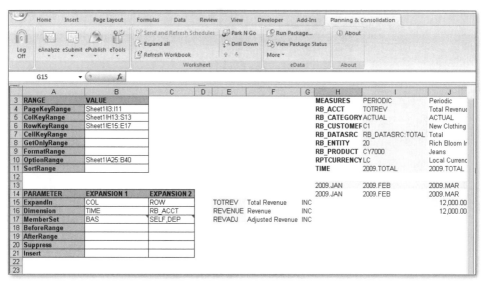

Figure 5.11 Creating an EvDRE Report—Part F

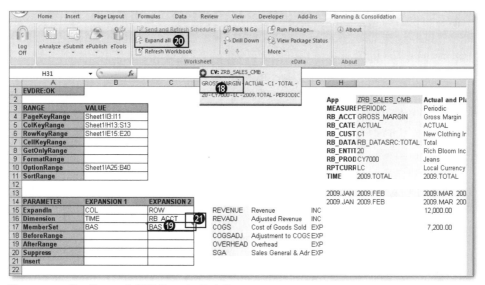

Figure 5.12 Creating an EvDRE Report—Part G

19. Now click on EVDRE: BUILDER FILTER to make the selections for the Account dimension (Figure 5.13, ㉒).

Figure 5.13 Creating an EvDRE Report—Part H

20. The FILTER dialog box is displayed to define the selections for the data. Here, you can specify the property value used as a basis for selecting data. The interface also allows you to specify the selection criteria in multiple lines, using "AND" or "OR" expressions (Figure 5.14, ㉓). After specifying the selections, click on APPLY (Figure 5.14, ㉔).

21. The selections you made in the filter are displayed in the MemberSet parameter for the Account dimension (Figure 5.14, ㉕). Now click on the EXPAND button to display the report (Figure 5.14, ㉖).

22. You're now ready to save the report. You can save it locally on your desktop by going to the EANALYZE menu and then selecting SAVE MY REPORTS.... Selecting this option makes the report is available only to you.

23. We'll save this report to the Company folder so that others in the organization can access it. From the ETOOLS menu option, select SAVE DYNAMIC TEMPLATES (Figure 5.15, ㉗). This opens the SAVE AS dialog box.

24. Select the COMPANY folder (Figure 5.15, ㉘). Specify the file name "Actual Sales Data for 2009" and click on SAVE (Figure 5.15, ㉙ and ㉚). This enables other users who have access to this folder to execute the report.

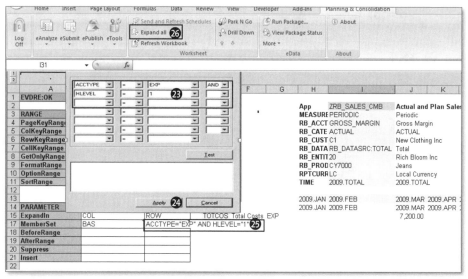

Figure 5.14 Creating an EvDRE Report—Part I

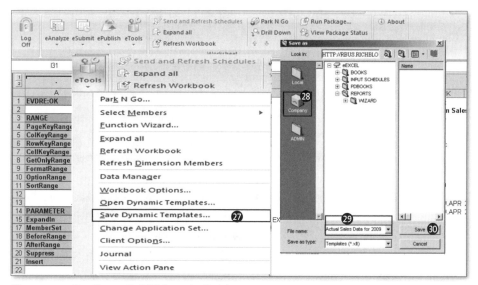

Figure 5.15 Creating an EvDRE Report—Part J

Now that we've discussed the creation of reports using EvDRE, we'll review some of the options available to format the report. The formatting of reports is done in the control panel.

5.1.6 Control Panel

All EvDRE reports in SAP BPC have a control panel where you can set expansion options, filter parameters, and formatting parameters. The following are the sections available in the control panel of a report:

- Range
- Parameter
- Options
- Format
- Sort

Range

In the Range section, you can specify the range of cells that will contain specific values. Table 5.3 describes the parameters.

Parameter	Description
PageKeyRange	Specifies the range of cells that contain the set of default dimension member values used to filter data for the page.
ColKeyRange	Specifies the range of cells that contains the keys for columns in the report.
RowKeyRange	Specifies the range of cells that contains the keys for rows in the report.
CellKeyRange	Specifies the range of cells that will overwrite dimension member IDs used in ColKeyRange and RowKeyRange.
GetOnlyRange	Specifies a range of cells in an input schedule that should only retrieve (not send) values. The cells are designated as read-only.
FormatRange	Specifies the range of cells that contain the instructions to format data in the report.
OptionRange	Specifies the range of cells that contain options that can be set in a report such as Show Comments, Hide Column Keys, and so on.
SortRange	Specifies the range of cells that contain instructions to define sorting of data in rows of the report.

Table 5.3 Range Parameters

Parameter

You can use the Parameter section to set parameters related to expansion and filters of a report or input schedule. We saw some examples of using these parameters when we developed the report using the EvDRE function earlier. Table 5.4 shows a list of parameters you can set in this section.

Parameter	Description
ExpandIn	Specifies whether the expansion of a dimension needs to be done by row (ROW) or column (COL).
Dimension	Specifies the dimension for which you want to set the expansion and filter parameters.
MemberSet	Specifies the set of dimension member values to use to filter and display data for rows or columns in a report. You can either choose a specific value or use one or more of the following keywords: ▶ **SELF**: The current member. If you define the MemberSet as SELF, the expansion occurs on the current member. If you leave MemberSet blank, the system suppresses the expansion. ▶ **DEP**: All children of the current member. You can enter DEP (parent) to return the dependent members of a specified parent rather than using the parent from the page key range or current view. ▶ **BASMEMBERS**: All base members in the dimension. ▶ **BAS**: All base members below the current member. ▶ **NOEXPAND**: Do not expand. ▶ **ALL**: All dependents and base members that fall under the current member.
BeforeRange	You use this parameter to dynamically insert rows and columns at the beginning of expansions.

Table 5.4 Parameters

Parameter	Description
AfterRange	You use this parameter to dynamically insert rows and columns of data at the end of expansions.
Suppress	Setting this parameter to Y allows you to suppress rows and columns that contain zero or null values.
Insert	Setting this parameter to Y allows you to dynamically insert an explicit set of members before a current row or column of a report or input schedule.

Table 5.4 Parameters (Cont.)

Options

Use the Options section to set parameters related to a report or an input schedule. Table 5.5 shows a list of options you can set.

Parameter	Description
AutoFitCol	Automatically adjusts the size of the columns containing the EvDRE ranges to fit the content after refreshing data.
Bottom	Shows only the specified number (*n*) of the lowest values in the entire data range.
DumpDataCache	Writes the content of the data cache to the log file *EvDre_log. txt*.
ExpandOnly	Disables the refresh action and performs only an expansion, when requested. The system does not retrieve data from the database.
HideColKeys	Hides the column key ranges.
HideRowKeys	Hides the row key ranges.
NoRefresh	Prevents the system from refreshing data from the database.
NoSend	Prevents the system from sending data to the database.
ShowComments	Adds an Excel comment in any DataRange cell with a formula, if the value retrieved from the database differs from the one displayed by the formula.

Table 5.5 Options

Parameter	Description
ShowNullAsZero	Fills all empty cells in the data range with zeros.
SortCol	Sorts a given column.
SumParent	Inserts new rows with subtotals.
SuppressDataCol	Performs suppression on the defined columns directly in Excel.
SuppressDataRow	Performs suppression on the defined rows directly in Excel.
SuppressNoData	Prevents the suppression of zero values in the report.
Top	Shows only the specified number (n) of highest values in the entire data range.

Table 5.5 Options (Cont.)

Format

The Format section contains instructions for formatting data in a report or an input schedule. Table 5.6 shows a list of the columns in the Format section.

Parameter	Description
Criteria	Defines criteria for formatting data. The following are valid values: ▶ **CALC**: Applies to calculated values ▶ **INPUT**: Applies to noncalculated values ▶ **DEFAULT**: Default format
Evaluate In	Defines the range for which the criteria must be evaluated. The following are valid values: ▶ **ROW**: Evaluate in rows ▶ **COLUMN**: Evaluate in columns ▶ **ROWCOL**: Evaluate in rows and columns ▶ **PAGE**: Evaluate in pages
Format	Lets you specify font attributes such as color, font size, font style, bordering, etc.

Table 5.6 Format Parameters

Parameter	Description
Use	Lets you specify which components of the formatting properties should be applied. The following are valid values: ▸ **ALL**: Apply all formatting properties ▸ **PATTERN**: Apply all pattern properties ▸ **NUMBER**: Apply all numbering properties ▸ **ALIGNMENT**: Apply all numbering properties ▸ **FONT**: Apply all font properties ▸ **FONTSTYLE**: Apply all font style properties ▸ **BORDER**: Apply all border properties ▸ **FRAME**: Apply all frame properties ▸ **STYLE**: Apply all style properties ▸ **CONTENT**: Apply all content properties ▸ **LOCK**: Apply LOCK property
Parameters	Lets you specify formatting instructions directly into text format.
Apply To	Lets you specify the sections of a report or input schedule to which a format should be applied. The following are valid values: ▸ **KEY**: Applies to row and column key ranges. ▸ **HEADING**: Applies to text associated with keys that exists between the keys and data. For example, a description associated with account derived using EVDES. ▸ **DATA**: Applies to data range. ▸ **BLANK**: Applies to keys, heading, and data.

Table 5.6 Format Parameters (Cont.)

These parameter options allow you to develop customized reports to meet specific reporting requirements.

Recall that earlier, we discussed the CV and said that the values selected in it determine the selection of data in the report. At the same time, we also studied the ability to specify filter values in the control panel of the report, for example, by specifying dimension member values in the MemberSet. In the context of EvDRE reports, it is important to understand the order of precedence of the CV to determine how the values of filters are applied to a report or input schedule.

In the next section, we'll look at the order of precedence the system uses to apply filter values to reports.

Order of Precedence of the Current View

If filter definitions conflict with one another, the system uses the following order of precedence, from lowest to highest, to determine filter values. For example, the cell key, if it exists, takes precedence over the row key; the row key takes precedence over the page key; and the page key takes precedence over the current view (CV bar). Refer to Table 5.7 for the order of precedence of the CV.

Rank	Description
1	The system CV, as defined by the CV bar.
2	The workbook CV, as defined in the workbook options.
3	The page CV, as defined in the PageKeyRange.
4	The column CV, as defined in the ColumnKeyRange.
5	The row CV, as defined in the RowKeyRange.
6	The cell CV, as defined in the CellKeyRange.

Table 5.7 Current View Order of Precedence

We've already discussed the steps to create and format reports using the SAP BPC for Excel interface.

5.1.7 Developing Reports Using the EVGET Function

In the previous section, we used the EVDRE function to develop a report. There are alternative functions to use in addition to EVDRE to report data in SAP BPC. We can use the EVGET function.

You use the EVGET function to retrieve data to a single cell based on the selection of dimension members. An EVGET function calls the database to retrieve the data for the selection. Note that when a report containing the EVGET function is refreshed, there will be as many calls made to the database as the number of cells in the report that contains this function.

The EVGET function allows data to be retrieved based on the parameters defined in this function. The selections for which the data is retrieved are specified in the function. In the EVGET function, the application name and the dimension values for the dimensions in the application are specified.

The syntax for using the EVGET function is as follows:

▶ EVGET(AppName,[dim:]member1,[dim:]member2,...[dim:]memberN)

▶ EVGET function can also be used inside an EVDRE type report

> **Note**
>
> If values are not specified for some dimensions in the EvGET() function, for those dimensions, the system uses the selection of dimension members in the current view to retrieve the data.

The EvGET function provides a lot of flexibility in reports to retrieve data. It also provides the ability to bring data from different applications within an application set. But it is inefficient in the way it is run because each function costs a call to the database when the data is refreshed.

Next, we'll discuss development of an EvDRE report that does not use the expansion option.

5.1.8 Development of EvDRE Report With "No Expansion"

When the layout of a report or input template is static and is not expected to change, you can use an EvDRE report with no expansion. You use a report with no expansion when you know the dimension members that you want to report in the rows and/or columns. You can also use this option if you can derive the members (using Excel functions) that are required in your rows and/or columns.

This report is created like any EvDRE report, you either do not specify the expansion range in the EvDRE function or you specify the NOEXPAND option in the MemberSet for rows and columns in the parameter section of report or input schedule.

In a report or input template without expansions, for those dimensions that are in the rows or columns that are set to NOEXPAND, changes made to selections of dimensions in the current view (CV) or page key range will not have any effect on the content of the report because the members entered in the row and column key ranges take priority for reporting. Recall the precedence of the current view that we discussed earlier in this chapter.

Let's look at an example to illustrate usage of an EvDRE report with NOEXPAND. Let's say you want to display rolling forecast data for accounts. We're in May 2010 when you want to display this data. The data in the rolling forecast should display the actual data for the periods January 2010 through April 2010 (periods elapsed) and the forecast data for periods May 2010 into the future.

The actual data and the forecast data reside in the same application. The category associated with actual data is ACTUAL, and the category associated to forecast data is FORECAST.

An easy way to develop this report is to copy actual data for the closed months to the forecast category. In this approach, the actual and forecast data resides in the same category (FORECAST), and it is easy to report on the same category using EvDRE with expansion.

Let's say we did not copy the actual data into the forecast category at the close of every period. We can still create a rolling forecast report provided we know the period up to which actual data is available. Let's assume that the category dimension has a member called ACTUAL and this member has a property called CURR_MONTH that is updated with the period up to which actual data is available. Because we are in the month of May 2010, we'll have the property CURR_MONTH for the ACTUAL member set to "2010.APR" to indicate that actual data is available until this period.

In a rolling forecast report, we want to display data for all of the forecast periods. But for periods that have already elapsed, we want to display the actual data. We'll list accounts along the row, and the category and time periods along the column. Figure 5.16 shows the format of the report. We take the following steps to define this report.

1. Define an EvDRE report with no expansions. The EvDRE command contains the application name, key ranges, and the expansion range as parameters. In this case, we do not specify the expansion range.

2. In the key range section, specify the row key and column key range. In the row key range, you define the range of cells that would contain rows data. We'll enter the list of accounts in the rows. In the column key range, define the range of cells that would contain column data. We'll enter "Category" and "Time" along the column.

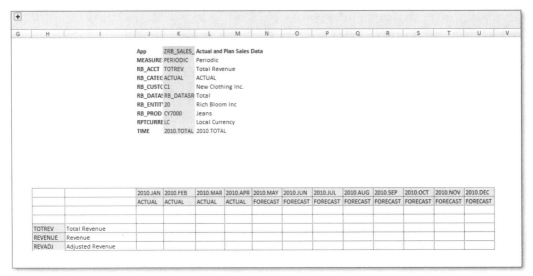

Figure 5.16 Rolling Forecast Report

3. Assuming your forecast is for a year, display 12 months of data. Display the actual data for the periods that have elapsed and forecast data for future periods.

4. The user selects the year for which the rolling forecast is to be displayed by choosing a time period in the year in the current view (CV). Define an EVCVW function in, let's say, cell D3 that would retrieve the period chosen by the user.

```
EVCVW(<application name>,"TIME")
```

5. Define an EVPROfunction in cell D4 to read the CURR_MONTH property in the Category dimension for the ACTUAL member.

```
EVPRO(<application name>, "ACTUAL", "CURR_MONTH")
```

6. Define another EVPRO function in cell D5 to look at the period obtained in the previous step (content of cell D4) and determine the TIMEID for the period from the Time dimension. We'll use this TIMEID to compare with periods in the current year to determine if we need to use the ACTUAL or FORECAST category for each period.

```
EVPRO(<application name>,$D$4,"TIMEID")
```

7. Define the static member in the row key range area. List the accounts for which you want to see the rolling forecast information in the cells defined by the row key range.

8. In the column key range, based on the year selected by the user, populate the 12 months in the cells that represent TIME. For example, in the current view, if the user selects 2010.TOTAL, using an Excel formula, determine the 12 months for the 12 cells in the column key range that represents TIME. We can use the MID Excel function as follows:

```
=MID($D$4,1,4)&."JAN", =MID($D$4,1,4)&."FEB" etc.
```

9. In the column key range, specify the following formula in each cell in the 12 columns that represent Category—whether ACTUAL or FORECAST. In the formula, we're reading the TIMEID property for the each of the 12 periods and determining whether the ACTUAL or FORECAST category would apply to the period.

```
=IF(EVPRO(<App Name>,<reference cell containing time period in
column>,"TIMEID")>$D$5, "FORECAST", "ACTUAL")
```

10. You've defined an EvDRE report with no expansions for developing the rolling forecast report.

In summary, you've seen how to define a rolling report to display actual data for elapsed periods and forecast data for current and future periods. You also saw how to use the function EvPRO to return the property value from a dimension number and use it in your report.

SAP BPC also provides an interface to develop and display reports on the Web. We'll now discuss the steps involved in doing so.

5.1.9   Developing Reports Using the SAP BPC Web Interface

From the SAP BPC Web interface, you can develop reports using drag-and-drop. This provides you with an easy-to-use interface for developing reports, and users can start developing reports with little training. These types of reports are used less frequently than Excel-based SAP BPC reports but can be used by users who prefer to report on the Web.

1. To build a report using drag-and-drop, click on the INTERFACE FOR THE WEB link in the list of available interfaces (refer back to Figures 5.1 and 5.2).

2. Figure 5.16 shows the web interface that displays. Click on LIVE REPORTING (Figure 5.17, ❶). This opens a new interface titled LIVE REPORTS LIST OPTIONS. Click on BUILD A REPORT USING DRAG & DROP (Figure 5.17, ❶ and ❷).

Figure 5.17   Creating a Report Using Drag-and-Drop—Part A

3. Drag the RB_ACCT dimension to the rows, select INHERIT MEMBER VALUE FROM CV, and click on the green checkmark to continue (Figure 5.18, ❸, ❹, ❺, and ❻).

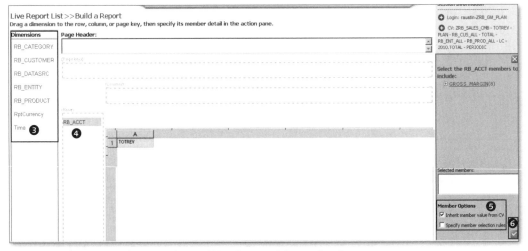

Figure 5.18   Creating a Report Using Drag-and-Drop—Part B

4. You've selected the RB_ACCT dimension for the rows. Now drag the Time dimension to the columns and select 2010.TOTAL in the right pane as the filter

for this report. Select SPECIFY MEMBER SELECTION RULES, and click on the green checkmark to continue (Figure 5.19, ❼, ❽, ❾, and ❿).

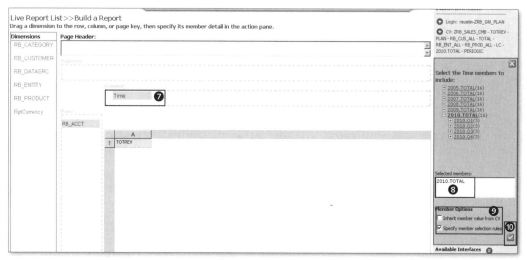

Figure 5.19 Creating a Report Using Drag-and-Drop—Part C

5. In the MEMBER SELECTION RULE—STEP 1 OF 2 section, select DEPENDENTS ONLY OF SELECTED, and click on the green checkmark to continue (Figure 5.20, ⓫ and ⓬).

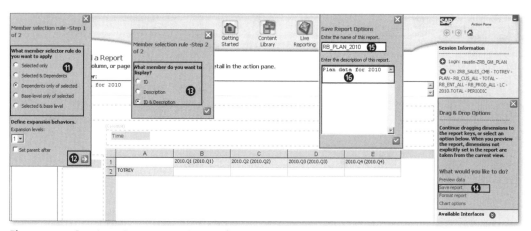

Figure 5.20 Creating a Report Using Drag-and-Drop—Part D

6. In the MEMBER SELECTION RULE—STEP 2 OF 2 section, select ID & DESCRIPTION, and click on the green checkmark to continue (Figure 5.20, ⓭).

7. You're now prompted by the question "What would you like to do?" Click on SAVE REPORT (Figure 5.20, ⓮). You're prompted to enter the technical name and description of the report. Enter "RB_PLAN_2010" for the technical name and "Plan data for 2010" as the description (Figure 5.20, ⓯ and ⓰). Then click on the green checkmark to continue.

8. You can now access the report from the LIVE REPORT LIST. Click on the report to display it (Figure 5.21, ⓱ and ⓲). You can click on the plus icons to drill down further into the report. For example, you can drill down on the totals displayed by quarter to see the data by month.

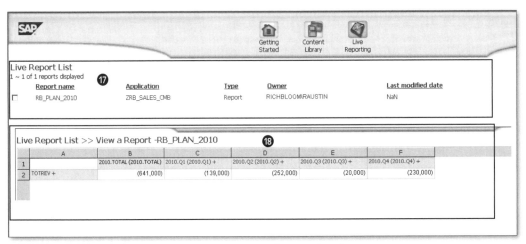

Figure 5.21 Creating a Report Using Drag-and-Drop—Part E

You've now seen how you can develop and deploy reports using the SAP BPC Web interface. In the next section, we'll provide tips to develop reports using structures and VB macros.

5.1.10 Developing Reports Using Structures and VB Macros

You may sometimes want to develop custom reports that group data displayed in each row using a specific criteria. For this, you can use structures. In some reports, you may also want to use VB macros to calculate certain values.

Usage of Structures in Reports

We'll now use the EvDRE function to create a report that displays the total revenue, total cost, and gross margin for all entities (grouped together) of our model company, Rich Bloom. There are many ways to develop a report to meet this requirement. We'll develop this report using structures to demonstrate this function. We can use structures to report groups of data.

To create the report, identify the dimensions that will be used to create the grouping, and include these dimensions in the rows. Identify the dimension to be displayed in the column.

1. Start by creating an EvDRE report, and include the Account and Entity dimensions in the rows, because you want to create a row for a combination of values, based on accounts and entities in your structure. Include the Time dimension in the column. Figure 5.22, ❶, shows the CV. All of the products have been selected because the report has to display the data for all of the products.

2. In the MemberSet parameter for the Account dimension, include the following accounts, each separated by a pipe sign. Each account will be displayed as a separate row in the report (Figure 5.22, ❷).

   "TOTREV|TOTCOS|GROSS_MARGIN"

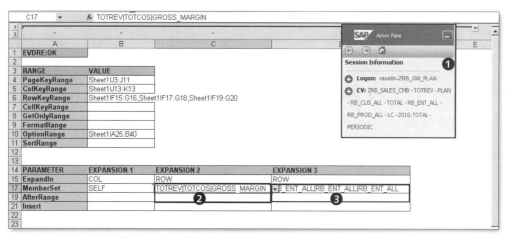

Figure 5.22 Creating a Structure in a Report—Part A

3. In the MemberSet for the Entity dimension, include the following entities, each separated by a pipe sign. Each entity will be displayed as a separate row in the report (Figure 5.22, ❸).

```
"RB_ENT_ALL|RB_ENT_ALL|RB_ENT_ALL"
```

4. Enter the following value in the RowKeyRange, as shown in Figure 5.23, ❹ and ❺. Every combination should include at least two rows. Then click on the Expand button to display the report.

```
=EVRNG(F15:G16,F17:G18,F19:G20)
```

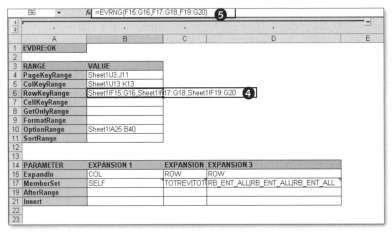

Figure 5.23 Creating a Structure in a Report—Part B

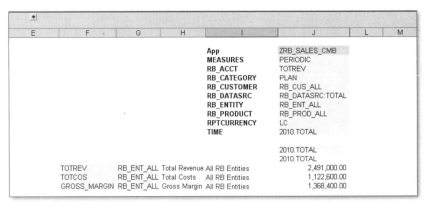

Figure 5.24 Creating a Structure in a Report—Part C

5. The report displays the data you requested (Figure 5.24), but notice that the descriptions associated with the Account and Entity dimensions are displayed in the report. If you want to display only one description for each row, hide some of the columns that you do not want to display.

6. You can hide the row keys by setting the HIDEROWSKEYS option to "Y" (Figure 5.25, ❻). This hides columns F and G. You can hide column H using the HIDE option in Excel (Figure 5.25, ❼).

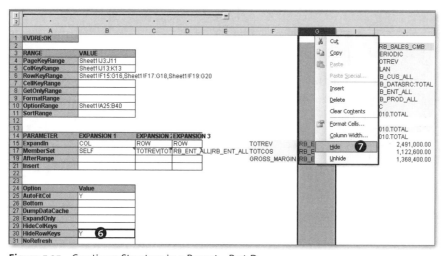

Figure 5.25 Creating a Structure in a Report—Part D

7. In the rows displayed in column I, enter the description for the row values (Figure 5.26, ❽). Save the report using ETOOLS • SAVE DYNAMIC TEMPLATE.

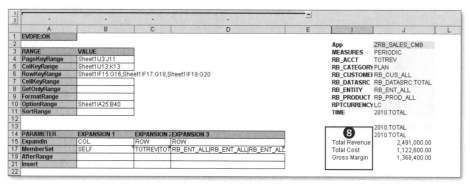

Figure 5.26 Creating a Structure in a Report—Part E

We've now created a report that groups data based on your requirements. Next, we'll see how to use VB macros in reports.

Usage of Visual Basic Macros in Reports

SAP BPC comes with several macros that you can use in reports and input templates. In addition, you can develop custom macros in SAP BPC and assign them to buttons in reports and input schedules. When you click the button, the macro will be executed. You can also develop macros and assign them to specific functions such as AFTER_REFRESH, AFTER_CHANGECVW, and so on. If a macro is coded under the AFTER_REFRESH function, then the macro code is executed after a user refreshes data in a report or input template.

You can also run SAP-supplied macros within custom macros. Please find below an example of a command for running the SAP-supplied macro to refresh data in a report or input template.

```
Application.Run "MNU_ETOOLS_REFRESH"
```

With the following macro, users are not prompted to save the workbook when they exit an input schedule.

```
Private Sub Workbook_BeforeClose(Cancel As Boolean)
 Me.Saved = True
End Sub
```

Let's look at an example of creating a custom macro. We have an account called Gross Margin created as a member in the Account dimension. This account is set as a node of income and expense accounts. The gross margin is calculated by aggregating the values in the accounts. Now, instead of using the hierarchy for calculating the gross margin, we want to use a VB macro that subtracts total cost from total revenue to derive the gross margin.

To perform this calculation, we must develop a macro using VB. Any time data is expanded in SAP BPC; for this, the function AFTER_EXPAND is executed. We can include VB code in this function to perform certain specific tasks. In our example, we'll use this function to derive the gross margin. The AFTER_EXPAND function should be in a separate module (Figure 5.28, ❿ and ⓫).

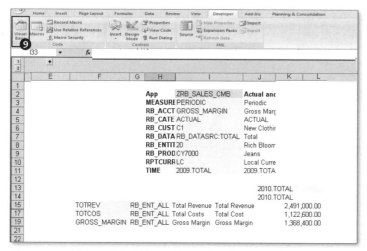

Figure 5.27 Usage of Visual Basic Macros in a Report—Part A

1. From the menu, select TOOLS and, under the MACRO submenu, select the VISUAL
   BASIC editor (Figure 5.27, ➒). Then create a new module and include the code
   shown in Figure 5.28, ⓬.

Figure 5.28 Usage of Visual Basic Macros in a Report—Part B

2. This code reads the total revenues value in cell J15 and the total cost value in
   J17 and populates the gross margin in cell J19.

3. The last statement in the code sets the cursor in cell J15.

In this example, we coded our macro in the AFTER_EXPAND function. Depending on business requirements, you can execute a custom operation in any of the functions shown in Table 5.8.

Function
BEFORE_CHANGECVW
AFTER_CHANGECVW
BEFORE_REFRESH
AFTER_REFRESH
BEFORE_SEND
AFTER_SEND
BEFORE_EXPAND
AFTER_EXPAND

Table 5.8 Functions Where VB Macros Can Be Coded

The name of the function tells you when the function will be executed; for example, the AFTER_CHANGECVW function is executed after changing CV values.

You should now understand how to create a report using VB macros. We coded the formula for the gross margin and populated a cell with this value.

Syntax for MemberSet

We'll conclude this section by providing a few tips for developing syntax to specify member values for a dimension in the MemberSet. You should use the conventions and guidelines shown in Figure 5.29 when developing the syntax.

After reading this section, you should now know how to create reports using standard templates. We discussed the usage of Ev functions to develop custom reports, and you learned how to develop and execute reports on the Web using drag-and-drop functionality. In the next section, we'll explain how to use input schedules to enter and modify data in an application.

Combination	Expression*	Example	Incorrect use case	Comment
Member ID + Member ID	[Member ID], [Member ID]	2006.Jan,2006.Feb ExtSales,ICSales	2006.Jan ,2006.Feb ExtSales ,ICSales	Space is not allowed.
Member ID + Flag	[Member ID],[Flag]	Actual,DEP ICSales,BAS(2006.TOTAL) SalesKorea,LDEP(2,BalanceSheet) BAS(2006.Q1),2006.Q1	Actual ,DEP SalesKorea , LDEP(2,BalanceSheet) BAS(2006.Q1) ,2006.Q1	Space is not allowed.
			Actual or DEP SalesKorea or LDEP(2,BalanceSheet) BAS(2006.Q1) or 2006.Q1	'AND'/ 'OR' is not allowed.
Member ID + Filter	[Member ID],[Filter]	ExSales,ACCTYPE="INC"	ExSales ,ACCTYPE="INC"	Space is not allowed.
			ExSales or ACCTYPE="INC"	'AND'/ 'OR' is not allowed.
Flag + Flag	[Flag],[Flag]	SELF,DEP BAS,DEP(2006.Q1) LDEP(2),BAS	SELF ,DEP BAS ,DEP(2006.Q1) LDEP(2), BAS	Space is not allowed.
Flag + Filter	[Flag] **and** [Filter]	BAS(2006.Q1) and LEVEL="MONTH" Budget and Period="2006" LDEP(2,BalanceSheet) and Year="2007" SELF,,DEP and ACCTYPE="INC",ID=Account:SalesKorea MEMBERS and Group="ACTUAL"	Budget , Period="2008" MEMBERS , Group="ACTUAL" LDEP(2,BalanceSheet) , Year="2007"	Comma is not allowed.
			Budget or Period="2006" MEMBERS or Group="ACTUAL" LDEP(2,BalanceSheet) or Year="2007"	'OR' is not allowed.
Flag + ParentAfter	[Flag],[ParentAfter]	SELF,ParentAfter DEP(2006.Total),ParentAfter,SELF ParentAfter,MEMBERS and Acctype="INC" and Group="Profit & Loss"	SELF ,ParentAfter DEP(2006.Total) ,ParentAfter , SELF	Space is not allowed.
			SELF or ParentAfter DEP(2006.Total) or ParentAfter or SELF	'AND'/ 'OR' is not allowed.
Filter + Filter	[Filter] **and/or** [Filter]	AccType="INC" or AccType="EXP" and calc="N" Year="2007" or Period="2006"	CALC="Y" and [YEAR="2006" or PERIOD="TOTAL"]	Bracket is not allowed.
			YEAR="2006" CALC="Y"	Comma is not allowed.

Figure 5.29 SAP AG Usage and Considerations of EvDRE for SAP BPC 7.0M

5.2 Planning in SAP BPC Using Input Schedules

An input schedule is used for entering and modifying data in an application. For input schedule reports, data entered in the report can be validated and updated in the database.

The following are some of the uses and features of input schedules:

▶ **Entry of data at the base member level**
When you use input schedules, the dimension member to be updated cannot be a hierarchy member. The rows in the input schedule should be base members. For example, if the Revenue account is a hierarchy member and is a parent of several base members, it cannot be directly used in the input schedule. The data needs to be entered only for the base members that make up the hierarchy member.

▶ **Concurrency lock**
When data on an input schedule is sent for updating, the locks on the data are checked. These locks are called *concurrency locks* and are designed to prevent two users from updating the same set of data at the same time. If two users enter data for the same selection and try to send the data to the database at the same time, only the user who obtained the lock first will be able to update the data. The user who sends the request for a lock later will get an error message stating that another user has already obtained the lock and that the update cannot happen at this time.

▶ **Work status**
Work status can be configured to prevent changes from being made to data; for example, the plan data for 2010 can be set to the locked status so that no further changes can be made to it. When a user attempts to modify data for a region that is locked, he receives a message indicating that the data cannot be modified due to work status locks. We'll discuss work status in detail in Chapter 7.

▶ **Validation of data**
SAP BPC for NetWeaver supports creating validations in the SAP NetWeaver BW system. For example, a validation can be set up to ensure that transaction data entered for an entity located in the United States accept U.S. dollars as the currency. If data for an entity located in the United States is entered with euros as the currency, the validation test fails and the data is rejected. Transaction UJ_VALIDATION is available for configuring validations in the SAP NetWeaver BW system. This is a new functionality that is available only in SAP BPC for NetWeaver.

ABAP can be used to create custom logic to enforce validations when you use this transaction. The validation mechanism can be used to configure validation rules that are checked before data is entered or updated. We'll discuss how to use and set up validations in Chapter 6.

5.2.1 Standard Templates for Input Schedules

Similar to the standard templates used for reporting, standard templates are available for entering data. The standard templates for input schedules are also based on the EvDRE function. Table 5.9 shows a list of standard templates used for input schedules.

Template Name	Description
Account Trend	The Account Trend input schedule is used for displaying and modifying the current trend of data based on the Time dimension. The account members are displayed in the rows, and time data is displayed in the columns.
Consolidating	The Consolidating input schedule contains Account Type members in the rows and Entity members in the columns.
Entity Trend	The Entity Trend input schedule is set up similarly to the Account Trend template. The only difference is that the Entity Trend input schedule contains Entity members in the rows, and the Account Trend input schedule contains account members in the rows.
Nested Row	The Nested Row input schedule is set up so that no more than one dimension can be specified in the rows.
Comparative	The Comparative input schedule is defined to display account members in the rows and category members in the columns.

Table 5.9 Standard Templates for Input Schedules

5.2.2 Workbook Options

Before we go into creating an input schedule, it will be helpful to look at the various workbook options that are applicable for reports and input schedules. You can set the workbook options by selecting WORKBOOK OPTIONS from the ETOOLS menu. The available selections provide additional control and further customization features that may be required in a report or an input schedule. The settings for these options are available in WORKBOOK OPTIONS and are outlined in Table 5.10.

225

Workbook Option	Description
Type	The type indicates whether a workbook is a report or an input schedule. If the user needs to modify and update the data in an application, the report should be set as an input schedule report.
Refresh and Expansion	The following options are available to refresh data: ▸ Refresh Workbook on Worksheet Update: This option refreshes the data when a change is made to an affected data cell. ▸ Refresh After Data Send: When the workbook is an input schedule, a refresh is performed after sending the data. ▸ Expansion on Workbook Open: When this option is selected, the expansion is automatically executed when the workbook is opened. ▸ Expansion on Current View Change: When this option is selected, the expansion is executed automatically when there is a change to the expansion member in the current view. ▸ Refresh by Sheet: When multiple worksheets are opened, selecting this option refreshes worksheets individually.
Allow Users to Change Options	If you select this option, nonadministrators can also change the workbook options. If this option is not selected, only administrators can change workbook options.
Drilldown	This option specifies drill-down behavior. There are two options: ▸ Expand by Overwriting Rows: When this option is selected, the expanded members display the data below the expanded member, clearing the existing members. ▸ Expand by Inserting Rows: When this option is selected, the existing members are displayed below the expanded members. The existing members are not cleared.
Read Options for Comment	This option can be used to specify how a comment entered in SAP BPC is displayed: ▸ Within Cell: Text is displayed inside the cell. ▸ As Excel Popup: Text is displayed in an Excel dialog box.

Table 5.10 Workbook Options

Workbook Option	Description
Set Maximum Expansion	This option is available to set the maximum columns and rows that can be displayed in the workbook. This option is used for performance reasons: ▶ The default number of columns is set to 100. ▶ The default number of rows is set to 1,000. ▶ The maximum number of columns is 255. The maximum number of rows is 65,000. This setting determines the maximum rows and columns in the report.
Override Current View Settings	The workbook always uses the dimension members selected in the CV settings to display the report or input schedule. If you want to override the current view settings, you can specify a two-range dimension containing the dimension and member values. If you do so, the value of the dimension members specified here is used and overrides the current view settings. This applies only to EvDRE templates.
Save the Session CV with the Workbook	When you're running different reports in a session, the value in the CVs is used for all reports. When you want to use different member values for the same dimension in different reports, you can select this option.
Set Worksheet Password	A specific SAP BPC password may be set to secure the workbook. This password works differently from the Excel-based password. Do not use the Excel-based password in SAP BPC, because expansions may not work properly.
Lock Status	The status below this heading indicates whether a workbook is open or locked. A workbook can be locked by selecting the Park N Go option from the eTools menu.

Table 5.10 Workbook Options (Cont.)

5.2.3 Developing an Input Schedule

We'll now explain how to create an input schedule to manually enter and modify data.

1. The creation of an input schedule is similar to the creation of a report. First, create a report using the EvDRE function that has the Account dimension in the row and the Time dimension in the column. Alternatively, you can use the DATA INPUT task that is available in the available task categories (refer back to Figure 5.1, ❸) to create the input schedule. Figure 5.30, ❶, shows the selections of dimension member values.

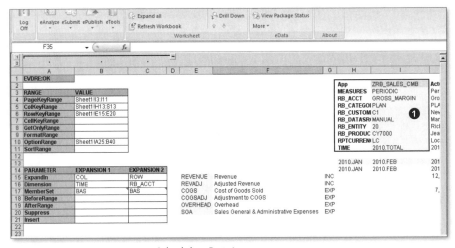

Figure 5.30 Creating an Input Schedule—Part A

2. After creating the report, select the ETOOLS menu and then select WORKBOOK OPTIONS. Select INPUT SCHEDULE as the workbook type (Figure 5.31, ❷). This allows users to use the workbook to enter or modify data in an application.

3. The REFRESH OPTIONS automatically refresh the data when changes to CV selections are made (Figure 5.31, ❸). Click on the OK button (Figure 5.31, ❹) after you have set the options.

4. After selecting the type of report to be an input schedule, click on SEND AND REFRESH SCHEDULE (Figure 5.32, ❺). This is required before the report can be used as an input schedule.

5. Enter "2,000" as the amount for February 2010 (Figure 5.32, ❻). Then click on the SEND AND REFRESH SCHEDULE button again to send the data to the database.

This opens the SEND AND REFRESH SCHEDULES dialog box. Select ACTIVE WORK-BOOK and click on the REFRESH button (Figure 5.32, ❼).

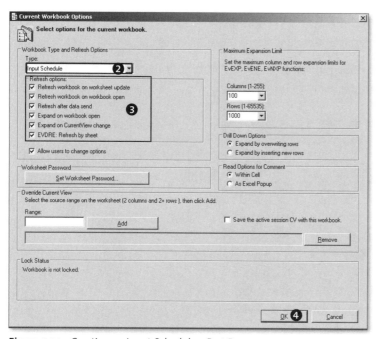

Figure 5.31 Creating an Input Schedule—Part B

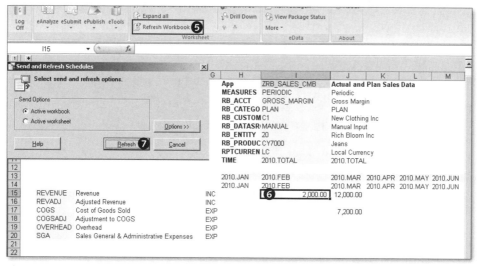

Figure 5.32 Creating an Input Schedule—Part C

6. The BUSINESS PLANNING AND CONSOLIDATION dialog box is displayed, indicating the number of records that will be sent to the database and asking you to confirm the update to the database (Figure 5.33, ❽).

7. After you confirm the action to continue, a message log displays the details of the records updated in the database (Figure 5.33, ❾).

You should now understand how to create an input schedule. We'll now discuss the EvSNDl option to create an input schedule.

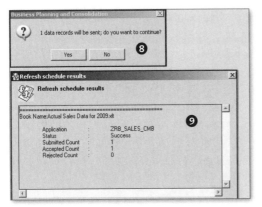

Figure 5.33 Creating an Input Schedule—Part D

5.2.4 Developing an Input Schedule Using EvSND

In the last section, we discussed development of input schedules using EvDRE function. In this section, we will see how we can use the EvSND function to send data from an input template to the database. The EvSND function syntax includes the application name, the dimension values that represent the selection for which data is sent, and the reference cell that contains the value to be updated.

The syntax for using the EvSND function is as follows:

```
EvSND(ValueReference,AppName,[dim:]member1,[dim:]member2,...[dim:]
memberN)
```

where ValueReference is the reference cell that contains the signed data.

You can send the data only for a base member, and a member value should be specified for every dimension in the application. You can also use the EvSND function inside an EvDRE input schedule.

The EvGET and EvSND functions provide a lot of flexibility in reports and input templates to retrieve and send data. They also provide the ability to bring data from different applications within an application set. But they are inefficient in the way that they are run because each function costs a call to the database when the data is refreshed or sent. Please exercise caution when using these functions.

We'll now discuss additional properties that you can set for reports and input schedules.

5.2.5 Worksheet Dimension Lock Option

In the previous example, we used the selection of dimension member values in the CV for the input schedule. If you want to override the selection of dimension member values in the CV with other specific values for a report or input schedule, you can use the worksheet dimension lock options. The values specified here override the CV settings for the member and any settings specified in the workbook options of a report or input schedule.

The worksheet dimension lock options are available under DATA INPUT • AVAILABLE TASK CATEGORIES • SCHEDULE TASKS (Figure 5.1, ❸).

5.2.6 Park N Go

Park N Go is a function that is available in SAP BPC to lock either the CV or both the CV and the data in a report or input schedule. You can also use this function to take a workbook offline. This feature is useful when you want a user of a particular report or input schedule to use specific dimension member value selections when executing this report and to prevent him from refreshing the data. Another application of this functionality is to take an input schedule offline, send it to a user who does not have access to SAP BPC, have him enter data, and then bring the input schedule online for updating the data entered by the user.

You can access Park N Go by selecting ETOOLS • PARK N GO and set one of the following options (Figure 5.34):

▶ **Live**
This is the default setting for a report or input schedule.

▶ **Live Data and Static Current View**
This option locks the CV in a report or input schedule. When a user changes the CV selections, the selections for the report or input schedule are not changed.

▶ **Static Data and Static Current View**
This option not only locks the CV in a report or input schedule but also prevents the data in the report or input schedule from being refreshed.

▶ **Offline (No Connectivity)**
With this option, a workbook can be taken offline and distributed to users who do not have access to SAP BPC. After these users have made changes to the data, the workbook can be brought online again by selecting the LIVE option.

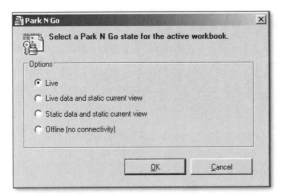

Figure 5.34 Park N Go

5.3   Summary

In this chapter, we explained the steps for reporting, planning, and analyzing data in SAP BPC. We discussed examples of how to use dynamic templates and create a custom report using the Ev functions and explained how to create and deploy reports on the Web. We then went on to create an input schedule, and explained how to use it for entering and modifying data in an application.

In Chapter 6, we'll introduce different types of business logic that can be configured in SAP BPC and see how it automates several tasks related to planning and consolidation. Here, you'll learn how to configure business rules, develop K2 scripts, and set up validation.

In this chapter, we discuss options available in SAP BPC to apply business logic. Dimension formulas, script logic, business rules, and BAdIs can be used to define business logic and perform calculations in planning and consolidation applications.

6   Developing Business Logic in SAP BPC

Every organization has rules and policies that guide its business processes and must be incorporated into IT applications; this is no different for planning and consolidation applications. In this chapter, we'll discuss the options available in SAP BusinessObjects Planning and Consolidation (BPC) for defining logic and automating the process of deriving data and enforcing business rules.

In Section 6.1, you'll learn how to use dimension formulas to perform calculations in SAP BPC applications.

In Section 6.2, we'll discuss the usage of K2 logic or script logic in SAP BPC, and you'll learn how to use it to perform functions related to data management. (*Script logic* is a code-based logic that is used to meet complex business process requirements.)

In Section 6.3, we'll discuss business rules and their usage in SAP BPC. We'll briefly look at how they are used to perform certain common tasks related to planning and consolidation. (We'll also discuss business rules in Chapter 9, when we discuss the process of consolidating financial data for an organization.) In this section, we'll explain how to perform currency translation, which is used in the context of planning and consolidation. Currency translation is a requirement for an organization that does business in more than one country and/or has transactions in different currencies.

In Section 6.4, we'll discuss allocation. Organizations commonly use allocation to apportion expenses incurred by a common entity, such as a corporate entity, to other units based on certain drivers.

In Section 6.5, we'll review the usage of BAdIs to define business logic in SAP BPC. BAdIs are coded using the ABAP language, which provides additional flexibility when there is a need to write custom code. It also helps to leverage ABAP expertise in the organization when implementing SAP BPC applications.

In Section 6.6, we'll discuss validation of data in SAP BPC, explaining how to use driver dimensions to define validation rules and enforce data integrity.

We'll start by discussing how to use dimension formulas to automatically calculate values in an SAP BPC application.

6.1 Dimension Logic

In the past few chapters, we discussed how to use dimensions in SAP BPC. We went through the process of defining a dimension and loading data into it and talked about how to integrate it into an application and use it in reporting. In Chapter 3, we explained that a dimension can have a property with a technical name of Formula, which means that it contains formulas that aid in the automatic calculation of data. This process is referred to as *dimension logic*.

6.1.1 Dimension Formulas

To use dimension formulas, you must include a property with the technical name Formula to the dimension. This property contains a formula; for example, in the Account dimension, there could be a Gross Margin dimension member that has the formula property filled with a formula called Total Revenues−Total Cost.

> **Note**
>
> Ensure that your formula property is set to be long enough that it can accommodate the formula defined for the member.

The following rules apply to the formula property of a dimension:

▸ Formulas can be set only for base members, not for hierarchy members, of a dimension.

▸ When a formula is defined for a dimension member, you cannot directly enter any data for that member.

▶ In the formula, the name of the dimension should be used to refer to dimension members, but the dimension name is not required for the Account dimension. For example, the formula property of dimension member Product 3 can be set as follows:

```
[PRODUCT].[Product1] + [PRODUCT].[ Product2]
```

Note the usage of the technical name of the PRODUCT dimension in the formula.

▶ The dimension formula for the dimension member applies to all applications containing the dimension in the application set.

▶ SAP BPC supports the use of addition, subtraction, multiplication, and division operators when defining formulas.

▶ You can use multidimension expressions when defining formulas; these are especially useful for complex formulas. The list of available MDX expressions can be displayed by executing the BAPI_MDPROVIDER_GET_FUNCTIONS function module in the SAP NetWeaver BW system. The ApShell comes with a list of standard MDX formulas, available in the file *Mdxlib.lgf.* When maintaining dimension members to include MDX formulas, specify the name of this library file in the options sheet of the dimension member maintenance screen.

▶ The syntax of the formula is checked when dimension members are activated using the Process dimension option.

▶ When a formula is defined for a dimension member, the system calculates the result for the dimension member based on the formula at runtime. Including formulas for a dimension member can cause data retrieval to take more time depending on the amount of data on which the formula has to work.

6.1.2 Solve Order

In the context of defining dimension formulas, it is important to understand the *solve order keyword*. In some reports, you may display more than one dimension member that is calculated based on a dimension formula, and the solve order function helps resolve conflicts between two formulas used in a report. In this situation, it sets the priority for which formula should be used.

For example, let's look at a scenario where you have the Account dimension with members Account 1, Account 2, and Account 3 in an application set. Account 3 is defined as a calculated member based on the following formula:

```
Account3 = [ACCOUNT].[Account1]/[ACCOUNT].[Account2]
```

Assume that the same application set includes another dimension, Product, with the members Product 1, Product 2, and Product 3. The Product dimension is defined as a calculated member based on the following formula. SAP BPC evaluates the member with the highest solve order first, and calculates it last. Zero is the highest priority.

```
Product 3 = [PRODUCT].[Product1] + [PRODUCT].[Product2]
```

Here, we have two calculated members, Account 3 for the Account dimension and Product 3 for the Product dimension. For these dimension formulas, we can set the solve order function to set which formula should take precedence over the other. A formula that has the solve order defined as a lower value takes priority over others with a higher value; a formula that has the solve order defined as a value of 0 takes the highest priority. In SAP BPC release 7.5, when we add the FORMULA property to a dimension, the SOLVEORDER property is also added to the dimension. We'll define the formulas to include the solve order function as follows:

```
Account3 = [ACCOUNT].[Account1]/[ACCOUNT].[Account2];SOLVE_ORDER=5
Product 3 = [PRODUCT].[Product1] + [PRODUCT].[ Product2];SOLVE_ORDER=50
```

Consider a report that contains the accounts in rows and products in columns. Table 6.1 shows the format of such a report.

	Product 1	Product 2	Product 3
Account 1	120	130	250
Account 2	5	5	10
Account 3	24	26	50

Table 6.1 Demonstration of Solve Order

Now look at the value of the cell that intersects Account 3 and Product 3. The result is 24 + 26 = 50, not 250/10 = 25. This is because the Account formula takes precedence over the Product formula, because the value of the solve order for the Account formula is less than that of the Product formula.

Now, let's create a Gross Margin dimension member in the Account dimension. We'll calculate the gross margin by subtracting the total cost from the total revenue. Recall from Chapter 3 that we set the gross margin as a hierarchy node of total revenue and total cost. To demonstrate the use of the Dimension formula, we'll no longer have the gross margin as a hierarchy node. Instead, we'll use gross margin as a base dimension member and define a dimension formula that calculates the gross margin.

We'll now create a dimension formula for the Account dimension in our planning application.

1. Log in to the SAP BPC Admin Console, select the ZRB_GM_PLAN application set, and select the ZRB_SALES_CMB application.

2. From the DIMENSION LIBRARY, select the RB_ACCT dimension, and then click on the DIMENSION MEMBERS task in the right pane. You'll see the list of dimension members for the Account dimension displayed.

3. The GROSS_MARGIN account was set as the parent for the TOTALREV and TOTALCOS members. Remove the parent relationship from the TOTREV and TOTCOS accounts, because we'll be using a dimension formula to derive the value for the GROSS_MARGIN account.

4. Then, go to the cell that is associated with the formula property for the GROSS_MARGIN account, and enter the formula as shown in Figure 6.1.

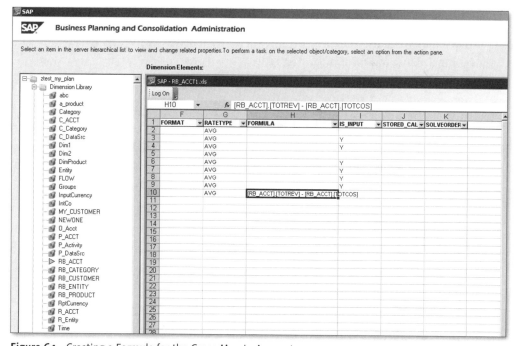

Figure 6.1 Creating a Formula for the Gross Margin Account

5. After entering the formula, process the changes for the Account dimension, and then run a report that shows the gross margin account. The application now uses the formula to derive this value (Figure 6.2).

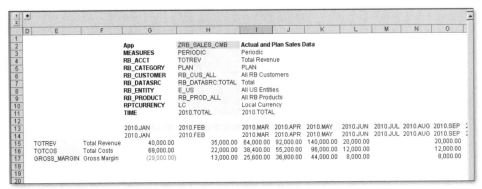

Figure 6.2 Reporting the Gross Margin Account Using the Dimension Formula

In this section, we explained how to use dimension formulas to automatically calculate values. We also discussed the importance of using solve order when defining a formula and how to use it when multiple formulas are in conflict.

In the next section, we'll explain the use of script logic in SAP BPC and see how it can help us satisfy detailed business requirements that cannot otherwise be met using a standard SAP BPC configuration.

6.2 Script Logic

Sometimes a business process may be so complex that a standard configuration is not enough to satisfy a requirement, or it may not be feasible to use dimension formulas. In these cases, you can use script logic, or K2 logic, to meet the requirement.

Consider a business scenario where you're planning sales for a future period. You copied last year's actual sales data as the basis of planning for the current year; however, due to changes in current demand, it is now necessary to adjust revenue based on the realities of the market by, say, accepting a percentage value from the user to either increase or decrease revenue. This is a good candidate for script logic because it is not possible to meet this requirement using the standard SAP BPC application or dimension logic. Script logic, on the other hand, can be used to increase or decrease revenues by a certain percentage for certain selections.

The script language provides full-fledged language support to write custom logic to meet a specific business requirement. The language constructs are similar to 4GL and can be easily included in an SAP BPC application. They are powerful and efficient, especially when a lot of data needs to be processed.

A script file is used to create the code and is stored with the extension .lgf. We'll now look at some of the common instructions used in script logic.

6.2.1 Script Logic Construct

In this subsection, we'll discuss some of the commands used when developing script logic.

Pass Specific Dimension Members

It may be necessary to pass specific members to apply in the script logic. You can achieve this using the following coding instruction, which overrides any members selected for the dimension in the CV or prompt statements for that dimension. This will be helpful if you want to use only a specific member list in your script logic; you can specify more than one member when using this statement.

```
*XDIM_MEMBERSET {dimension name} = {member set}
```

The following instruction will use the member set ACTUAL, BUDGET for the Dimension category when processing the script file:

```
*XDIM_MEMBERSET CATEGORY = ACTUAL,BUDGET
```

You can also use the *XDIM_MEMBERSET instruction with the "not equal to" operator, as follows:

```
*XDIM_MEMBERSET CURRENCY<>USD
```

If you want to read all of the members of a dimension, you can use the keyword <ALL>, as follows:

```
*XDIM_MEMBERSET INTCO = <ALL>
```

Adding Members to Existing Member Sets

A *member set* is a set of dimension member values that is selected for processing from an application in a script. You can add members to an existing member set using the following instruction:

```
*XDIM_ADDMEMBERSET {dimension} = {member set}
```

This will add the members specified in the instruction to the list of existing selections.

```
*XDIM_ADDMEMBERSET CURRENCY = LC
```

For example, if the user has selected the USD and EUR currency dimension members, the above instruction will also add the LC currency to the list of dimension members. This is helpful when you want to make sure a dimension member is always included in the list of members for that dimension.

Threshold for Maximum Number of Dimension Members Processed for a Dimension

In some cases, when the number of dimension members selected for processing is too high, the execution performance of the script logic may be impacted. In these cases, it may be necessary to break the queries into more than one to improve performance. The following instruction can be used to specify the threshold for the maximum number of dimension members before the query has to be split:

```
*XDIM_MAXMEMBERS {dimension} = {max number of members}
```

In the following instruction, if the number of entities to be processed exceeds the limit of 20 members, the query processor will break the query into multiple queries of no more than 20 entities each:

```
*XDIM_MAXMEMBERS Entity = 20
```

Storing and Retrieving Variable Values

You can build a dynamic set of members and store it in a variable using the following instruction, which enables the values of a particular dimension member ID or property value to be stored in a variable. The values stored in the variable can be used later in the logic.

```
*SELECT ({variable}, {what}, {from}, {where}
```

The following example shows how to store data in a variable using the *SELECT instruction:

```
*SELECT(%REPORTING_CURRENCIES%, ID, CURRENCY, [GROUP] = 'REP')
```

In this instruction, the user can retrieve the ID of all members in the CURRENCY dimension, where the GROUP property has the value REP. The <variable> is the %REPORTING_CURRENCIES%, the <what> is the ID that will be stored in the variable, the <from> represents the dimension to use, and the [GROUP] (<where>) represents the property to pull the data from the dimension specified in the <from>.

The values stored in the variable using the instruction can be used to set the member values for a dimension, as follows:

```
*XDIM_MEMBER_SET CURRENCY=%REPORTING_CURRENCIES%
```

In this case, %REPORTING_CURRENCIES% is the variable containing the values.

Members Passed to a Dimension

You can use the %SET% keyword can be used to determine the members that are passed for a dimension. Add additional members using the following instruction:

```
*XDIM_MEMBERSET ENTITY = %ENTITY_SET%, SPECIAL_ENTITY
```

In this example, the SPECIAL_ENTITY entity is added to the entity dimension list.

Looping—WHEN/ENDWHEN Statement

You use the WHEN/ENDWHEN structure when it is necessary to update the current record and/or generate new records. The syntax of this structure is as follows:

```
*WHEN {criteria}
*IS {valid condition1}[,{valid condition2},…]
*REC([FACTOR|EXPRESSION={Expression}][,{dim1}={member},{dim2}=…])] [*R
EC([FACTOR|EXPRESSION={Expression}][,{dim1}={member},{dim2}=…])]] ….
[*ELSE] … …
*ENDWHEN
```

An example of usage is as follows:

```
*WHEN ACCOUNT.RATETYPE
*IS "AVG", "END"
*REC(FACTOR=-1, ENTITY=INTCO.ENTITY)
*ENDWHEN
```

In this example, the script logic reads all records that have the RATETYPE property equal to AVG or END and generates a new record that has a value equal to the current value, times the FACTOR. In addition, the value of the ENTITY dimension in the new record is set to the ENTITY property value associated with the INTCO dimension member of the current record. Values of all other dimensions are the same as that of the current record.

When there is no criterion to test, you can use the following instruction:

```
*WHEN *
*IS *
*REC(…)
*ENDWHEN
```

Looping—FOR/NEXT Statement

FOR/NEXT is a looping statement that allows you to apply logic to a specific set of records. The logic module supports any level of nesting of FOR…NEXT loops in the body of the logic files. The *FOR/NEXT structure can also be included inside a *WHEN/ENDWHEN structure to create new records.

The syntax for the FOR/NEXT loop is as follows:

```
*FOR {variable1} = {set1} [ AND {variable2={set2}]
{text}
{text} …
*NEXT
```

The FOR/NEXT loop also supports up to two variables iterating on two independent sets of members. Here is an example:

```
*FOR %MYTIME% = %TIME_SET%
// logic content
*NEXT
```

COMMIT Statement

You can use the commit instruction anywhere in the code to commit or update the data to the database.

```
*COMMIT
```

Revaluing Using an MDX Statement

You can use the following MDX statement in an expression to revalue revenues to increase them by 10%.

```
[Account].[#Revenue] = [Account].[Revenue] * 1.10
```

The # sign is used to redefine the value posted to an account member. All calculated members should have ID preceded by the number sign (#).

LOOKUP/ENDLOOKUP Statement

You can use the LOOKUP/ENDLOOKUP statement in conjunction with a WHEN/ENDWHEN structure to retrieve ("lookup") values that may be needed either to calculate a new value or to define criteria to be evaluated. The lookup can be performed in the current application or in a different application.

The lookup mechanism defines a relationship between the current record being processed and another record in a corresponding user-defined record set. For example, when performing currency translation, you may want to look up, in the RATE application, the value of the rate based on current entity, category, and period.

The syntax is:

```
*LOOKUP {App}
*DIM [{LookupID}:] {DimensionName}="Value" | {CallingDimensionName}
[.{Property}] [*DIM …]
*ENDLOOKUP
```

where {App} is the name of the application from which the values are searched; {DimensionName} is a dimension in the lookup application; {CallingDimension-Name} is a dimension in the current application; and {LookupID} is an optional identifier of the "looked-up" amount. This is only required when multiple values must be retrieved. Refer to the following example:

```
*LOOKUP RATE
*DIM R_ENTITY="GLOBAL"
*DIM SOURCECURR:INPUTCURRENCY=ENTITY.CURRENCY
*DIM DESTCURR1:INPUTCURRENCY="USD"
*DIM DESTCURR2:INPUTCURRENCY="EURO"
*DIM R_RATE=ACCOUNT.RATETYPE
*ENDLOOKUP
```

In this example, three values are retrieved from the INPUTCURRENCY dimension (the rate of the currency of the current entity, the rate of the EURO currency, and the rate of the USD currency). Each of these values has been assigned a specific identifier (SOURCECURR, DESTCURR1, and DESTCURR2) that will be used somewhere in the WHEN/ENDWHEN structure.

Any dimension not specified in the lookup instruction is assumed to match a corresponding dimension in the source application. In the example, the following instructions have been omitted because they are redundant:

```
*DIM CATEGORY=CATEGORY
*DIM TIME=TIME.
```

In SAP BPC 7.5 for SAP NetWeaver, script logic has been enhanced to include additional keywords, as discussed below.

Time Offset

A new keyword, TMVL, is available to calculate offset time values from a given time period. The format for this parameter is as follows:

```
TMVL(offset, base_period)
```

For example, you could use the following statement to offset the time period by four months, starting in January 2010:

```
TMVL(4, 2010.JAN)
```

▶ Offsets can be either negative or positive.

▶ The base period can be a hard-coded value, as in the previous example. You can also use a time script variable, %TIME_SET%, or a data manager variable prompt variable such as $NEWPER$.

▶ You can use TMVL in:

  ▶ FACTOR/EXPRESSION within REC

  ▶ FOR/NEXT loops

  ▶ IS conditions inside WHEN/ENDWHEN

  Nested TMVL parameters such as `TMVL(-1, TMVL(-3, 2009.JAN)))` are not supported.

Copy Data Across Applications

The keyword DESTINATION_APP is available to copy data from a source application to a destination application. The destination application may not contain all of the dimensions available in the source application. In these cases, you must add the following key word to skip those dimensions:

```
*SKIP_DIM= {dimension name}[,{dimension name},…]
```

If the destination application contains dimensions that are not available in the source application, they can be added by using the ADD_DIM keyword and specifying a dimension name and value.

```
*ADD_DIM {dimension name}={value}[,{dimension name}={value},…]
```

If the dimension names in the destination application are named differently than in the source application, they can be renamed using the RENAME_DIM keyword. You use the RENAME_DIM key word as follows:

```
*RENAME_DIM {dimension name}={value}[,{dimension name}={value},…]
```

You can add multiple dimension names to the instruction, separated by commas, when using the SKIP_DIM, ADD_DIM, and RENAME_DIM keywords.

When the DESTINATION_APP keyword is defined in a script, all of the subsequent statements used for writing data are directed to the application referenced in the DESTINATION_APP keyword.

The following is an example taken from SAP Help on using the DESTINATION_APP keyword in a script file. To explain DESTINATION_APP with SKIP_DIM, ADD_DIM, and RENAME_DIM, let's say that another application, DETAIL_PLAN is created by copying the PLANNING application from the delivered APSHELL. It is then necessary to do the following:

▶ Create new the dimensions PRODUCT and MARKET, and add these to the DETAIL_PLAN application.

▶ Replace P_ACCT with P_ACCTDETAIL.

▶ Remove the P_ACTIVITY dimension from the DETAIL_PLAN cube.

The following is the syntax for using the DESTINATION_APP command in your script file:

```
*XDIM_MEMBERSET TIME = 2006.AUG
*XDIM_MEMBERSET CATEGORY=ACTUAL
*DESTINATION_APP=DETAIL_PLAN
*SKIP_DIM = P_ACTIVITY
*ADD_DIM P_DATASRC=INPUT, PRODUCT = NO_PRODUCT, MARKET = NO_MARKET
```

```
*RENAME_DIM P_ACCT=P_ACCTDETAIL
*WHEN CATEGORY
*IS "ACTUAL"
*REC(EXPRESSION=%VALUE%)
*ENDWHEN
```

In this example, DETAIL_PLAN is the target application, which has all dimensions of PLANNING except for P_ACCT. This dimension is replaced with P_ACCTDETAIL. Also, DETAIL_PLAN has two additional dimensions: PRODUCT and MARKET. The script logic sets the values of the target Application DETAIL_PLAN as follows:

▶ PRODUCT and MARKET are set to NO_PRODUCT and NO_MARKET, respectively.

▶ The value of P_DATASRC is set based on INPUT.

▶ The value of P_ACCT is copied to P_ACCTDETAIL.

You now know a few commands you can use when developing script logic. In the next section, we'll explain how to execute script logic.

6.2.2 Executing Script Logic

You can execute script logic two ways. It can be either included in the file DEFAULT. LGF and automatically executed when users enter or load data to an application, or it can be executed using a data manager package.

DEFAULT.LGF is a special type of script logic file that is executed when you load data or enter data using an input template. The SAP BPC system runs the default logic indicated in the DEFAULT.LGF file of the application.

You can also execute a script logic file from the data manager. Using a data manager package, you can develop script logic to perform specific data management tasks and execute the script logic.

In the next section, we'll explain how Rich Bloom uses script logic to revalue plan data.

6.2.3 Creating Script Logic to Revalue Plan Data

Rich Bloom wants to revalue the plan data for specific products, so we'll explain how this is done using script logic. In this example, we'll create script logic that will allow a user to select specific products and specify a percentage by which to revalue the plan. The change in revenue will be posted to the REVADJ account.

We'll first create a script logic file in SAP BPC that contains the logic to perform revaluation. Then we'll create a process chain in SAP NetWeaver BW that can be used to execute script logic. Finally, we'll configure a data management package in SAP BPC that is associated with the script logic file and process chain and can be executed as needed.

1. Log into the SAP BPC Admin Console and select the ZRB_GM_PLAN application set.

2. In the left pane, under ZRB_SALES_CMB, click on SCRIPT LOGIC (Figure 6.3, ❶); the action pane related to script logic is displayed on the right. Click on CREATE NEW LOGIC (Figure 6.3, ❷).

3. In the NEW LOGIC dialog box, enter "REVALUE_PLAN" for LOGIC NAME and click on OK (Figure 6.3, ❸ and ❹).

Figure 6.3 Creating Script Logic to Revalue Plan Data—Part A

4. Next, you can enter the script logic for revaluing the plan data. Enter the code as shown in Figure 6.4, **❺**. The script is used to prompt the user to enter a percentage for revaluing revenue, and the increase or decrease in revenue is posted to the revenue adjustment account (REVADJ); it is calculated by multiplying the percentage increase/decrease (entered by the user) and the revenue amount. After entering the code, click on VALIDATE AND SAVE (Figure 6.4, **❻**).

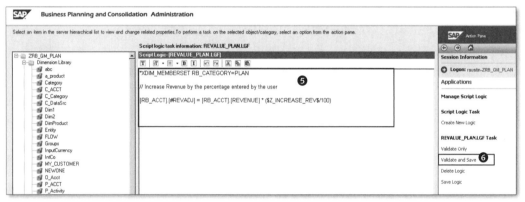

Figure 6.4 Creating Script Logic to Revalue Plan Data—Part B

5. Create a new process chain using Transaction RSPC in the SAP NetWeaver BW system, as shown in Figure 6.5. In this step, we'll show you how to create a process chain for running script logic. But in SAP BPC 7.5, you do not have to create a separate process chain for running script logic. You can use process chain /CPMB/DEFAULT_FORMULAS, which is delivered with SAP BPC for NetWeaver. The process chain will include the Start process type and the following process types that are specific to SAP BPC:

▶ Modify Dynamically

▶ Run Logic

▶ Clear BPC Tables

> **Note**
>
> In SAP BPC 7.0 for NetWeaver, the process chains used to create data manager packages were unique and not reusable in another data manager package. SAP BPC 7.5 for NetWeaver provides the ability to reuse process chains across data manager packages.

> **Note**
>
> The Clear BPC Tables process type is used in many SAP BPC process chains to clear temporary tables during processing.

6. Make sure you include the process types in the same order as shown in Figure 6.5. Every process type will be associated with a variant, and the variant for the Start process has to be unique for every process chain in the system. Create a new process variant for the start type.

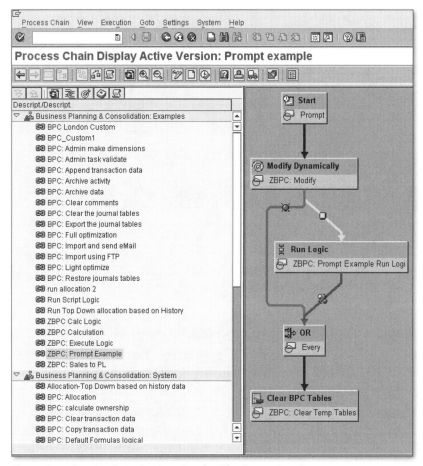

Figure 6.5 Creating Script Logic to Revalue Plan Data—Part C

7. Now, associate this process chain with a data package in SAP BPC. To do this, go to SAP BPC Excel, and log into the ZRB_SALES_CMB application. In the Excel interface, from the EDATA menu, select ORGANIZE PACKAGE LIST to create a new data package, and associate the process chain you created in the previous step with this package (Figure 6.6).

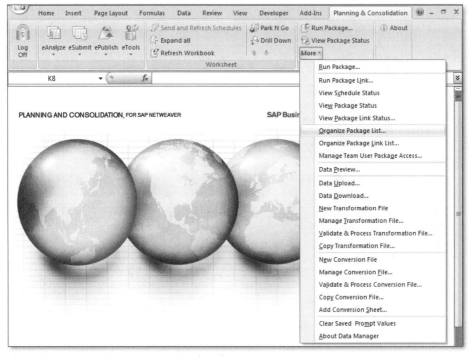

Figure 6.6   Creating Script Logic to Revalue Plan Data—Part D

8. This will open a new dialog box where you can maintain and create new packages. We'll add this package under the System Administrative group. (This is just an example; you can place it into any group you want.) Click on the ADD PACKAGE icon (Figure 6.7, ❼).

9. Using the dropdown list, select the ZRB_PROMPT process chain you created in the earlier step in the SAP NetWeaver BW system (Figure 6.8, ❽). This process chain is run when this data package is executed. Enter "Increase Plan Revenue" as the package name (Figure 6.8, ❾). Select the group where this package should belong using the dropdown box, and enter "Package to Increase Plan Revenue" for the description (Figure 6.8, ❿ and ⓫).

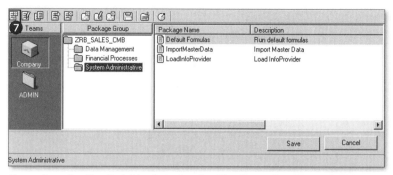

Figure 6.7 Creating Script Logic to Revalue Plan Data—Part E

10. To give appropriate access to the package, specify whether users will be authorized to execute it. If you select USER PACKAGE, users can execute the package. If you select ADMIN PACKAGE, only administrators can execute it (Figure 6.8, ⑫). After specifying the selection, click on the ADD button (Figure 6.8, ⑬).

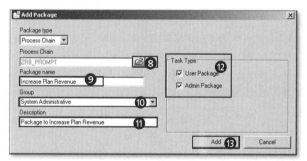

Figure 6.8 Creating Script Logic to Revalue Plan Data—Part F

11. After you add the package, you'll see the new package named INCREASE PLAN REVENUE. Click on the SAVE button to save the package (see Figure 6.9, ⑭).

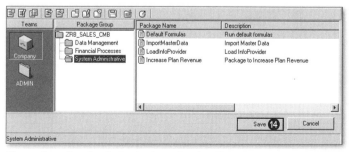

Figure 6.9 Creating Script Logic to Revalue Plan Data—Part G

12. Next, you need to associate the script logic file with the data management package. From the EDATA menu, select the ORGANIZE PACKAGE list to modify the data package you created. Select the INCREASE PLAN REVENUE package and right-click on MODIFY option. The MODIFY PACKAGE dialog box displays; click on the icon (Figure 6.10, ⓯) to modify the package and save (⓰).

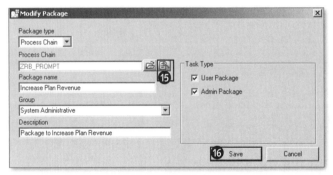

Figure 6.10   Creating Script Logic to Revalue Plan Data—Part H

13. The DATA MANAGER PACKAGE VIEW & DYNAMIC SCRIPT EDITOR dialog box displays. Click on ADVANCED to specify the package settings (Figure 6.11, ⓱).

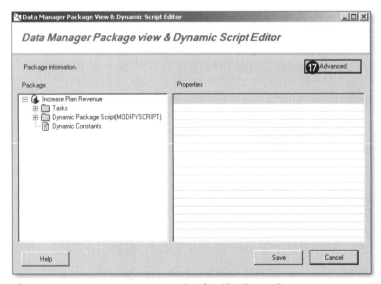

Figure 6.11   Creating Script Logic to Revalue Plan Data—Part I

14. Enter the code as shown in Figure 6.12, ⓲. The code is also provided here:

```
PROMPT(SELECTINPUT,,,,"%ENTITY_DIM%,%CATEGORY_DIM%,%CURRENCY_
DIM%,%TIME_DIM%,%DATASRC_DIM%,RB_CUSTOMER,RB_PRODUCT")
PROMPT(TEXT,%Z_INCREASE_REV%,"Input Revenue Increase in Percent",)
INFO(%EQU%,=)
INFO(%TAB%,;)
TASK(ZBPC_PROT_EXP_RUN_LOGIC,TAB,%TAB%)
TASK(ZBPC_PROT_EXP_RUN_LOGIC,EQU,%EQU%)
TASK(ZBPC_PROT_EXP_RUN_LOGIC,SUSER,%USER%)
TASK(ZBPC_PROT_EXP_RUN_LOGIC,SAPPSET,%APPSET%)
TASK(ZBPC_PROT_EXP_RUN_LOGIC,SAPP,%APP%)
TASK(ZBPC_PROT_EXP_RUN_LOGIC,SELECTION,%SELECTION%)
TASK(ZBPC_PROT_EXP_RUN_LOGIC,LOGICFILENAME,REVALUE_PLAN.LGF)
TASK(ZBPC_PROT_EXP_RUN_LOGIC,REPLACEPARAM,Z_INCREASE_REV%EQU%%Z_
INCREASE_REV%)
```

15. You can also copy the settings from a file. Note that in this setting, we're prompting the user to enter selection values for the ENTITY, CATEGORY, CURRENCY, TIME, DATA SOURCE, CUSTOMER, and PRODUCT DIMENSIONS fields. We're also prompting the user to enter a percentage in the %Z_INCREASE_REV% field for revaluation. The name of the process variant we used in the process chain for the Run Logic task is ZBPC_PROT_EXP_RUN_LOGIC. In this code, we're also passing the values entered by the user to the process chain.

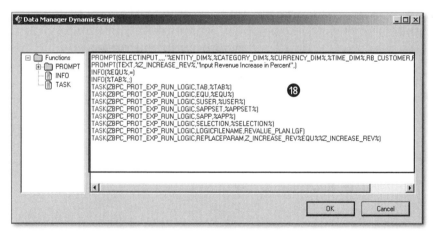

Figure 6.12 Creating Script Logic to Revalue Plan Data—Part J

16. Run a report to see the data before the revaluation is done (Figure 6.13).

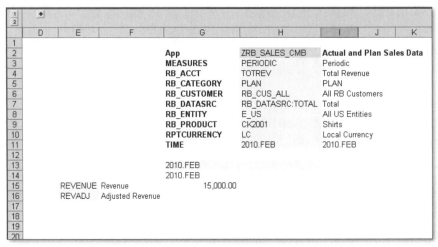

Figure 6.13 Creating Script Logic to Revalue Plan Data—Part K

17. You're now ready to execute the package to increase the plan revenue. From the EMENU menu option, select RUN PACKAGES. Select the INCREASE PLAN REVENUE package and click on RUN (Figure 6.14).

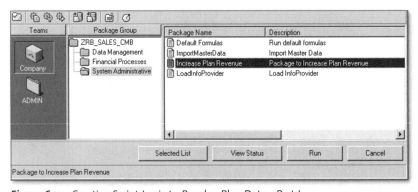

Figure 6.14 Creating Script Logic to Revalue Plan Data—Part L

18. Enter the revenue increase percent you want to effect and click on the NEXT button (Figure 6.15).

Figure 6.15 Creating Script Logic to Revalue Plan Data—Part M

19. You're prompted to enter the member value selections for the dimensions. Select RUN NOW and click on the NEXT button (Figure 6.16). Enter the selections for which you want to increase revenue, and click on NEXT to run the report. Note that we selected product CK2001 for revaluation.

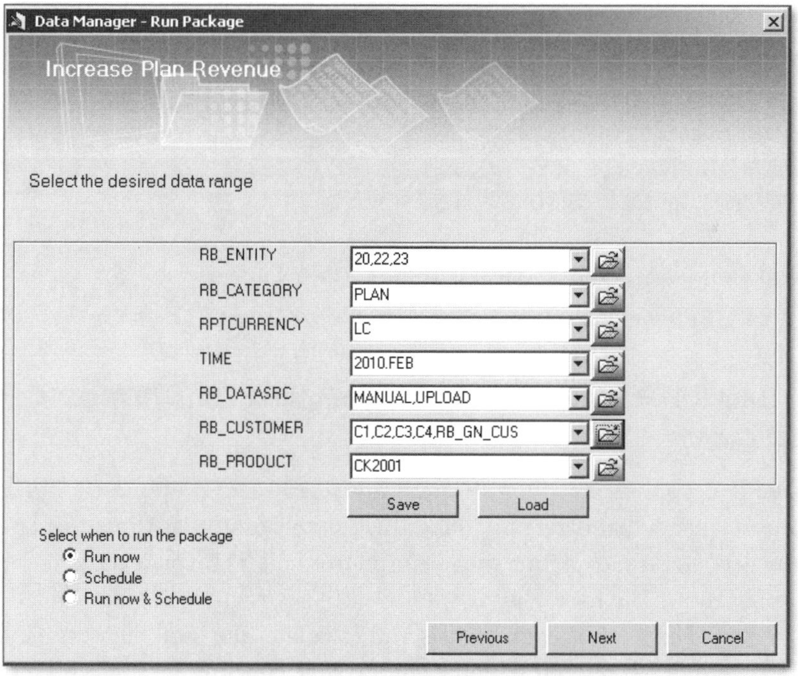

Figure 6.16 Creating Script Logic to Revalue Plan Data—Part N

20. Click on Run Now. You'll see that product CK2001 has an amount posted to the revenue adjustment account, as shown in Figure 6.17. This amount represents revaluation to the revenue.

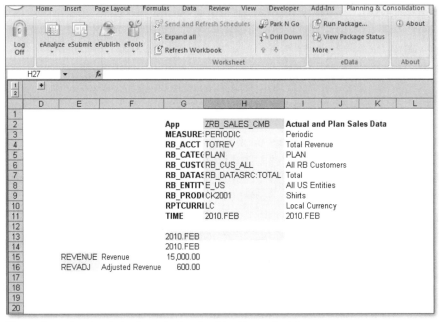

Figure 6.17 Creating Script Logic to Revalue Plan Data—Part O

You should now understand how to use script logic to revalue revenue for a specified period in an application.

6.2.4 Creating Script Logic to Push Data from the YTD to PERIODIC Applications

You may have two applications in your application set—a YTD application that contains consolidated actual data and a PERIODIC application that contains plan data. You may need to push data for a single period from the YTD application to the PERIODIC application. The following script logic can be used to meet this objective. For income and expense accounts, the script calculates the periodic values by subtracting YTD values of previous period from the YTD values of the single period entered by user. For balance sheet accounts, the script pushes the ending balances for the single period entered by user. The name of the destination application that contains the plan data is PLAN_APP. The script logic is created and executed in the application that contains the YTD consolidated actual data.

```
//Push data for a single period from YTD application to PERIODIC
application
*SELECT(%PYEAR%,"[YEAR]","TIME","[ID]=%TIME_SET%")
//Prevents multiple periods in time set
*SELECT(%PPERIOD%,"[ID]","TIME","[ID]=%TIME_SET%")

//Scope-in prior period and selected period
*XDIM_MEMBERSET TIME=TMVL(-1,%PPERIOD%),%PPERIOD%

//Scope-in ACTUAL that needs to be pushed
*XDIM_MEMBERSET CATEGORY=ACTUAL
// Push data to PLAN_APP application
*DESTINATION_APP = PLAN_APP

*WHEN TIME.YEAR
//Used for month of January - Prevent processing of December
//of prior year
*IS %PYEAR%
  *WHEN TIME
  *IS %PPERIOD% // Period selected by user

    *WHEN ACCOUNT.ACCTYPE
     *IS AST,EXP
      *REC(FACTOR=1)
     *IS LEQ,INC
      *REC(FACTOR=-1)
     *ENDWHEN // ACCOUNT.ACCTYPE

// Period previous to period selected by user
  *IS TMVL(-1,%PPERIOD%)         *WHEN ACCOUNT.ACCTYPE
       *IS EXP
        *REC(FACTOR=-1, TIME=%PPERIOD%)
       *IS INC
        *REC(FACTOR=1, TIME=%PPERIOD%)
       *ENDWHEN // ACCOUNT.ACCTYPE
  *ENDWHEN // TIME

*ENDWHEN // TIME.YEAR
```

Listing 6.1 Push Data for a Single Period from YTD Application to PERIODIC Application

6.2.5 Script Logic Files Provided by SAP

SAP BPC provides a library of standard script logic functions, all of which have the file extension .lgf. Table 6.2 shows some of these script logic files, which you can view in the SAP NetWeaver BW system by executing Transaction UJFS.

	Script File	Description
1.	Allocation.lgf	Runs allocation logic.
2.	Calcaccount.lgf	Runs account transformation business rule.
3.	Consolidation.lgf	Runs a legal consolidation business rule.
4.	Copy_Opening.lgf	Runs a balance carry forward business rule.
5.	FX_Trans.lgf	Runs currency conversion.
6.	ICBooking.lgf	Runs the IC Booking business rule. Based on business rules, this script automatically books mismatches in intercompany entries entered by an entity and its trading partner.
7.	ICData.lgf	Performs intercompany reconciliation. The script creates entries that allow users to match intercompany transactions.
8.	ICElim.lgf	Runs intercompany elimination.
9.	MDXlib.lgf	Library of MDX financial functions.
10.	System_Constants.lgf	Stores constant values for use within a script logic. The system constants file is located in the \\root\ Data\Webfolders\<AppSet>\AdminApp\<App> folder.
11.	System_Library.lgf	Includes basic examples of a set of keywords.
12.	Validation.lgf	Runs a validation business rule.

Table 6.2 Script Logic Files Provided by SAP

> **Note**
>
> We can use Transaction UJKT to debug script logic. This transaction allows us to test the execution of script for a particular data region.

In the next section, we'll discuss business rules and explain how to use them in an application.

6.3   Business Rules—High-Level Overview

In the previous section, you saw how you can code script logic to perform certain data management tasks. Instead of writing code, you can configure *business rules* to perform certain tasks related to planning and consolidation. The code is already available in SAP function modules; you just need to call them in a script and pass the appropriate parameters to perform the preferred function.

In this section, we'll will provide a brief introduction to the business rules you can configure in SAP BPC. We'll discuss setting up business rules to perform currency translation. (We also discuss business rules in detail in Chapter 9, when we discuss the process for consolidating data in SAP BPC.)

To begin, we will discuss the different business rules that can be configured in SAP BusinessObjects Planning and Consolidation.

6.3.1   Currency Translation

This is required when an organization executes business in more than one country, and when multiple currencies are used for transacting business. When an organization uses multiple currencies, they need to convert transactions in different currencies to one or more reporting currencies. Currency translation is used in both planning and financial consolidation applications. Business rules can be set up to perform currency translation. We'll discuss the steps and configuration for setting up business rules for performing currency translation in this chapter.

6.3.2   Carry Forward

The carry forward of balances is an essential step in the creation of a balance sheet for an organization; it is when the closing balance of accounts for a fiscal period is transferred as the opening balance of a subsequent fiscal period. The carry forward balance rules can also be used to close current period net income and post to balance sheet to create a fully balanced balance sheet. The set up for this process is taken care of in SAP BPC with the use of a business rules table. We'll discuss the steps and configuration for setting up this business rule in Chapter 9.

6.3.3 Account Transformation

There are some scenarios where accounts are consolidated or transformed into another account, an activity that is used extensively in cash flow applications. Account transformation business rules are used to aggregate values posted to specific combinations of source Account, Flow, Category, and Data Source and post them to aggregated destination Account, Flow, Category, and Data Source. We'll discuss the steps and configuration for setting up this business rule in Chapter 9.

6.3.4 Intercompany Matching/Booking

Intercompany matching/booking is applicable for an organization that has entities that do business with each other. When intercompany transactions exist, it is important to ensure that they are matched between entities before running the intercompany elimination process. For example, if an entity within an organization reports an intercompany sales transaction the trading partner associated with this transaction should post an intercompany expense transaction. The two transactions will need to be matched under a matching currency. This is required to produce accurate consolidated results. The intercompany booking business rule allows us to post/book differences in amounts reported by the entities so that intercompany transactions match. We'll discuss the steps and configuration for setting up this business rule in Chapter 9.

6.3.5 Intercompany Elimination

This is applicable for an organization that has entities that do business with each other. A consolidated balance sheet of the organization shows transactions that relate to external companies. The transactions such as sales and COGS or receivables and payables that result from exchange of goods or services within the organization should not be counted. In these cases, it is essential to eliminate the intercompany transactions, The intercompany eliminations process creates entries that eliminate intercompany transactions. There are two methods of performing intercompany elimination, one using U.S. elimination and the other using automatic adjustments. Both of these methods use business rules. We'll discuss the steps and configuration for setting up these business rules in Chapter 9.

6.3.6   Validation

The validation rules functionality in SAP BPC is a check mechanism that enables an organization to ensure accuracy of data. For example, using the validation rule table, an organization can set up business rules that will compare balances in assets and liabilities/owner's equity accounts for a given period, and report variances, if any, for that period. The variances can be posted to a validation account. We'll discuss the steps and configuration for setting up this business rule in Chapter 9.

6.3.7   Automatic Adjustments

We discussed the usage of the automatic adjustments business rule to perform intercompany elimination. This business rule is also used for consolidation of investments. The automatic adjustment business rule supports the calculation and generation of these postings. We'll discuss the steps and configuration for setting up this business rule in Chapter 9.

6.4   Currency Translation

In this section, we'll discuss currency translation using SAP BPC. An organization may have businesses in more than one country and conduct business transactions in many currencies. The currency translation business rule is used to translate all business transactions to one or more reporting currencies.

The transaction data in SAP BPC is stored in the currency in which the transaction is performed. This currency is referred to as the *transaction* currency. The currency that is associated with an entity is referred to as the *local* currency. These transactions are converted using the currency translation business rule to one or more reporting currencies and/or group currencies.

We'll now explain how to use the currency translation business rule to translate all financial transactions to one or more reporting currencies. First, we'll explore the contents of the RATE application that is used in the currency translation process.

RATE Application

SAP BPC provides an application called the RATE application. This is a supporting application used by financial and consolidation applications to store exchange rates that support currency conversion. It is important that the Category and Time dimensions in the RATE application are identical to the respective dimensions in the application that uses the RATE application for performing currency translation. The RATE application has the following dimensions:

```
CATEGORY
INPUTCURRENCY
R_ACCT
R_ENTITY
TIME
```

Enter exchange rate data into the RATE application either by using input templates or by loading the data.

The value of the CATEGORY dimension specifies the category to which the exchange rate is applicable. Sometimes we may maintain data for several categories in our planning or consolidation applications, and it may not be feasible to maintain exchange rates for each of the categories in the RATE application, especially if the exchange rates for all categories for an exchange rate type and period are going to be the same. In this case, we can maintain exchange rates for a generic category in the RATE application. In the planning and consolidation applications that contain the source records that will need to be translated, we can set the RATE_CATEGORY property of the CATEGORY dimension to this generic value. The currency conversion process will then look for the exchange rate in the RATE application based on this property associated with the CATEGORY of the source record.

The value of R_ENTITY specifies the entity to which the exchange rate is applicable. We can set this value to "GLOBAL" and can use it for currency conversion across all entities. In this case, when we call the program to perform currency translation, we specify RATEENTITY = GLOBAL.

The value of R_ACCT is the account rate type for which the exchange rate is applicable for currency conversion. The RATE application contains the currency translation exchange rate to use for different periods and for different exchange rate types. The exchange rate type signifies the type of rate—for example, average rate or month-end rate. The business rules table for currency conversion defines logic for currency conversion based on the account rate type.

The value of the TIME dimension is the period for which the exchange rate is valid. We can use the RATE_YEAR and RATE_PERIOD properties of the CATEGORY dimension to determine the year and period that the source records would look up during currency conversion to determine exchange rates. If these properties are filled in the CATEGORY dimension, then during currency conversion, based on the CATEGORY of the source record, the currency translation process would look up the values in these properties to determine year/period for determining the exchange rate.

The INPUTCURRENCY dimension within the RATE application must include the MD property, whose values can be either M (to multiply rates) or D (to divide rates).

The currency exchange rate is maintained for each currency. In the RATE application, if the exchange is with respect to U.S. dollars, then the rate for USD is set to 1. The rate for EUR is set to 0.75.

Next, we'll understand the process of currency translation.

Currency Conversion

The process of currency translation entails the following steps:

1. Data for each entity is either entered or loaded into the SAP BPC system in local currency (CURRENCY=LC). If group dimension (type=G) is used in the data model, when loading or entering data, the value of group dimension is set to NON_GROUP where NON_GROUP represents the dimension member of the group dimension that has CURRENCY_TYPE property set to N (Non Group). Group dimension is used in legal consolidation applications.

2. The reporting/group currency(ies) to which local currency data must be translated are determined based on selection used when running data manager package to run translation.

3. When currency translation process is run for a data region, the system reads all records for the data region that were entered or loaded in local currency and determines the local currency of each record based on CURRENCY property associated to the entity.

4. The RATETYPE to be used for currency translation is based on the RATETYPE property of the account in the record read.

5. When the currency translation process runs, it looks up business rules that pertains to the RATETYPE. The business rules table has the logic to perform the currency translation. The process creates records that have the translated values with reporting/group currency(ies) in the currency dimension. If currency translation is run for a group, the value of the GROUP dimension is set with ID of group.

Let's look at some important setup that relates to the translation of currency:

▸ The application that requires currency translation must be created as a financial or consolidation application.

▸ An application can include only one dimension for indicating currency type. This is the dimension that states whether the transaction is in the local or reporting currency.

▸ The Entity dimension has a Currency property that denotes the local currency associated with an entity.

▸ Set the CURRENCY_TYPE property of the currency dimension—L for Local Currency and R for Reporting. For example, the CURRENCY_TYPE property of Local Currency (LC) is set to L and US dollars (USD) is set to R.

▸ Set the REPORTING property of the currency dimension. If a currency is marked as reporting (REPORTING=Y), currency translation can be used to convert transactions from the local currency to this reporting currency. For example, REPORTING property of US dollars (USD) is set to Y.

▸ The Rate Type property of the Account dimension specifies the type of rate to be used for the translation.

▸ The TIME dimension must include the YEAR, PERIOD, TIMEID, and MONTH-NUM properties.

▸ The Data Source dimension must include the following properties:

  ▸ DATASRC_TYPE, whose values include the following:

    — I: Input

    — M: Manual adjustment

    — A: Automatic adjustment or elimination

    — L: Data source level (use only for consolidation)

  ▸ IS_CONVERTED, whose values include the following:

    — N (or blank): These members are ignored in the conversion.

    — Y: These members are converted from the local currency (LC) into the preferred currency.

    — G: These members are copied from the reporting currency of the group that is being translated into the currency member corresponding to the given group.

▶ The Flow dimension is not mandatory for currency translation, but if it is included, the dimension must include the FLOW_TYPE property. This property is used in the currency translation business rule to perform "force closing." In this case, an additional entry is generated where the destination flow is set to a flow whose FLOW_TYPE is equal to CLOSING.

▶ CATEGORY dimension. When we discussed the RATE application, we discussed certain properties of the CATEGORY dimension related to currency conversion such as RATE_CATEGORY, RATE_YEAR, and RATE_PERIOD. In addition, we can use the FX_SOURCE_ CATEGORY of the CATEGORY dimension to determine the category of source data to be used for currency conversion. The FX_DIF-FERENCE_ONLY property, if set to Y, is used to post differences between the calculated (default) value and the source (simulated) value.

You can run the currency translation program in two modes: reporting currency mode and group currency mode. In reporting currency mode, transactions are translated from the local currencies to the reporting currencies. You should include the following script:

```
*RUN_PROGRAM CURR_CONVERSION
CATEGORY = %C_CATEGORY_SET%
CURRENCY = %RPTCURRENCY_SET%
TID_RA = %TIME_SET%
RATEENTITY = GLOBAL
......
*ENDRUN_PROGRAM
```

The group currency mode is used in an organization that is composed of a group of subsidiaries and where the subsidiary data should be converted to one or more group currencies.

A consolidation group represents the relationship of entities for a given consolidation result. The relationship between the entities is stored in the OWNERSHIP application. In this case, the group dimension is added to the data model. We will study OWNERSHIP application in detail in chapter 9. The following properties must be set in the group dimension to enable currency translation:

▶ Set the CURRENCY_TYPE property for members in the group dimension – G for group currency, N for non-group (group input), and L for local currency.

▶ Set the GROUP_CURRENCY property for the groups – for example, USD, EUR etc. The currency translation process translates data in local currency to group currency that is specified in the GROUP_CURRENCY property of the group dimension for the group.

```
*RUN_PROGRAM CURR_CONVERSION
CATEGORY = %C_CATEGORY_SET%
GROUP= %GROUPS_SET%
TID_RA = %TIME_SET%
RATEENTITY = GLOBAL
......
*ENDRUN_PROGRAM
```

In addition, you maintain the currency conversion business rules table to define the rules for currency translation. When the currency translation data manager package is run, the rules defined in this table are used during the currency translation process.

The following keywords are used in the FORMULA field of the business rules table. These keywords are used to determine the amount to post during currency translation.

```
AS_IS—Do not change existing value in target currency
AVG—Average Rate as stored in the RATE application
COPYLC—Translate the local currency to reporting/group currency with
factor=1
END—Month-end rate as stored in the RATE application
OPEEND—END rate of last period of prior year
OPEAVG—AVG rate of last period of prior year
```

Table 6.3 explains the details for setting up the business table for currency conversion.

Field Name	Description
Account Rate Type	Specify the account rate type to use in the currency translation. Examples of account rate type for an account are AVG, END, HIST.

Table 6.3 Currency Translation Business Rules

Field Name	Description
	When the rate type of the source account is the same as defined in the rule, the criteria for using the business rule is met.
Source Flow	Specify the source flow as additional criteria to use in the translation. The value specified in this field can be one of the following: ▶ Base member ▶ Parent member ▶ A list of members is defined and filtered using a value of the DIMLIST property in the Flow dimension. Balance sheet accounts, such as inventory accounts, have an opening balance at the beginning of a period, additions and transfers for the period, and a closing balance for end of the period. The Flow dimension helps break the account into various flow types such as opening, additions, transfers, and closing
Destination Account	Specify a base member as the destination account. If no value is specified for the destination account, the value of the source account is used.
Destination Flow	Specify a base member for the destination flow. If no value is specified for the destination flow, the value of the source flow is used.
Formula	Specify an arithmetic expression to define calculation of the amount during currency translation. In the Formula field, we can specify formulas as follows: END-AVG. In this case, the difference between the month-end rate and average rate is calculated and used by the currency conversion process.
Force Closing	When the Force Closing checkbox is selected, an additional entry is generated where the destination flow is the closing balance. This is applicable for members in the Flow dimension where the property FLOW_TYPE is equal to the value CLOSING.

Table 6.3 Currency Translation Business Rules (Cont.)

Field Name	Description
Apply to Periodic	When the application is a YTD application and must perform the currency translation based on periodic values, select the Apply to Periodic checkbox. When this checkbox is selected, the difference between the current period and prior period amounts is calculated, and the formula is applied on the resulting amount. The result is added back to the prior period's value as written in the current period.
Entity FX Type	When a value is specified in Entity FX Type, the rule will be applied to all of the entity members that have a matching value in the FX_TYPE property of the Entity dimension.
Remark	A brief description of the business rule.

Table 6.3 Currency Translation Business Rules (Cont.)

Please refer to Table 6.4, which displays business rules.

Account Rate Type	Source Flow	Destination Account	Destination Flow	Formula	Force Closing
AVG				AVG	
ENDFLOW	F_OPE		F_DIFF	END-OPEEND	

Table 6.4 Currency Translation Business Rules (sample)

The first business rule would look for all accounts in the source data that have RATE_TYPE property = AVG and perform currency translation based on the exchange rate for R_ACCT = AVG in the RATE application.

The second business rule would look for all accounts in the source data that have RATE_TYPE property = ENDFLOW and Flow = F_OPE and perform currency translation. The business rule would post the difference between the END (current month-end) rate and OPEEND (END rate of last period of prior year) to the same account and flow F_DIFF. In the example that we're going to illustrate, we do not have the FLOW dimension. However, this rule helps us understand the usage of the business rules if we use FLOW dimension in our data model.

We'll now use an example to demonstrate how currency translation is set up and performed in SAP BPC. One of the required dimensions for currency translation is DataSource. The planning application we use for our model company, Rich Bloom, includes the DataSource dimension. The objective is to understand how to convert currency data from the British pound (GBP) to the U.S. dollar (USD).

We would normally load exchange rate data provided by a third-party vendor to the rate application. But for our illustration, we'll enter this information directly into the rate application.

1. Log into SAP BPC for Excel, and access the rate application of your application set. Create an input schedule and enter the exchange rate for Jan 2010, as shown in Figure 6.18. The average rate (AVG) for Jan 2010 is entered for the GBP and USD currencies. We want to translate the data from GBP into USD, so we enter a factor of 1 for USD and a factor of 1.50 for GBP. Save the exchange rate data.

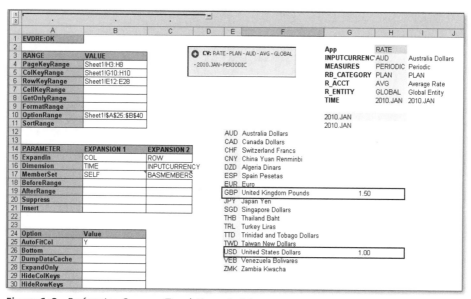

Figure 6.18 Performing Currency Translation—Part A

2. Log into the SAP BPC Admin Console, and select the application for which you want to perform currency translations. Enter the following code (Figure 6.19) in the FXTRANS.LGF file:

```
*RUN_PROGRAM CURR_CONVERSION
CATEGORY = %RB_CATEGORY_SET%
```

```
CURRENCY = %RPTCURRENCY_SET%
TID_RA = %TIME_SET%
RATEENTITY = GLOBAL
OTHER = [ENTITY=%RB_ENTITY_SET%]
//For more than one other scope parameter:
//OTHER = [ENTITY=%ENTITY_SET%;INTCO=%INTCO_SET%...]
 *ENDRUN_PROGRAM
```

Save and validate the logic file.

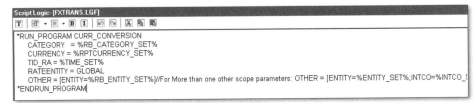

Figure 6.19 Performing Currency Translation—Part B

3. Execute a report to see the data before the currency translation is executed. Figure 6.20 shows the data associated with entity C2000, in local currency. The RATE_TYPE associated with accounts REVENUE and COGS is set to "AVG."

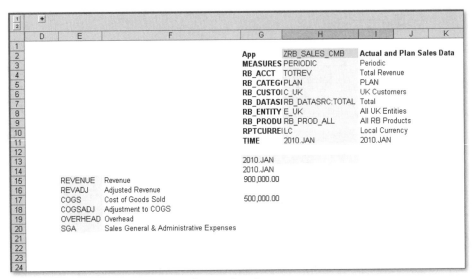

Figure 6.20 Performing Currency Translation—Part C

4. You're now ready to execute the FX Restatement currency translation data package (Figure 6.21).

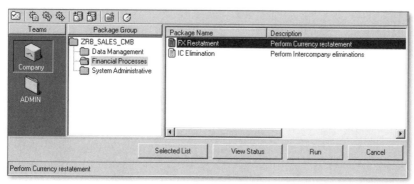

Figure 6.21   Performing Currency Translation — Part D

5. Execute the FX Restatement data package. The system will prompt you to enter parameter values (Figure 6.22). Our objective is to translate transactions in local currency to U.S. dollars. Select USD for the report currency.

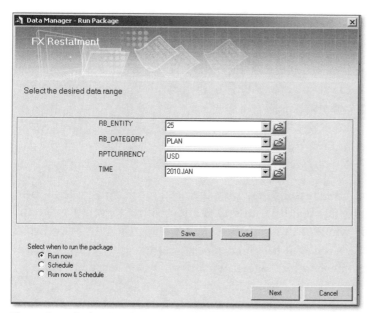

Figure 6.22   Performing Currency Translation — Part E

6. After you execute the data package, you'll see that the data from the local currency has been translated to U.S. dollars, based on the exchange rate specified in the rate application (Figure 6.23).

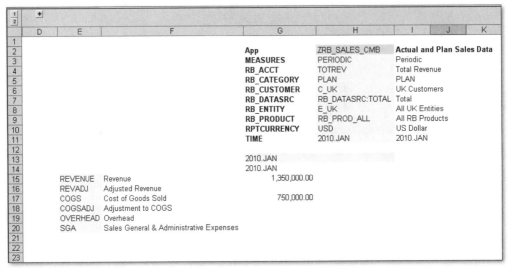

Figure 6.23 Performing Currency Translation—Part F

You now know how to translate financial transactions that are maintained in a local currency to reporting/group currency. In this section, you've seen the different types of business rules you can set up in SAP BPC. In the next section, we'll explain how you can perform allocations.

6.5 Allocations

There are several business reasons that drive the need for using allocation logic. Let's say, for example, that you have an organization with a corporate office and additional locations where it does business. When the corporate office incurs an expense, such as overhead, it has to be allocated to the other office locations based on criteria that depend on usage or work done by the corporate office for the other offices.

SAP BPC supports a robust interface for allocating data. The allocation definition is coded as a script file and can be called from a data manager package. The script for allocating data is based on a table interface for the developer to specify how the allocation should be performed. This process provides the developer with an intuitive interface through which he can satisfy the business requirements for allocation.

An allocation is always made up of the following components:

▸ What needs to be allocated

▸ Where the results of the allocation must be written

▸ What driver should be used to perform the allocation

▸ How the allocation driver should be used; that is, what factor must be applied to the source amounts during the allocation process

You should have a clear understanding of these components before you begin coding the allocation logic. When you know what needs to be allocated, you can use the following syntax to code the allocation:

```
*RUNALLOCATION
*FACTOR={expression}
*NAME={allocation name}
*APP [WHAT={app name};] [ WHERE={ app name };] [USING ={ app name }]
*DIM {dim name} WHAT={set}; WHERE={set};[USING ={set};] [TOTAL={set}]
*DIM …
*ENDALLOCATION
```

Now let's discuss the following instructions in the code: *FACTOR and *DIM. The *FACTOR instruction can be used to define any arithmetic expression (written in the {expression} parameter) and may contain operands, parentheses, constants, and one or both of the keywords USING and TOTAL, representing, respectively, the amount coming from the USING region (i.e., the amount of the driver) and the amount coming from the TOTAL region (i.e., the sum of the drivers):

```
*FACTOR=USING/TOTAL
```

Another keyword supported by this parameter is COUNT, which represents the number of members into which one amount must be allocated. For example, when evenly allocating a yearly value into all months of a year, the administrator may use just the COUNT keyword.

```
*FACTOR=1/COUNT
```

With the *DIM keyword, you can define the set of members that each dimension should read for each specific region of the allocation (the WHAT, the WHERE, the USING, and the TOTAL regions).

Using the same logic, if you had to allocate rent expenses incurred by a corporate entity called Admin to other entities based on the respective percentage usage, you would have to code the following in your script logic. Note that the percentage is maintained in the application for each entity.

```
*RUNALLOCATION
*FACTOR=USING/100
*DIM ENTITY WHAT=ADMIN; WHERE<>ADMIN; USING<>ADMIN
*DIM ACCOUNT WHAT=RENTAL; WHERE=RENTAL; USING=PERCENTAGE
*ENDALLOCATION
```

To demonstrate this concept, we'll perform allocations so that Rich Bloom can allocate the overhead expenses incurred at its corporate office (entity 22) to other entities in the United States, based on the revenue they generated for the period.

1. Looking at the plan data for Jan 2010, Rich Bloom's corporate office has planned overhead expenses for $20,000 (Figure 6.24). This has to be allocated to the other entities in the United States, based on their total revenue for the same period.

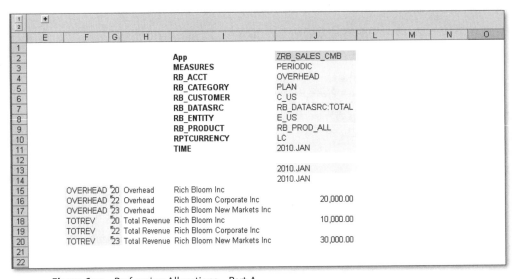

Figure 6.24 Performing Allocations—Part A

2. Enter the following code in the ALLOCATION.LGF script file for the application:

```
*RUNALLOCATION
*FACTOR=USING/TOTAL
*DIM RB_ACCT WHAT =OVERHEAD;WHERE=<<<;USING=REVENUE;TOTAL=<<<;
*DIM RB_ENTITY WHAT=22;WHERE=>>>;USING=>>>;TOTAL=BAS(E_US);
*DIM RB_CATEGORY WHAT=PLAN;WHERE=<<<;USING=<<<;TOTAL=<<<;
*DIM TIME WHAT=2010.JAN;WHERE=<<<;USING=<<<;TOTAL=<<<;
*ENDALLOCATION
```

Save and validate the script file (Figure 6.25). The logic allocates the overhead data for the period Jan 2010 from entity 22 to the other entities in the United States, based on their sales revenue for that period.

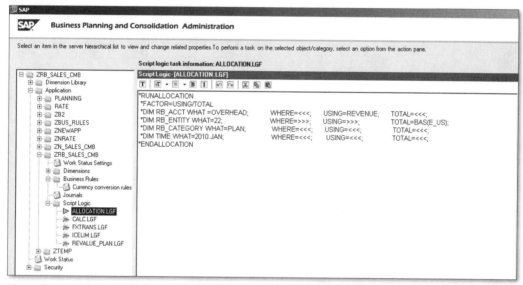

Figure 6.25 Performing Allocations — Part B

3. You're now ready to execute the Allocation data manager package (Figure 6.26).

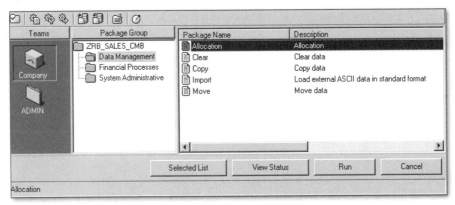

Figure 6.26 Performing Allocations—Part C

4. After executing the package, run the report to see how the allocation logic has worked (Figure 6.27). The overheads have been allocated from the corporate entity to the other entities, based on revenues.

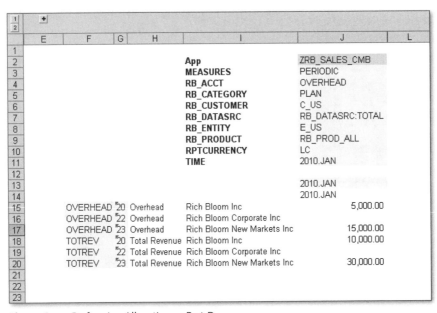

Figure 6.27 Performing Allocations—Part D

> **Note**
>
> The allocation process does not normally zero-out the amounts from the source accounts, but in this example, the source account was set to zero because of the driver that was used to perform the allocation. We allocated overheads to all base entities in the United States based on each entity's revenue, and because the corporate entity did not have any revenue, the allocation process calculated the overhead account of the corporate entity to zero.

In this section, you've seen how to perform allocation in SAP BPC. In the next section, we'll discuss areas where you can write ABAP code to meet specific business requirements.

6.6   Using BAdIs to Code Logic

Some business processes require the use of additional logic to complement the existing SAP BPC application framework. You can use SAP Business Add-Ins (BAdIs) for this purpose and create them using ABAP in the SAP NetWeaver BW system. The rich language constructs in ABAP make it excellent for use in SAP BPC applications. ABAP may also provide performance benefits when used in certain application scenarios.

You'll need a basic understanding of object-oriented ABAP before you can develop BAdIs in SAP BPC applications. We're just providing the high-level steps to create a BAdI. An ABAP programmer in your organization will be able to help in this area.

1. Use Transaction SE19 to create a BAdI, which should be based on enhancement UJ_CUSTOM_LOGIC and is provided for use in SAP BPC applications. You're prompted to create a transport when you create a custom BAdI.

2. Specify the filter values for the BAdI implementation. These are the values that pass to the BAdI.

3. The UJ_CUSTOM_LOGIC~EXECUTE method is automatically created for the BAdI, because it is based on the UJ_CUSTOM_LOGIC enhancement. Enter the code for the BAdI here. The internal table CT_TABLE contains the data passed from the SAP BPC application, which can be modified based on the business requirement.

4. Save and activate the objects created.

5. Create a script file in SAP BPC to call the BAdI you've created. Refer to the following example:

```
Syntax:
*START_BADI <BADI_Name>
<key1> = <value1>
<key2> = <value2>
..
*END_BADI
```

where <BADI_Name> is the name used in the BAdI. You can also pass the additional parameters <key1> and <key2>.

The execution of the BADI performs a default query and automatically writes back to the application. Set the QUERY parameter to OFF if you want to perform your own read inside the BAdI implementation; set WRITE to OFF to turn off the automatic write back of query results. You may code to write to another application from the BAdI.

6. Create a data manager package and assign process chain /CPMB/DEFAULT_FOR-MULAS to the package. This data manger will be used to run the script logic described in the last step. In the data manager package, adjust the prompts for the script to be executed.

7. You're now ready to execute the data manager package. This will execute the package and prompt for any parameters you specified in the BAdI.

You now know the steps for developing logic using BAdIs in SAP BPC.

You can also use BAdIs to write logic in Start Routine and End Routine that is associated with data loading. Start Routine is logic that is executed before transformation is executed during data loading. End Routine is a logic that is executed after transformation is executed during data loading.

First, create a BAdI implementation for UJD_ROUTINE. Develop the logic in separate filters—one for Start Routine and another for End Routine. In the Options section of the transformation file associated with a data load, specify the filters of the BAdI that contain the logic as follows:

```
STARTROUTINE=<BAdI filter name1>
ENDROUTINE=<BAdI filter name2>
```

In the next section, we'll discuss rules you can configure to ensure data accuracy.

6.7   Validation

With the introduction of SAP BPC for NetWeaver, a new and powerful feature has been introduced to enforce business rules and to prevent incorrect records from being entered or updated in the system. This ensures the accuracy of data in an SAP BPC application. Recall that we discussed usage of the Validation business rule to perform validations of data. This business rule compares values in two accounts, and if differences exist posts to a control account. The validation that we'll discuss in this section is used to validate combinations of dimensions. For example, we can set up a validation rule to ensure that corporate expenses are only posted to corporate entity dimension members.

The following rules apply to validation:

- Validation is performed in the SAP NetWeaver BW system using Transaction UJ_ VALIDATION. You'll need access to this transaction to access this interface.
- Only one dimension can be marked as the Driver dimension.
- Any dimension in an application can be specified as the Driver dimension for validation. Different applications in a given application set can use any dimension as the Driver dimension.
- In the planning and consolidation application, the Account dimension is usually marked as the Driver dimension.
- Rules are defined so that only those records that meet the criteria can be saved to the application. Every time a record is updated for the application, including a Driver dimension, the rules are checked before the data is updated.
- When data is updated in SAP BPC, if the data does not comply with the rule defined, the record is rejected and an error message displayed.
- If the same dimension is used as the Driver dimension by more than one application in the application set, any rules created for that Driver dimension apply to all of the applications that share it.
- You can turn off the validation's functionality for an application using Transaction UJ_VALIDATION. When the validation is turned off, the rules for the application are not checked when data is updated. Validations can be set to apply to journals, manual updates, and data manager packages.
- Setting up validation rules does not require knowledge of ABAP, but to set up advanced logic using code, the BAdI implementation is available. This provides additional ABAP functionality when a standard configuration for validation

does not fully meet the requirement or when the process is complex enough to require the use of BAdIs.

▶ Validation rules configured in the development system can be transported across the landscape.

We'll now look at an example of setting up validation rules in the SAP NetWeaver BW system.

1. Log into the SAP NetWeaver BW system and execute Transaction UJ_VALIDA-TION. Identify the application set for which you want to set validation rules, and then click on ASSIGN DRIVER DIMENSION (Figure 6.28, ❶ and ❷).

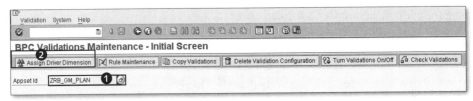

Figure 6.28 Creating a Validation Rule—Part A

2. All of the applications associated with the application set are displayed. Enter the dimension for the application for which you want to set the Driver dimension, and click on SAVE DRIVER DIMENSION SETTINGS (Figure 6.29, ❸ and ❹). In our example, we're setting RB_ACCT as the Driver dimension for our planning application.

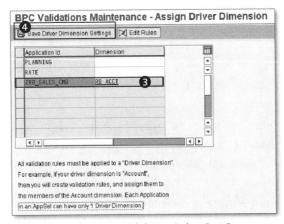

Figure 6.29 Creating a Validation Rule—Part B

3. After you have saved the Driver dimension settings, click on the back arrow. Here, you can create a new rule. Click on CREATE RULE to create a new validation definition (Figure 6.30, ❺).

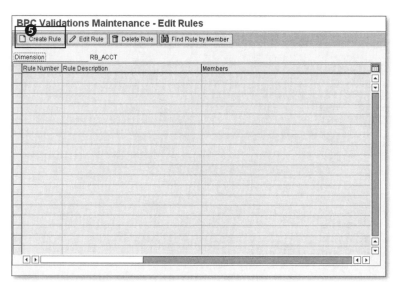

Figure 6.30 Creating a Validation Rule—Part C

4. Create a new account for corporate expenses and call it CORPORATE_EXP; this is the member for which you'll be setting the validation. Select CORPORATE_EXP as the member of the Account dimension (Figure 6.31, ❻). Then click on ADD DIMENSION (Figure 6.31, ❼). Enter the following values in the first row for the columns:

```
Dimension  <RB_ENTITY>
Operator   <=>
Value      <22>
```

This defines the member value for the entity that can post values for this account. Entity 22 is the corporate office of Rich Bloom under which corporate expenses are recorded (Figure 6.31, ❽). Other entities should not be able to charge corporate expense amounts.

5. Click on SAVE RULE, and click on the back arrow to go back to the previous screen (Figure 6.31, ❾).

6. You'll now see the validation rule you created (Figure 6.32).

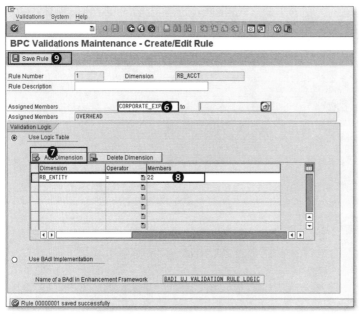

Figure 6.31 Creating a Validation Rule—Part D

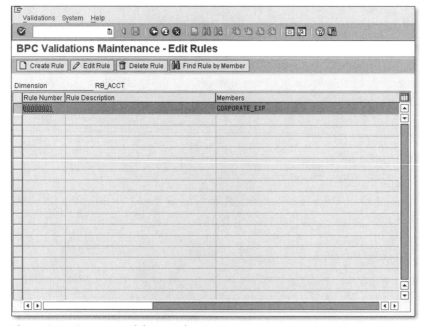

Figure 6.32 Creating a Validation Rule—Part E

7. Click the green arrow to go back to the initial screen of Transaction UJ_VALIDA-TION, and click on the TURN VALIDATION ON/OFF button to activate the validation rules (Figure 6.33, **❿**).

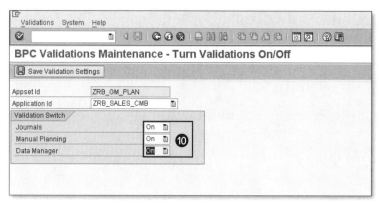

Figure 6.33 Creating a Validation Rule—Part F

8. Create an input schedule. Select 20 as the entity and OVERHEADS as the account member. Enter a value for CORPORATE_EXP, and send the data to the database (Figure 6.34). The system should disallow this transaction based on the validation rule created earlier.

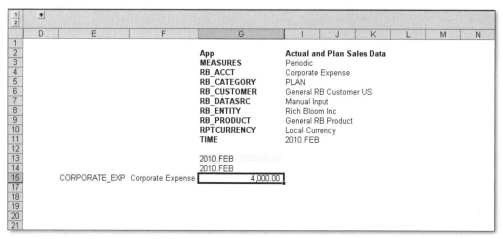

Figure 6.34 Creating a Validation Rule—Part G

9. You'll receive an error message saying that the data failed the validation rule, because corporate expenses can only be posted to corporate entity 22 (Figure 6.35).

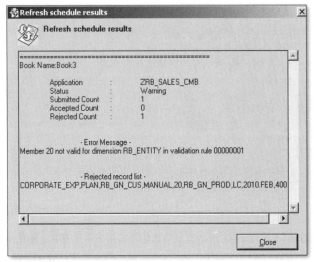

Figure 6.35 Creating a Validation Rule—Part H

You now know how to set up validation rules in the SAP NetWeaver BW system. This powerful functionality enforces data integrity in SAP BPC applications.

6.8 Summary

In this chapter, you learned about the options available to define logic in an SAP BPC application. First, you saw how to define formulas as a property of a dimension member to automatically calculate values. Then, you learned about script logic and saw how it provides a rich collection of statements to handle complex logic in applications.

We then discussed business rules to execute common planning and consolidation tasks and explained how to use them in place of developing detailed script logic. We showed examples of performing currency translation using the RATE application and business rules. We also showed how to perform allocations based on certain drivers.

We then saw how BAdIs can be used with SAP BPC for NetWeaver. This is especially useful for coding complex application business requirements using ABAP.

Finally, we explained how to define validation rules in the SAP NetWeaver BW system to ensure accuracy of data.

In the next chapter, we'll review the tools available in SAP BPC to support collaboration. Specifically, we'll review the *work status*, which you use to monitor the planning and consolidation process and protect data from further changes. We'll also discuss options available to post comments, distribute and collect financial data, and develop a user interface using menus.

This chapter discusses implementation of work status, addition and viewing of comments, distribution of data in reports and input templates, and creation of menu based application to facilitate the planning and consolidation process.

7 Process Management and Collaboration

This chapter introduces the collaboration tools and features available in SAP BusinessObjects Planning and Consolidation (BPC) that facilitate the sharing and exchange of data. The objective of using these tools is to promote team dynamics and to enable users to make informed decisions on different business aspects.

Section 7.1 discusses how to configure work status to monitor and restrict changes to the data in an application. In particular, we'll explain how you can use work status in a scenario where the current plan needs to be locked against further changes.

Section 7.2 explains how to add and view comments in SAP BPC. You use comments to provide context to information and to share perception and reasoning behind information in an application.

Section 7.3 explains how you can distribute data or input schedules in SAP BPC to users as offline reports and how these reports can then be uploaded back into SAP BPC after users make changes to them.

SAP BPC can be used not only with Excel, but also with PowerPoint and Word. Section 7.4 shows steps involved in integrating SAP BPC data with Word and PowerPoint documents.

Section 7.5 discusses the functions available in SAP BPC for creating a menu-based application. Menus help users view and execute periodic tasks in a planning or consolidation process.

We'll begin by explaining the use of work status and how to configure it to restrict changes to the data in an application.

7.1 Work Status

In SAP BPC, work status serves the important function of protecting changes to data stored in an application. It enables a subset of data, also referred to as a region of data, to be assigned a work status and helps you monitor the status of the data throughout the planning cycle.

Work status can be set for any region of data, based on the dimensions selected for maintaining work status for an application. (If you're familiar with SAP planning tools such as SAP NetWeaver Business Planning and Simulation and SAP NetWeaver BW Integrated Planning, you may have heard the term *data slices* used in those environments to describe the same thing.)

Work status helps you meet the objective of protecting and monitoring data as follows:

▶ Work status gives an organization more control over its data and defines the tasks that each user can perform. It differs from standard data access in SAP BPC in that, after the work status is set as locked, even users who have write access to the data are restricted from performing data updates. For example, the data can be restricted from being updated by anyone in the organization after the plan data is approved by management.

▶ For each application set, you can define different work statuses such as unlocked, submitted, approved, and so on, depending on the process flow the organization uses. All of the applications in the set use the work status defined for an application set.

▶ You can also create a new work status, reorder the work status, edit the description of the work status, or delete a work status for an application set.

▶ Work status can be applied to the following activities:
  ▶ Data manager (DM)
  ▶ Journals (JRN)
  ▶ Manual entry (MAN)
  ▶ Comments (COMM)
  ▶ Documents (DOCS)

▶ Work status applies to a set of data in an application, which is called a data region. For each application in the application set, you configure a set of dimensions to use for setting the work status. Only the dimensions selected in this configuration can be used to define the data region for setting the work status.

▶ To use work status, you have to select a minimum of three and a maximum of five dimensions in each application.

▶ When you're defining the dimensions for work status in an application, the system requires one dimension to be specified as the Owner dimension, which should include the Owner property. The members listed in this dimension should be updated with a user ID or team ID in the Owner property so that the IDs can be used for setting work status.

▶ You can select a region of data for setting the work status. For example, if you want the plan data for all of 2010 to be locked from any changes in an application, you can set this region of data as locked.

▶ For a combination of work status and activity, you can define the following types of access:

▶ All: When the work status for a data region is set to All, any user who has write access to the data region in the application can update data for the data region.

▶ Locked: When the work status for a data region is set to Locked, no user can update data for the data region.

▶ Owner: When the work status for a data region is set to Owner, only the user ID or team ID listed under the Owner property of the Owner dimension can update the data for the data region.

▶ Manager: When the work status for a data region is set to Manager, only the user ID or team ID associated with the parent of the dimension member can update the data for the data region.

▶ You can set multiple owners as values in the Owner property of a dimension. Separate owner names with a semicolon. The owner name can be a user ID or team ID.

▶ SAP BPC for NetWeaver supports the inclusion of the Account dimension for work status settings. The previous version of SAP BPC did not support this.

▶ Work status also lets you monitor updates to unstructured data such as documents.

▶ Administrators at both the application set and application levels set work status configuration, so administrators should be familiar with the business process and the work status steps to perform this role. Administrators define the work statuses and the types of users who can update data for a given work status. This serves the purpose of defining the users who can update data for a given work status.

▶ Changes to the work status definition remove any existing work statuses set by users for all applications in the application set.

▶ Before you can use the dimension identified as the Owner dimension in setting a work status, you have to specify a hierarchy for it. The web administration parameter APPROVALORG—which is an application-level parameter—identifies the hierarchy (H1, H2, H3, ... , Hn) to use in the work status. We'll discuss setting this parameter in Chapter 8, when we discuss web administration parameters.

▶ When data is written back to an SAP BPC application, the work status is checked for each record that is updated. If, for example, one of the records in the update failed the work status check, that record is rejected. The other records are updated successfully.

▶ In SAP BPC for NetWeaver 7.5, functionality is available to generate and send email messages when there is a change to a work status. (You'll find more information on this new version of SAP BPC for NetWeaver in Chapter 10.)

Let's take a look at a common scenario that requires the use of work status, using our sample company. In this scenario, the sales managers of Rich Bloom enter the sales plan for the next year, which is then submitted to management for approval. After the plan has been approved, it should be protected from changes by anyone other than the owner of the entity, as follows:

1. Log into the ZRB_GM_PLAN application set and click on WORK STATUS in the left pane (Figure 7.1, ❶).

2. In the center pane, you'll see the work statuses in the rows and the activities in the columns. The intersection identifies who can update the data for the combination of work status and activity (Figure 7.1, ❷). The work status defined here applies to all of the applications in the application set.

3. In the right pane, you can see the options to maintain work status for an application set (Figure 7.1, ❸). You can also create a new work status using the options listed here.

4. Select OWNER for manual activity (MAN) to ensure that only the owner of an entity can modify the data when the work status is set to Approved (Figure 7.1, ❹).

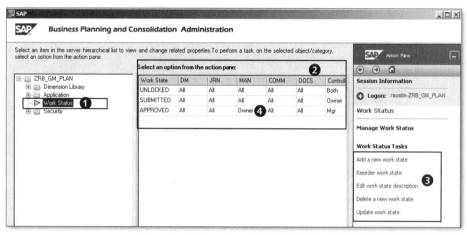

Figure 7.1   Configuring Work Status to Lock Data—Part A

5. Select the sales plan application, ZRB_SALES_CMB, and identify the Category, Entity, and Time dimensions as the dimensions to be used for setting work status for the application (Figure 7.2, ❺). As discussed earlier, you can select a maximum of five dimensions to set work status, and you are required to set one dimension as the Owner dimension, which should include an Owner property. We selected the Entity dimension as the Owner dimension in our example.

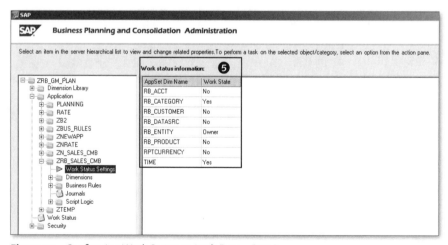

Figure 7.2   Configuring Work Status to Lock Data—Part B

6. Select the RB_ENTITY dimension under Dimensions in the left pane, and enter the owner value for the members in the dimension. The Owner property identifies who is the owner of the entity. In our example, SHILL (Shawn Hill) is identified as the owner (Figure 7.3, ❻). You can also enter a team in the Owner property or multiple owners separated by semicolons.

D	E	F	G	H	I	J	K
					STORED_CAL		
1 CURRENCY ▾	ELIM ▾	FX_TYPE ▾	INTCO ▾	OWNER ▾	C ▾		
2 USD				RBLOOM\SHILL			
3 USD				RBLOOM\SHILL			
4 USD				RBLOOM\SHILL			
5 USD				RBLOOM\SHILL			
6 USD				RBLOOM\SHILL			
7 GBP				RBLOOM\SHILL			
8 GBP				RBLOOM\SHILL			
9 EUR				RBLOOM\SHILL ❻			
10 EUR				RBLOOM\SHILL			
11							
12							

Figure 7.3 Configuring Work Status to Lock Data—Part C

7. Let's say you have different entity members that fall under a higher-level hierarchy node. The owner property value associated with the higher-level entity node is the implied manager of the entities that fall under the node. The hierarchy used to maintain this relationship of owner and manager is known as the *approval organization hierarchy*. We can use the SAP BPC Web interface to set the APPROV-ALORG parameter for the ZRB_SALES_CMB application (Figure 7.4, ❼).

Figure 7.4 Configuring Work Status to Lock Data—Part D

8. Select H1 as the APPROVALORG for this application (Figure 7.5, ❽). In this case, hierarchy H1 of the Entity dimension is used to determine the implied manager of entities.

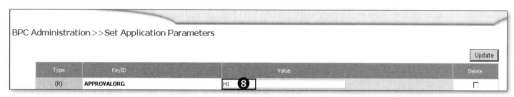

Figure 7.5 Configuring Work Status to Lock Data—Part E

9. From SAP BPC for Excel, in the eSubmit menu, select Modify Work Status (Figure 7.6, ❾).

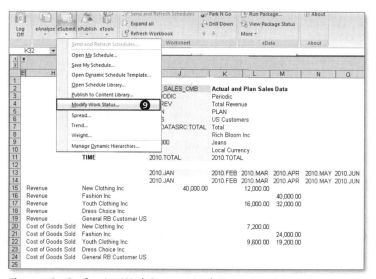

Figure 7.6 Configuring Work Status to Lock Data—Part F

10. You'll now be directed to the Web interface and required to authenticate your SAP BPC credentials. Specify the member values to use for specifying the work status, and make the selections specified in Figure 7.7, ❿, as follows:

   ▶ Category: Plan

   ▶ Entity: 20

   ▶ Time: 2010.Total

   Click on the green checkmark to continue.

11. Include all of the children for the selections by selecting Include Children in the Data Region (Figure 7.7, ⓫). This will apply the work status selection

for all of the time periods in 2010. Select APPROVED as the work status and click on ENTER.

Figure 7.7 Configuring Work Status to Lock Data—Part G

12. Now, from SAP BPC for Excel, create an input schedule and enter or modify plan data for entity 20 for the Jan 2010 period (Figure 7.8, ⓬). Then send the data to the database.

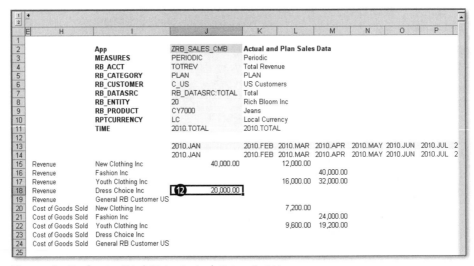

Figure 7.8 Configuring Work Status to Lock Data—Part H

13. You'll notice that the update fails with an error message indicating that the work status check has failed. Because the work status is Approved, only the owner of the entity, Shawn Hill, can modify the data (Figure 7.9).

Figure 7.9   Configuring Work Status to Lock Data—Part I

In this section, we explained how to define work status types and select the dimensions to be used when assigning work status for an application. We also reviewed the steps for setting the work status for a data region and explained how to use work status to lock data from being changed in an SAP BPC application.

In the next section, we'll discuss how to use comments in SAP BPC.

7.2   Comments

Comments serve an important purpose in SAP BPC; they enable users to enter free-form text about the data in an application. Information users enter as comments can be viewed by others and helps users make better decisions. The following are important points about comments:

▶ You can access the Comments interface from the SAP BPC for Excel, SAP BPC Web, SAP BPC for Word, and SAP BPC for PowerPoint interfaces.

▶ You can set a comment for a specific current view selection from the SAP BPC for Excel interface.

▶ A comment can be up to 265 characters. This is the Excel limit for a comment.

▶ You can create a comment for unstructured documents such as Word or Power-Point documents that are available in the content library of SAP BPC.

▶ Users should have authorization to add, view, or delete comments. Authorization for these two tasks is necessary to add and manage comments: AddComment and ManageComment.

▶ When you create a comment, you can assign a keyword and priority to it. You can then search for comments using either partial or full criteria based on these two parameters.

▶ You can run a report to get a detailed list of comments by history.

▶ In SAP BPC for Excel, the EvCOM function sends comment to a database for a specific set of member values. The EvCGT and EvCGP functions retrieve comments based on a specific set of member values.

▶ The value of the Comment application-level parameter determines whether comments can be maintained for an application. The parameter should be set to ON before comments can be posted for an application. We'll discuss this setting in detail in Section 8.3, Web Administration Parameters.

7.2.1   Add Comments

There are two ways to add comments from the SAP BPC for Excel interface. You can add a comment either manually or by using the EvCOM function for a particular selection of dimension member values. Follow these steps:

1. To add a comment manually, open a report or input schedule using the SAP BPC for Excel interface. Click on the ADD NEW COMMENT task under BPC TASKS in the action pane on the right (Figure 7.10).

Figure 7.10   Adding Comments—Part A

2. The system displays a dialog box, Enter a New Comment—Step 1 of 2, with the following options to create a comment (Figure 7.11):

   ▶ The Active Report or Schedule Cell: You can select this option if a report or input schedule is open. Otherwise, this option is grayed out.

   ▶ The Active Current View: When this option is selected, the comment is associated with the values defined in the current view.

   ▶ Custom Current View: You can select this option if you want to create a comment based on a custom CV. If this option is selected, the system prompts you to optionally select the dimension values to which the comment should apply. If a dimension is not selected, that dimension is ignored for the comment.

For our example, select Custom Current View. Select only the Category, Entity, and Time dimensions for the comment. Select the following member values for entering the comment:

   ▶ RB_CATEGORY: PLAN

   ▶ RB_ENTITY: 20

   ▶ RB_TIME: 2010.TOTAL

Then click on the green arrow button.

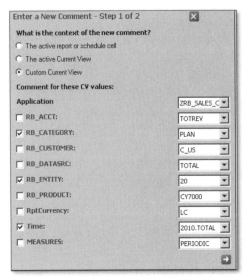

Figure 7.11 Adding Comments—Part B

3. In the next screen, select the priority of the comment (Figure 7.12). The values HIGH, MEDIUM, LOW, and NO PRIORITY can be selected.

4. You can optionally associate a keyword with the comment (Figure 7.12), which you can use later to retrieve the comment. You can enter a keyword of up to 30 characters.

5. Enter the comment (Figure 7.12).

Figure 7.12 Adding Comments—Part C

6. Click on the green checkmark. This is the last step in the process of adding comments; the comment is then stored in the database.

We've now added a comment for a combination of dimension member values. Next, we'll explain how to view comments.

7.2.2 Viewing Comments

Follow these steps to view comments:

1. Open a report or input schedule using the SAP BPC for Excel interface and click on the VIEW COMMENTS task under BPC TASKS in the action pane on the right (Figure 7.10).

2. A dialog box, VIEW COMMENTS—STEP 1 OF 3, is displayed (Figure 7.13). You can view a comment based on one of the following selections:

   ▶ THE ACTIVE REPORT OR SCHEDULE CELL: This option is available only if a report or input schedule is already open. Otherwise, this option is grayed out.

   ▶ THE ACTIVE CURRENT VIEW: The system returns a comment associated with the selections in the active CV.

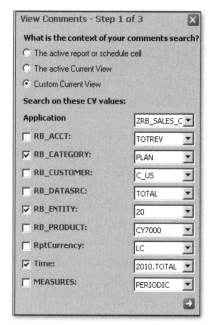

Figure 7.13 Viewing a Comment—Part A

▶ CUSTOM CURRENT VIEW: You can select this option if you want to view a comment based on dimension values that are different from what is shown in the CV. If this option is selected, the system prompts you to select the dimension values to retrieve the comments. If no values are selected for a dimension, that dimension is ignored in the retrieval process.

> **Note**
>
> Only the dimensions you selected when creating the comment should be selected when retrieving the comment.

After making your selections, click on the green arrow to move to the next step.

3. A new dialog box is displayed (Figure 7.14), and the system asks: "Do You Want to Include Comment History?" If you want to view the history of the comments associated with this selection, select the SHOW COMMENT HISTORY checkbox.

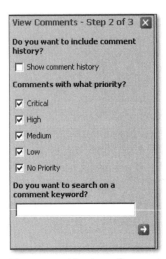

Figure 7.14 Viewing a Comment—Part B

4. Select the priority level of the comments you want to view.

5. Select the keyword criteria to use when searching for comments. You do not need to enter the complete keyword, and you can use a partial keyword in the search for comments. After making your selections, click on the green arrow to proceed to the next step.

6. You'll now be prompted to select an option based on the origin of the comment (Figure 7.15):

   ▶ COMMENTS FROM ANYONE: This selection returns all comments that were entered by all users. For our example, use this option.

   ▶ COMMENTS FROM MYSELF: This selection returns only the comments you entered (based on your user ID).

   ▶ COMMENTS FROM ANOTHER: This selection returns comments added by a specific user. When you select this option, you have to select the particular users whose comments you want to view.

7. You can also specify a date criteria if you want to search comments by a date range. Now, click on the green checkmark.

Figure 7.15 Viewing a Comment—Part C

8. The comments page opens on the Web (Figure 7.16). Before the page is displayed, you must authenticate your credentials by entering your user ID and password. The comments page is composed of two tables:

   ▶ DATA REGIONS WITH COMMENTS: This table displays the dimension members that were selected in the criteria for displaying comments. This table can include more than one row based on the selection criteria and will display only the selections for which comments exist.

▶ COMMENTS FOR THE SELECTED DATA REGION: This table displays all of the comments associated with a given data region as displayed in the DATA REGIONS WITH COMMENTS table. Click on a row in the DATA REGIONS WITH COMMENTS table to display the associated comments in this table. The following information is displayed for each comment displayed in this table:

▶ COMMENT: Displays the comment the user entered for this selection.

▶ PRIORITY: Denotes the priority of the comment.

▶ KEYWORD: Displays any keyword associated with the comment.

▶ ORIGINATOR: Displays the user who originally created the comment.

▶ DATE: Denotes the date when the comment was originally created.

9. On the right side of the action pane (Figure 7.16), you'll find options to add a new comment, report on comments, delete selected comments, or update comments. To delete a comment, select a comment displayed in the comments for the selected data region, and click on DELETE SELECTED COMMENTS. Here, you can also update the description of a comment, its priority, or its keywords and then click on UPDATE COMMENTS to effect the updates.

You now know how to maintain and view comments. In the next section, we'll explain how to report on comments.

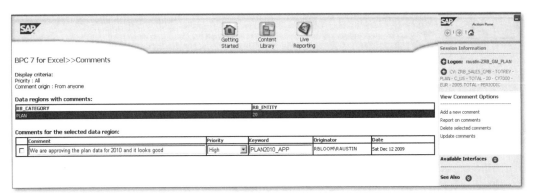

Figure 7.16 Viewing a Comment—Part D

7.2.3 Report on Comments

You can also view comments by selecting the LAUNCH BPC SYSTEM REPORTS option from the SAP BPC Web interface for your application (Figure 7.17, ❶). The menu option to run system reports is located under BPC TASKS.

Click on LAUNCH BPC SYSTEM REPORTS and you'll see COMMENTS REPORT under the APPLICATION REPORTS tasks in you're the left pane (Figure 7.17, ❷).

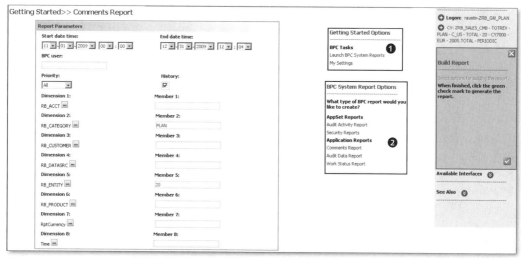

Figure 7.17 Reporting a Comment—Part A

You can generate a report of comments based on the following selections:

▸ START DATE: Specify the start date when the comment was created.

▸ START TIME: Specify the start time when the comment was created.

▸ END DATE: When you specify the start date, you can specify the end date for comments to be included in the report.

▸ END TIME: When you specify the start time, you can specify the end time for comments to be included in the report.

▸ SAP BUSINESSOBJECTS PLANNING AND CONSOLIDATION USER: If you want the report to include comments for only a particular user, you can specify the user's ID.

▸ HISTORY: Select this option if you want the report to include not only the latest comment but also a history of all of the comments for a selection.

▸ PRIORITY: Select the priority of comments to be included in the report.

▸ DIMENSION VALUES: Specify the dimension member values if you want to see comments based on specific values. A blank for a dimension member indicates that you want all values for that dimension to be reported.

▸ SET PORTRAIT: This setting indicates how you want to display the report. The available options are PORTRAIT and LANDSCAPE.

After you make your selections, click on the green checkmark in the action pane to display the comment report (Figure 7.18).

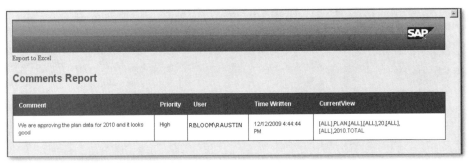

Figure 7.18   Reporting a Comment—Part B

You now know how to create comment reports. Next, we'll review some of the Ev functions that are available to maintain and view comments.

7.2.4   Ev Functions for Comments

You can use the following standard Ev functions in SAP BPC for Excel to create, update, or display comments:

▸ **EvCOM**
You can use the EvCOM function to send a comment to the database. The values specified in this function should reference the application name and dimension values with which this comment must be associated. If a member value is not specified, the value for the dimension is automatically taken from the CV of a report or schedule.

▸ **EvCGT**
You can use the EvCGT function to retrieve a comment from the database for an application and member values. Similar to the EvCOM function, if a dimension

member value is not specified, the value for the dimension is automatically taken from the CV of that report or schedule.

You should now know how to add and view comments, including how to use SAP BPC reports from the SAP BPC Web interface. In the next section, we'll explain how distribution and collection is used to distribute reports and input schedules. We'll also explain how to use the Distribution and Collection interface to update data from an offline input schedule into SAP BPC.

7.3   Distribution and Collection

The Distribution and Collection interface in SAP BPC allows a user to share the data in SAP BPC with other users who may or may not have access to the system. It also enables the data to be entered in offline mode and be reloaded back into SAP BPC.

You can access the distribution and collection menu options from the SAP BPC for Excel interface via the EPUBLISH menu. You must have the necessary authorization to use this functionality.

The process of sending a report or input schedule in offline mode is referred to as *distribution* in SAP BPC. The data included in this report can be used by others who may need access to this information for analysis and decision-making. Sometimes users who travel may not be able to connect to SAP BPC to access information in an application; distribution facilitates the process of getting data to the necessary users via email and aids in collaboration.

A user can update the data in an input schedule in offline mode and push the changes back to the SAP BPC system. The process of updating the data from an offline input schedule back to SAP BPC is referred to as *collection*.

The report or input schedule generated using the distribution list is a snapshot of the data at a specific point in time. When a user sends a report or an input schedule using a distributor, the data can be placed in a folder or sent as an email to users. If the report or input schedule is sent via email, the SAP BPC system should be configured to send email to users.

The process of defining reports or input schedules for distribution is managed using distribution lists. You can specify more than one report or input schedule when defining the distribution list; if you're sending data as an email message, you can list the users who should receive the report and what data should be sent. A distribution list with the definition of the reports or input schedules can be saved in XLS or XLT format.

After a distribution list is created, it can be executed to generate the reports and input schedules defined in it and be executed immediately or scheduled in the background. This job is executed on the machine of the user who schedules the job.

When data is generated using the distribution option, the access available for the user who schedules the distribution governs the content of the report or input schedules. Ensure that the user executing the distribution list has sufficient member access to the data requested in the distribution list. If the user does not have access to the data, the distribution list fails to execute and returns a message saying the user does not have sufficient authorization to run the reports. A report or input schedule generated using distribution can be viewed directly in Excel; there is no need to use any of the interfaces.

When a file is created or sent as an email after the generation of reports or input schedules using the distribution process, anyone who has access to that file or email can view the generated data, because the information is offline at that time. This has to be taken into consideration when data is distributed using this process, especially if the generated data is sensitive and should be kept confidential.

There are three primary interfaces that can be used to distribute and collect data:

▶ **Distribution lists**
This interface is used to create and maintain distribution lists. The list identifies the reports, schedules, and selections for generating the data.

▶ **Offline Distribution Wizard**
This interface is used to schedule execution of the distribution list. The job can be scheduled to run immediately, or it can be scheduled as a future job to be run later.

▶ **Collection**
This interface is used only for input schedules that were distributed earlier. With this interface, data entered or modified into an offline input schedule can be updated in the planning application.

7.3.1 Creating a Distribution List

We'll now explain how to create a distribution list for the input schedule displayed in Figure 7.19. Recall that we created this input schedule in Chapter 5.

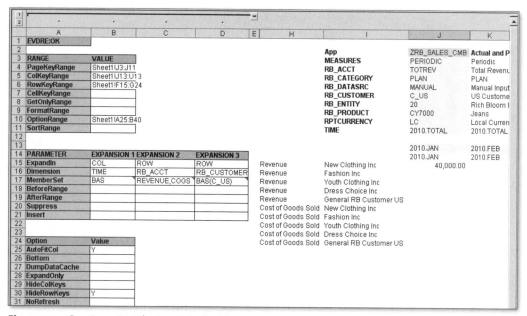

Figure 7.19 Creating a Distribution List—Part A

To access the distribution list, log into the SAP BPC for Excel interface. You need access to the MANAGE DISTRIBUTOR LIST task under COLLABORATION to maintain distribution lists.

1. Go to the EPUBLISH menu. Select MANAGE DISTRIBUTION LIST and select NEW. You're prompted to select a template to create the new distribution list. (Figure 7.20).

2. This opens up the distribution template (Figure 7.21), which contains a place-holder to enter the name of a book. This applies to the entire distribution list. A distribution list can include multiple sections, and each section denotes a report or an input schedule. Enter the following parameters for the distribution template:

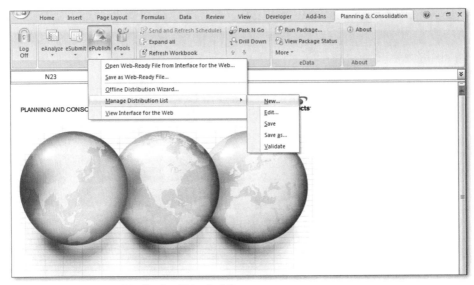

Figure 7.20 Creating a Distribution List—Part B

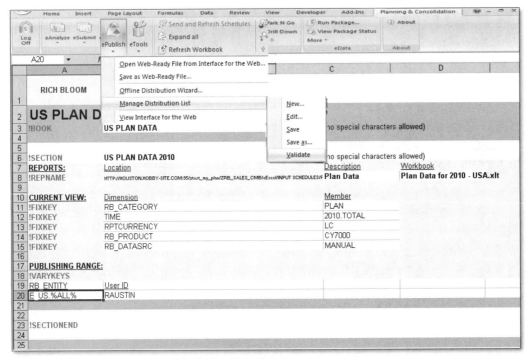

Figure 7.21 Creating a Distribution List—Part C

- ▸ BOOK: Every distribution list has a name assigned to it. Specify the name of the book here.

- ▸ SECTION: A distribution template can contain one or more sections, and a section is defined for each report or input schedule. Enter the name of the section here.

- ▸ REPNAME: In this parameter, specify the report or input schedule you want to use in a section of the distribution list.

- ▸ FIXKEY: This field specifies fixed filters for the report; specify the static selections. You can have more than one FIXKEY field for the different dimensions in your application; for example, you may need to always run a report for the PLAN category. In this case, the FIXKEY is used to specify the fixed values you want to use to run the report.

- ▸ VARKEY: The VARKEY field specifies the dimension values to use to burst the report. You can specify more than one dimension in this field. If you want a user to receive the report, specify the user here. The user receives the report for the selections corresponding to that user, which allows you to only send users the data they really need. (This is applicable only if you are distributing your report as an email message.) If multiple values are selected for a dimension specified in the VARKEY field, multiple reports are created when executing the report. In the example shown in Figure 7.21, a report will be generated for each entity that is under the E_US hierarchy.

- ▸ SECTIONEND: This denotes the end of the section.

The email configuration in SAP BPC should be set if you want to email reports or input schedules using the distributor. Also, email addresses should be maintained and current for the user in SAP BPC.

> **Note**
>
> If you do not specify a dimension available in your application in the FIXKEY or VARKEY fields, the values for the dimension are taken from the CV of the user who is scheduling the report.

3. Validate the distribution list you just created. When the distribution list is validated, the system checks to see whether all mandatory fields are entered and checks the syntax of the distribution list.

4. Save the distribution list. A user who wants to create a distribution list and save it to the company folder needs access to the UPDATE TO COMPANY FOLDER task that falls under FILE ACCESS.

Now that we've created a distribution list, we can execute and distribute it as an offline report or input schedule.

7.3.2 Offline Distribution Wizard

Before using the Offline Distribution Wizard, ensure that you have the necessary access. You'll need access to the PUBLISHOFFLINE task that falls under COLLABORATION.

1. Go to the EPUBLISH menu and select OFFLINE DISTRIBUTION WIZARD (Figure 7.22). You're prompted to select either the distribution or the collection process. Under DISTRIBUTION, there are two options for running the template:

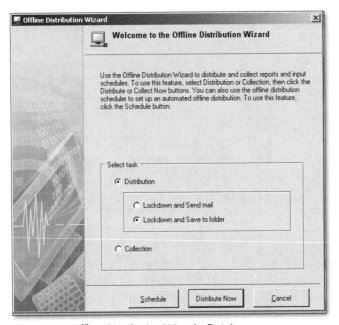

Figure 7.22 Offline Distribution Wizard—Part A

▶ LOCKDOWN AND SEND MAIL: When this option is selected, the system prompts you to select a distribution list and then requires you to specify the sender, subject, and body details of the email message. Additional options are available if you want to receive confirmation that the message was received or if you want to send the report as a ZIP file.

▶ LOCKDOWN AND SAVE TO FOLDER: When this option is selected, the system prompts the user to select a distribution list and specify a folder location where the reports or schedules selected in the distribution list should be saved.

2. Select the distribution list you want to execute, and specify the folder in which you want to the files to be created (Figure 7.23). Click on the NEXT button.

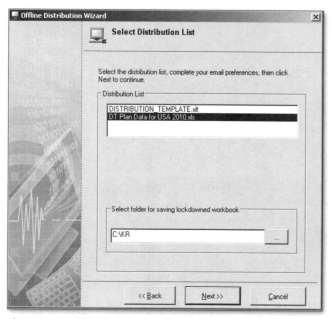

Figure 7.23 Offline Distribution Wizard—Part B

3. You're then prompted to select the sections in the distribution list you want to distribute (Figure 7.24). After making your selections, click on the NEXT button.

4. The next dialog box confirms the reports that will be created and the selections that will be used in creating the reports (Figure 7.25). Click on the PROCESS button to continue.

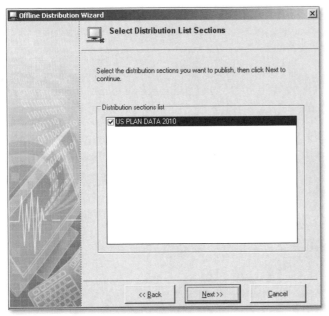

Figure 7.24 Offline Distribution Wizard—Part C

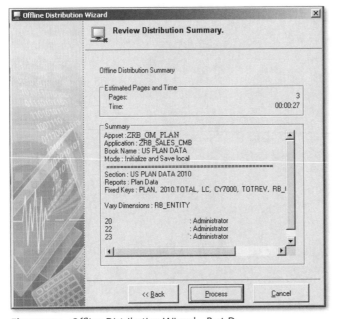

Figure 7.25 Offline Distribution Wizard—Part D

5. The distribution list is now executed on the client machine. In this case, the client is the user who is scheduling this process for execution. The reports and input schedules specified in the distribution lists are opened, the CV is changed based on the selections defined there, and the data is refreshed and saved in the folder specified when executing the list. A message confirms that the reports were distributed successfully. Click on FINISH to complete the distribution process (Figure 7.26).

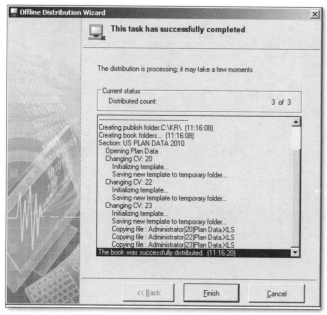

Figure 7.26 Offline Distribution Wizard—Part E

The files are generated in the folder specified in the distribution list (Figure 7.27). The naming convention of the reports or input schedules generated by the distributor is as follows:

► The report recipient or user ID name as specified in the VARKEY field in the distribution list.

► The VARKEY value specified in the distribution list section.

► The name of the report specified in the distribution section.

> **Note**
>
> More than one file or email may be generated based on the selections in the VARKEY field of the distribution list.

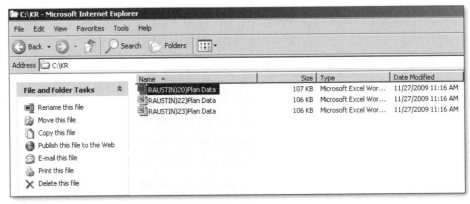

Figure 7.27 Offline Distribution Wizard—Part F

> **Note**
>
> Do not keep a distribution list open when you want to use the Offline Distribution Wizard to execute it.

7.3.3 Collection

Collection applies only to input schedules that were distributed using the Offline Distribution Wizard. Input schedules that are distributed as an offline report can be updated offline, and then the updates can be pushed back to SAP BPC.

You need sufficient authorization to collect data; specifically, you need access to the SubmitData task that falls under Analysis and Collection. The distribution list we ran included an input schedule; we'll now change one of the records in the input schedule and push the data back to SAP BPC using the Collect interface (Figure 7.28).

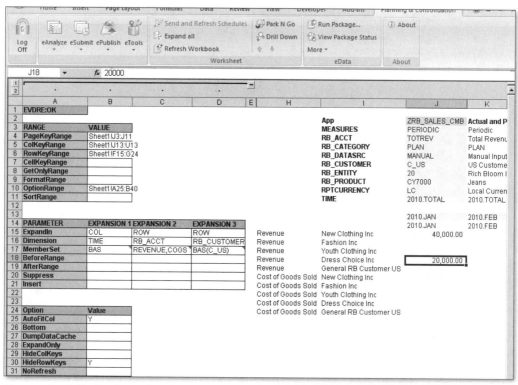

Figure 7.28 Collecting Data—Part A

1. Go to the EPUBLISH menu and select OFFLINE DISTRIBUTION WIZARD. You're prompted to select the distribution or collection task; select COLLECTION and click on the COLLECT NOW button to collect the data (Figure 7.29).

2. The next dialog box displays two options for collecting data (Figure 7.30):

   ▶ OUTLOOK MAIL BOX: When this option is selected, data is collected from an email message attachment.

   ▶ LOCAL FOLDER: When this option is selected, data is collected from a file located on your local computer. When you specify a folder, you can specify the folder and files from which you want to collect the data. You can select more than one file in this step.

3. Select the files to collect and click on the NEXT button.

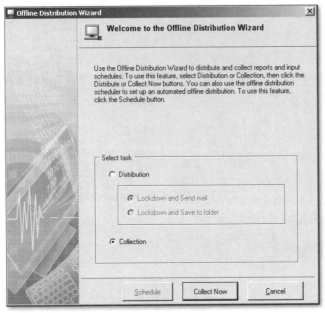

Figure 7.29 Collecting Data—Part B

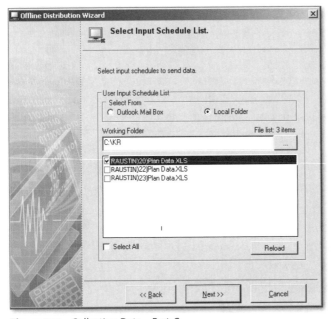

Figure 7.30 Collecting Data—Part C

4. After the files are selected, a dialog box indicates that the data in the files will be processed (Figure 7.31). Click on the PROCESS button.

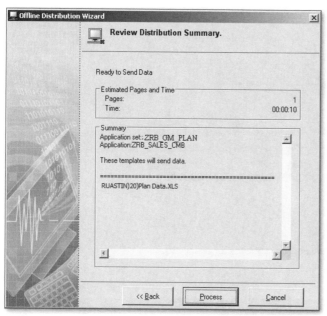

Figure 7.31 Collecting Data—Part D

5. During the update process, all of the validations defined for the application are checked before the data is processed. The number of records processed is displayed in the dialog box (Figure 7.32).

6. All of the processed files are moved to the SUCCESSFULLYPROCESSED folder, as shown in Figure 7.33.

You've now seen how the distribution and collection functionality works in SAP BPC. It is a powerful feature for generating and distributing reports and can be tailored to run multiple reports for different selections from a single distribution template. The ability to distribute input schedules in offline mode, and the ability to update those schedules offline and push them back into SAP BPC, is another key feature of the interface. Although data is entered offline, all of the validations for the application are enforced when the data is pushed back to SAP BPC.

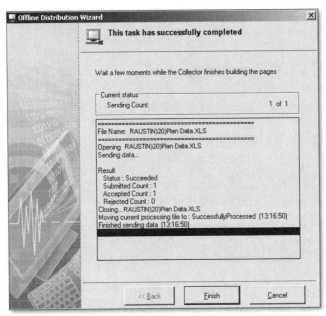

Figure 7.32   Collecting Data—Part E

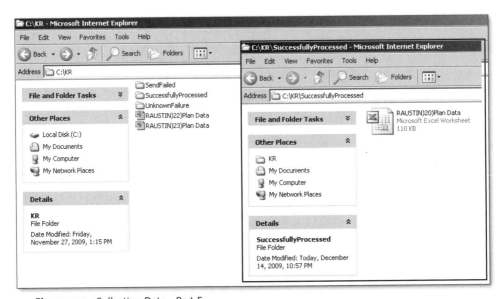

Figure 7.33   Collecting Data—Part F

In the next section, we'll explain how the Word and PowerPoint interfaces are used to integrate SAP BPC data into those types of documents.

7.4   Integrating SAP BPC Data into Word and PowerPoint

SAP BPC allows you to not only integrate data into Word and PowerPoint, but also to embed objects such as input schedules into these documents. You can also add and view comments from this interface. The following tasks are available when you use the Word and PowerPoint interfaces:

▶ **Insert Data**
You use the INSERT BPC DATA task in the action pane for inserting SAP BPC data into a Word or PowerPoint document. After you add the Insert BPC Data object into a document, the placeholder represents the dimension members specified in the current view. You can view the selection by placing the cursor on the object.

▶ **Insert Interface for Excel Object**
When this task is selected, a dialog box prompts you to select a report or input schedule. When an input schedule is inserted into a document, the changes can be updated in SAP BPC.

▶ **Comments**
The ADD NEW COMMENT and VIEW COMMENT tasks in the action pane can be used to add and view comments.

▶ **Retrieve All Data**
When you have inserted a link for the data in the CV using the INSERT BPC DATA task, you can retrieve the value for this selection using the RETRIEVE ALL DATA task.

▶ **Expand All**
When you insert an SAP BPC for Excel object in a document, you can click on the EXPAND ALL task in the action pane to use the expansion functions in SAP BPC.

▶ **Send All Data**
When an input schedule created in SAP BPC for Excel is inserted into a document, the change made to the input schedule can be updated to the database.

When an object is inserted into a document, you can only retrieve the data from SAP BPC; you cannot use it to update the data. We'll now use a simple example to show you how you can use the SAP BPC for Word interface to insert SAP BPC data into a document. You can access the SAP BPC for Word and SAP BPC for PowerPoint interfaces from the SAP BPC Admin, SAP BPC Excel, and SAP BPC Web interfaces.

1. Access the SAP BPC for Word interface. A list of menu options under TASKS and DOCUMENT TASKS is displayed (Figure 7.34).

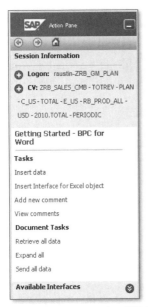

Figure 7.34 Integrating SAP BPC Data into Word—Part A

2. Open a new Word document as shown in Figure 7.35. Then click on INSERT BPC DATA, and insert this object into your Word document. The member selections in your CV are used to retrieve the data. Place the cursor on the object to view the selections SAP BPC will use to retrieve the data.

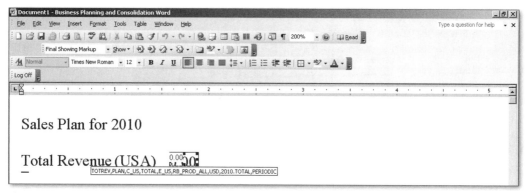

Figure 7.35 Integrating SAP BPC Data into Word—Part B

3. You can right-click on the object inserted in the previous step to display the object's properties (Figure 7.36).

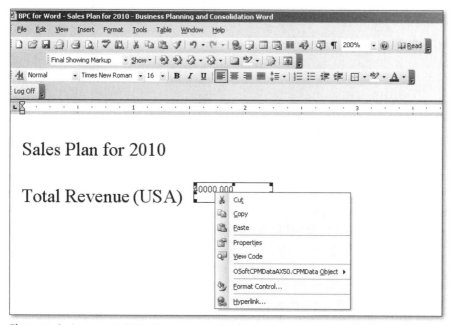

Figure 7.36 Integrating SAP BPC Data into Word—Part C

When you click on the RETRIEVE ALL DATA task under DOCUMENT TASKS in the action pane, the data from SAP BPC is retrieved and displayed for the objects inserted in the Word document, as shown in Figure 7.37.

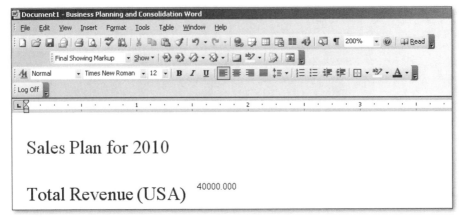

Figure 7.37 Integrating SAP BPC Data into Word—Part D

In this section, we explained how to interface SAP BPC data into Word and PowerPoint documents. In the next section, we'll explain how you can use menus to view and execute tasks in planning or consolidation processes that need to be performed on a periodic basis.

7.5 Menus

SAP BPC provides a standard set of EvMNU functions that you can use in SAP BPC for Excel to launch common tasks such as opening a report or executing a data package.

Two options are available when you use the EvMNU functions: You can create them as standard Excel functions or include them inside a VB macro. The following is the syntax for using the EvMNU function as an Excel formula:

▶ **EvMNU**
MacroName, DisplayName, Parameter.

▶ **MacroName**
This is the menu command for executing a common task such as setting the member value in the CV for a dimension or updating data from an input schedule to the database.

▶ **Display Name**
This is the text the user clicks on to launch the menu task. It is an optional parameter.

▶ **Parameter**

Some macro commands require additional parameters. For example, to execute a report, the name of the report to be run is required as a parameter in the command.

Table 7.1 lists the menu commands used in SAP BPC.

Menu Command	Description
MNU_eANALYZE_REFRESH	Recalculates reports.
MNU_eANALYZE_OPENMY	Opens the MyReports report folder.
MNU_eANALYZE_OPENSTANDARD	Opens the report library in the eExcel/Reports directory.
MNU_eANALYZE_SAVEMY	Saves the report to the MyReports folder.
MNU_eANALYZE_REPORTWIZARD	Launches the dynamic template report dialog box.
MNU_eSUBMIT_REFSCHEDULE_SHEET_NOACTION	Sends data without clearing or refreshing.
MNU_eSUBMIT_REFSCHEDULE_SHEET_REFRESH	Sends data and refreshes the worksheet.
MNU_eSUBMIT_REFSCHEDULE_SHEET_CLEARANDREFRESH	Sends data and clears and refreshes the worksheet.
MNU_eSUBMIT_REFSCHEDULE_BOOK_NOACTION	Sends data without clearing or refreshing the worksheet.
MNU_eSUBMIT_REFSCHEDULE_BOOK_NOACTION_SHOWRESULT	Sends data without clearing or refreshing the worksheet, and shows the result in a window on successful send.
MNU_eSUBMIT_REFSCHEDULE_BOOK_REFRESH	Sends the workbook and refreshes the data.
MNU_eSUBMIT_REFSCHEDULE_BOOK_CLEARANDREFRESH	Sends the workbook, clears the data, and refreshes the workbook.
MNU_eSUBMIT_REFRESH	Refreshes data from the database in a report or input template.

Table 7.1 List of EvMNU Functions

Menu Command	Description
MNU_eSUBMIT_OPENSTANDARD	Opens the schedule library.
	No parameter is allowed for SAP NetWeaver; the default settings open the eExcel directory.
MNU_eSUBMIT_OPENMY	Opens the MySchedules folder.
MNU_eSUBMIT_SAVEMY	Saves the input schedule to the MySchedules folder.
MNU_eSUBMIT_SCHEDULE	Opens the dynamic schedule template dialog box.
MNU_eSUBMIT_MODIFY	Opens the work status action pane in SAP BPC Web.
MNU_ePUBLISH_OPENPUBLICATION	Opens the SAP BPC Web directory.
	Parameter = directory path.
MNU_ePUBLISH_PUBLISHSHEET	Publishes a worksheet to SAP BPC Web.
MNU_ePUBLISH_OFFLINE_WIZARD	Opens the Distribution Wizard.
MNU_ePUBLISH_OFFLINE_NEW	Creates a new offline report.
MNU_ePUBLISH_OFFLINE_EDIT	Edits offline options.
MNU_ePUBLISH_OFFLINE_SAVE	Saves the offline report.
MNU_ePUBLISH_OFFLINE_SAVEAS	Opens the Save As dialog box.
MNU_ePUBLISH_OFFLINE_VALIDATE	Validates an offline report.
MNU_ePUBLISH_VIEWeDASH	Opens SAP BPC Web.
MNU_eTOOLS_CHANGEAPP	Opens the Change Application Set dialog box.
MNU_eTOOLS_MEMBERSELECTOR_x	Opens the member lookup for the specified dimension type. The dimension types are:
	A: Account
	C: Category

Table 7.1 List of EvMNU Functions (Cont.)

Menu Command	Description
	E: Entity
	T: Time
	F: Measures
	I: Intercompany
	Dimension types D, S, and U are not supported.
MNU_eTOOLS_FUNCTIONWIZARD	Opens the Function Wizard to insert function.
MNU_eTOOLS_EXPAND	Expands all dynamic expansions.
MNU_eTOOLS_REFRESH	Refreshes reports and input schedules from the server.
MNU_ETOOLS_PARKNGO	Opens the Park N Go dialog box.
MNU_eTOOLS_JOURNAL	Opens the journal form (only available if journals are set up on the server).
MNU_eJOURNAL_QUERY	Opens the Journal Manager (only available if journals are set up on the server).
MNU_eJOURNAL_REPORT	Opens the Journal Report Wizard (only available if journals are set up on the server).
MNU_eTOOLS_OPENSTANDARD	Opens the template library.
MNU_eTOOLS_SAVESTANDARD	Saves to the template library.
MNU_eTOOLS_DRILLDOWN	Performs drill-down on the current cell.
MNU_eTOOLS_DRILLDOWN_BACK	Reverses the last drill-down.
MNU_eTOOLS_DRILLDOWN_FORWARD	Performs a drill-down that was undone by the DRILLDOWN_BACK task.
MNU_eTOOLS_DATAMANAGER	Opens the Data Manager and adds the eData menu.
MNU_eTOOLS_OPTION	Opens the Client Options dialog box.
MNU_eTOOLS_WBOPTION	Opens the Workbook Options dialog box.
MNU_eTOOLS_ABOUT	Opens the About BPC dialog box.

Table 7.1 List of EvMNU Functions (Cont.)

Menu Command	Description
MNU_eData_RUNPACKAGE	Opens the Data Manager Run Package dialog box. Allows users who have access to run database packages.
MNU_eDATA_VIEWSTATUS	Opens the Data Manager View Status dialog box.
MNU_eDATA_ORGANIZEPACKAGE	Opens the Data Manager Organize Package dialog box.
MNU_eDATA_MANAGESITEPACKAGE	Opens the Data Manager Manage Team User Package Access dialog box.
MNU_eDATA_DATAPREVIEW	Opens the Data Manager Data Preview dialog box.
MNU_eDATA_DATAUPLOAD	Opens the Data Manager Data Upload dialog box. Allows users who have access to upload data files to the server and perform data transformations.
MNU_eData_DataDownLoad	Opens the Data Manager Data Download dialog box. Allows users who have access to download data files from the server.
MNU_eDATA_NEWTRANSFORMATION	Creates a new data manager transformation sheet.
MNU_eDATA_OPENTRANSFORMATION	Opens the Data Manager Open Transformation dialog box.
MNU_eDATA_NEWCONVERSIONFILE	Creates a new data manager conversion file.
MNU_eDATA_OPENCONVERSIONFILE	Opens the Data Manager Open Conversion File dialog box.
MNU_eDATA_SAVECONVERSIONFILE	Saves the active conversion file.
MNU_eDATA_SAVEASCONVERSIONFILE	Opens the Data Manager Save as Conversion File dialog box.

Table 7.1 List of EvMNU Functions (Cont.)

Menu Command	Description
MNU_eDATA_CLEARPROMPTVALUE	Clears saved data manager prompt values.
MNU_eDATA_TESTTRANSFORMATIONWDATA	Opens the Data Manager Test Transformation with Data dialog box.
MNU_ETOOLS_TASKPANE	Shows the Action pane.
MNU_ESUBMIT_MANAGE_DYNAMICHIERARCHIES	Opens the Dynamic Hierarchies dialog box.
MNU_ESUBMIT_REFSCHEDULE_SHEET_NODIALOG_SHOWRESULT	Sends the active sheet without any dialog box. Shows the Result dialog box.
MNU_ESUBMIT_SENDDATA	Sends data only (not refresh data).
MNU_ESUBMIT_COMMENT	Sends comments only (not refresh comments).
MNU_ESUBMIT_SENDDATA_AFTER_COMMENT	Sends data first.
MNU_ESUBMIT_COMMENT_AFTER_SENDDATA	Sends comment first.

Table 7.1 List of EvMNU Functions (Cont.)

The following macro sets the CV for the Time dimension to 2007.Jan. Select a specific cell, and enter the command as a formula, as shown in Figure 7.38, ❶ and ❷.

```
EvMNU("SETCV", "SET TIME", "Time=2007.Jan").
```

When a user clicks on the cell, the Time dimension in the CV is set to 2007.Jan.

The following macro launches a report. Select a specific cell and enter the command as shown in Figure 7.38, ❸ and ❹).

```
EvMNU("OPENFILE", "View Plan Report", "Reports/Plan_2010.xls").
```

When a user clicks on the cell, the Plan_2010.xls report in the Reports folder is executed.

1. You can optionally assign a macro to invoke a command. From the EXCEL menu, select VIEW • TOOLBARS • FORMS to display the tool bar to add form objects. Click on the button object and add it into the Excel worksheet (Figure 7.39, ❺).

2. Right-click on the object and select EDIT TEXT to edit the text displayed for the object.

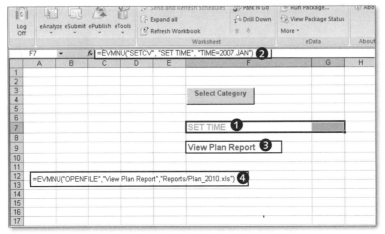

Figure 7.38 SAP BPC Menu Command

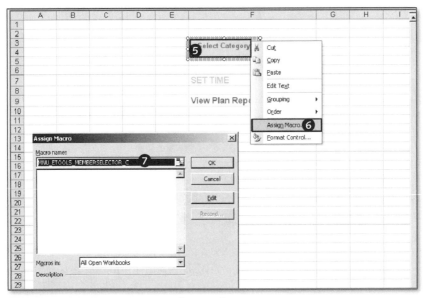

Figure 7.39 SAP BPC Assign Macro Command

3. To assign a menu command to the button, right-click on the object and select ASSIGN MACRO (Figure 7.39, ❻). This opens the ASSIGN MACRO, where you

specify the name of a macro (Figure 7.39, ❼). For example, the MNU_ETOOLS_ MEMBERSELECTOR_C macro command opens the member selection dialog box for the Category dimension and enables the user to select a value. When a user clicks on the button, the command is executed.

You can also invoke commands using a VB macro. When you include them inside a VB macro, you can include multiple EvMNU commands as a macro and make them available to users.

To create a VB macro, select VIEW • TOOLBARS • CONTROLTOOLBOX from the EXCEL menu; this displays the toolbar for adding objects. Click on the button object and insert it into the Excel worksheet. The following VB macro opens the DATA MANAGER RUN PACKAGE dialog box:

```
Private Sub CallDM_Click()
Application.Run ("MNU_eData_RUNPACKAGE")
End Sub
```

You now know how to develop menus that help users execute periodic planning and consolidation tasks.

7.6 Summary

In this chapter, you learned about key collaborative features available to monitor, lock, share, distribute, and collect data in SAP BPC. You learned how to use work status to lock data from changes and to enable workflow in applications. Next, you learned how to enter comments and view them in SAP BPC. We then discussed the distribution and collection features for distributing data, which allow users to update data and send it back into the planning application using the collection interface. We also discussed the SAP BPC interfaces for Word and PowerPoint. Finally, we discussed how to create a menu-based application for users to view and execute planning and consolidation tasks.

In the next chapter, we'll discuss the essential tools to help with the smooth functioning of your SAP BPC system. We'll explain the process of transporting objects from the development system to the quality assurance and production systems and discuss key topics such as locking, administration parameters, statistics, audits, and document management.

This chapter discusses the set of utilities to manage transport of objects across the system landscape, manage locks, maintain application set and application parameters, record statistics of usage, audit changes to objects and data, and configure and manage security.

8   Essential Tools for Building Applications

This chapter discusses the essential tools in maintaining an SAP BusinessObjects Planning and Consolidation (BPC) application. SAP offers a robust tool to manage changes to objects made in the development environment and provides an easy-to-use interface for moving them across the system landscape. The SAP BPC system is delivered with tools that are used to manage locking, enable statistics, activate audits, store unstructured data, and manage security.

In Section 8.1, we'll will explain how to transport SAP BPC objects from the development to the quality assurance and production systems. We'll explain the parameters and settings used to manage the transport process to help you gain a sound understanding of how to manage transports in your organization. In addition, you'll be able to identify the difference between transporting SAP BPC objects and standard SAP NetWeaver BW objects. We'll also discuss the back-up and restore tool that is available to address disaster recovery scenarios.

In Section 8.2, we'll explain the locking concept used in SAP BPC for NetWeaver and technical details about how the planning and consolidation application handles locks and maintains the integrity of data. We'll also look into the configuration tables that are available to customize the locking parameters for an application.

In Section 8.3, we'll discuss the parameters you can set for an application set and the applications that belong to an application set. You'll see how these parameters influence the functionality of an application.

In Section 8.4, we'll introduce how to enable statistics for an application and the benefits it provides in managing the performance of your application.

In Section 8.5, we'll introduce how to enable auditing for an application and the benefits it provides in monitoring the changes made in your application.

In Section 8.6, we'll discuss how to use the content management tool in SAP BPC to store, manage, and enforce the security of unstructured data.

In Section 8.7, we'll discuss security, which is an important component in any application. SAP BPC offers two types of security: one to manage the tasks a user can perform and one to determine the data-level access a user has in an application. In this section, you'll learn how to set up security for your applications in SAP BPC.

We'll start by looking at the interface used for transporting objects in SAP BPC and how it differs from the standard process of transporting objects in the SAP NetWeaver BW system.

8.1 Transporting SAP BPC Objects

SAP supports a landscape that includes development, quality assurance, and production systems to develop, test, and implement an application. The process of development begins, appropriately, in the development system. When development is complete, unit testing is performed, and the development objects are transported to the quality assurance system, where they are tested extensively to confirm that the functionality works as expected. This is normally the system where integration/user acceptance tests are performed. When the testing is completed successfully in the quality assurance system, the changes are moved to the production system. You should follow this process assiduously to avoid any issues of unintended changes going into production, leading to serious consequences. SAP BPC for NetWeaver supports the process of moving objects from one system to another via the transport mechanism.

In SAP BPC version 5.1, the transport mechanism was not available, because the product was not integrated with the NetWeaver system. The process used in this version moved or did a backup of objects in the development system and then restored them in the target system. With the integration of SAP BPC with NetWeaver, transport functionality is available to transport objects across the system landscape. The transport process in SAP BPC for NetWeaver leverages the existing framework in SAP systems to transport objects. Using this tool, you can identify objects that need to be moved across the landscape and send them in a streamlined and controlled fashion, reducing any problems in this process.

SAP Best Practices does not recommend doing any development-type activity in the production system because objects should be fully tested before they are moved; but there are cases where the customer needs to modify objects directly in the production system. In these scenarios, you can modify the configuration to make changes directly in production. This is especially true in reporting, where there may be a need to create ad hoc reports directly in the production system.

The transport mechanism involves the following steps:

1. Create or modify objects in the development system.

2. Perform unit testing in the development system.

3. Create a transport request in the development system for the objects created or modified.

4. Transport the request to the quality assurance system.

5. Perform integration/user acceptance testing in the quality assurance system.

6. Move the objects to the production system.

The existing framework in SAP NetWeaver BW is used for transports, and the mechanism now supports the ability to manage SAP BPC objects. But the process used for transport is different from what is used for transporting SAP NetWeaver BW objects; in the SAP NetWeaver BW system, Transaction UJBPCTR is used to create and manage transport requests for SAP BPC objects.

Only application sets can be transported in SAP BPC, but any application set, including the ApSHELL, can be transported. When an application set is transported, all of the subobjects under the application set are also transported. The application set must be offline before a transport request is created in the source system, and the application set in the target system should be offline before the transport is imported.

When a transport request is created for an application set, the system creates entries in two shadow tables, UJT_TRANS_HDR and UJT_TRANS_OBJ, and inserts the objects for the application set. The UJT_TRANS_HDR table contains an entry for the application set that is selected, and the UJT_TRANS_OBJ table includes the metadata for the application set objects. When the transport request is sent from a source system, the entries in the transport from these two tables are compared with the objects in the target system and synchronized.

Follow these steps to transport objects:

1. Execute Transaction UJBPCTR to create a transport and click on the green check-mark (Figure 8.1, ❶ and ❷). You're prompted to create the transport request in the following screen.

2. In the REQUEST TYPE section, select one of the three options for creating the transport request (Figure 8.1, ❸).

   ▶ INSERT/MODIFY REQUEST: This option lets you create a new transport request for an application set.

   ▶ DELETION REQUEST: This option lets you delete an application set in the target system you previously transported.

   ▶ ONLY UPDATE SHADOW TABLE: If you previously created a transport for an application set and have not yet released it, you can use this option to update the shadow tables for any changes made to the application set since that point.

3. In the PARAMETERS section, select the application set you want to transport (Figure 8.1, ❹).

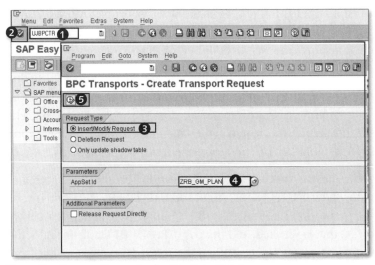

Figure 8.1 Transporting an Application Set—Part A

4. After a transport request is created, it has to be released. You can select the RELEASE REQUEST DIRECTLY option under the ADDITIONAL PARAMETERS section if you want to create a transport and immediately release it after making your selections.

5. After making the selections, click on EXECUTE (Figure 8.1, ❺).

6. The next screen prompts you to enter a description for the transport request. Enter a short description and click on the SAVE icon (Figure 8.2, ❻ and ❼).

Figure 8.2 Transporting an Application Set—Part B

There is a difference in the way SAP NetWeaver BW objects are transported and how SAP BPC objects are transported. For transporting SAP NetWeaver BW objects, you select the transport option in the administrator's workbench and select the options to transport the objects. Also, when a user creates a transport request for an SAP NetWeaver BW object, and another user modifies the same object before that transport is released, the transport is written as an additional task in the request created by the original user. But for SAP BPC, the system allows the second user to create a new request. The shadow tables UJT_TRANS_HDR and UJT_TRANS_OBJ include the updated entries for the application set, and, as a result, either of the transports can be released and sent to the target system. SAP NetWeaver BW objects are not included when you create an SAP BPC transport request. They are automatically created in the target system, based on the comparison of the objects included in the transport with the objects in the target system.

Table UJT_TRANS_CHG represents the object changeability table in SAP BPC and contains the entries for all subobjects in an application set (Figure 8.3, ❽). (Subobjects include applications, scripts, reports, journals, comments, security objects, etc.) The table includes a field called CHANGE_IND to indicate whether the object can be changed in the system (Figure 8.3, ❾). If this field is set to P for an object, it cannot be transported and is not included in a transport request. All objects that have the CHANGE_IND field set to D are transported when a transport request is created. You can modify the data in this table using Transaction SM30 to customize the transport process.

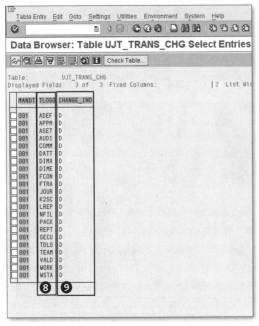

Figure 8.3 Object Changeability in SAP BPC—Part A

You can view the description of the objects in this table by double-clicking on a record (Figure 8.4). Position the cursor on the TLOGO field and click on the dropdown button to display the values for this field (Figure 8.4, ❿). This displays all of the text value descriptions for the objects (Figure 8.4, ⓫).

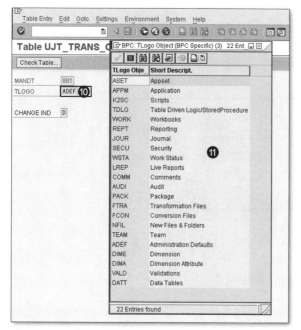

Figure 8.4 Object Changeability in SAP BPC—Part B

When an application is created in SAP BPC, the system creates directories and files in the background. The directories created during this process are used to store script files, journal templates, reports, input templates, and so on for an application. You can view the directories and files created under an application set using Transaction UJFS; this is the file service utility used in SAP BPC.

During the transport process, these files may need to be transported as well. The settings in Table UJT_TRANS_FIL determine the directories and files that are transportable (Figure 8.5). The TLOGO field in the table defines the type of object to be transported, and the PATTERN_ID field determines what is transported. When you double-click on a row in this table, you can see the pattern that indicates the files that are to be transported (Figure 8.5, ❷). Files/directories under subobject NFIL (new files and folders) are only transported to the target system when a new application is being created in the target system. Data manager files cannot be transported. Similar to the UJT_TRANS_CHG table, you can modify the entries in the table using Transaction SM30.

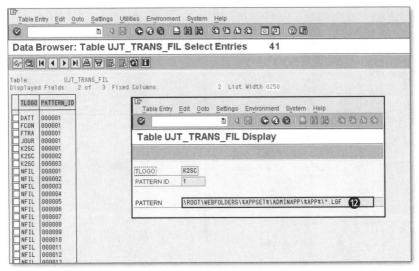

Figure 8.5 Directories and File Transport Options

You should not transport SAP BPC objects using the standard process for transporting SAP NetWeaver BW objects, because this will create errors in transport and issues when activating objects in the target system.

The standard configuration and authorization must be in place before transport requests can be released in the SAP NetWeaver BW system. After a transport request is created or released in the development system, you can view it using Transaction SE09 or SE10.

The transport administrators on the Basis team should perform the job of importing the request into the target system. After the transport is imported, you can view and display the logs, which provide detailed information on how the transport was processed in the target system, and errors, if any.

> **Note**
>
> The value of CHANGE_IND in Table UJT_TRANS_CHG determines which objects can be changed in the system. If this indicator is set to D, the object can be changed. This option is available so that customers can adjust the object changeability of objects in the production system.

You should now understand how to use the transport process to move objects from the development to the quality assurance and production systems.

The SAP BPC 7.5 NetWeaver SP 3 system provides Transaction UJBR for performing backup and restore of an application set. This tool is especially useful for addressing disaster recovery scenarios. It also provides an option to copy an application set from one system to another system. This transaction allows users to back up and restore objects, metadata tables, master data, and transaction data in an application set. You should use the transport mechanism outlined above to transport objects from the development system to quality assurance and production systems. You can use the backup and restore tool in disaster recovery scenarios and when you want to create a copy of an application set in another system.

Next, we'll review the locking process used in SAP BPC when data is updated for an application.

8.2   Concurrency Locking

Locking is an important concept to understand and consider during application development. The purpose of locking is to prevent two users from updating the same data at the same time. The application should prevent this from happening to avoid data inconsistency.

We'll first discuss the approaches to locking.

8.2.1   Approaches to Locking

Locking can be considered from two viewpoints. It can be granular; that is, locking can be set at the record level on the data that is updated. This approach has the advantage of locking only the records that are updated, but this is likely to take more time, because every record that needs to be updated is locked during the process. This option also consumes more memory, because you'll be acquiring locks for every record that is updated.

The second approach is to lock based on a range of data. With this approach, locking is based on the range of data the user is updating. This makes it faster for the system to acquire locks but has the disadvantage of making it easy for you to lock more records than necessary. Although the end objective is to prevent two users from updating the same region of data, it is necessary to achieve a balance when using these options.

SAP BPC for NetWeaver uses the concept of *concurrency locking,* which is based on a mixture of these options. We'll now discuss the locking features in SAP BPC for NetWeaver.

8.2.2 Locking Features in SAP BPC for NetWeaver

In SAP BPC, data is uploaded to the database when data is loaded using the data manager package and when data is updated via manual update using the interfaces for Excel, Word, and PowerPoint. (Data is updated even when journals are posted, which we'll discuss in more detail in Chapter 9.) During the update process, data integrity must be maintained so that two users do not update the same region of data at the same time. It is also important to ensure that one user does not overwrite data entered by another user.

SAP BPC for NetWeaver uses the concept of *concurrency locking* to lock data during updates. Concurrency locking comes into play only when a user sends data to update the database; no locks are obtained in SAP BPC prior to the update when the user enters data.

> **Note**
>
> Locking in SAP BPC is mandatory. There are no settings to bypass locking.

The concepts behind locking differ between SAP BPC and the other tools for planning used in SAP NetWeaver BW, namely SAP NetWeaver Business Planning and Simulation, and SAP NetWeaver BW Integrated Planning. In these tools, data is locked when a user opens the planning template to enter plan data for a particular selection. In SAP BPC, data is locked only when the plan/consolidation data is saved. But the same framework for locking is used by all three tools.

8.2.3 Locking Process in SAP BPC for NetWeaver

SAP BPC for NetWeaver obtains locks only when a user initiates the process to update data. This update is also referred to as the *write back* process. The request for update sent by the user is split into packets, and the default size of a packet is 40,000 records. This setting is governed by the PACKAGE_SIZE parameter in Table UJR_PARAM (Figure 8.6), and can be changed by modifying the default settings using Transaction UJR0 for an application in the application set.

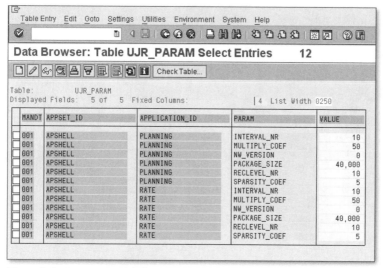

Figure 8.6 Parameter Table for Concurrency Locking

The packet of data for update is analyzed, and the region of data that should be locked is determined and set. The SAP BPC system determines whether it needs to perform record-level locking or to lock a range of data.

Record-Level Check

When the number of records to be updated is less than 10, record-level locking is used. The value of 10 is set in the parameter RECLEVEL_NBR in the UJR_PARAM table and can be configured to a different value for an application in the application set, based on the requirements of that application. To modify this parameter, execute Transaction UJR0 and click on the green checkmark (Figure 8.7). When the RECLEVEL_NBR parameter is set to a high number, updates may take longer to complete and result in higher memory usage due to the time it takes to obtain locks.

Sparsity Check

When the number of records is equal to or higher than the value in the parameter RECLEVEL_NBR, a sparsity check is performed. The sparsity check is carried out as follows:

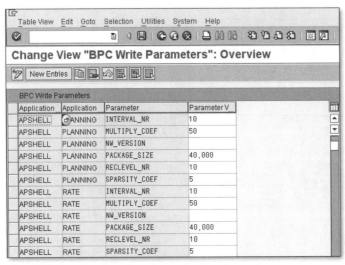

Figure 8.7 Customizing Concurrency Locking Parameters

First, the system determines the number of unique members in each dimension in the record set and then multiplies the number of unique member counts of each dimension to arrive at a value. For example, assume that there are four dimensions, and the numbers of unique dimension members in the dimensions are as follows:

▶ Account: 15

▶ Time: 3

▶ Category: 2

▶ Entity: 1

When you multiply these numbers, the value is 90. We'll call this value X. Next, the system multiplies the total number of records to be updated by the sparsity coefficient parameter SPARISITY_ COEF in Table UJR_PARAM. We'll call this value Y. The default value for the SPARISITY_ COEF parameter is 5. You can change the value of this parameter using Transaction UJR0.

If $X > Y$, the record set is considered to be sparse. If the number of records to be updated in this example is 14, the value of Y would be $14 \times 5 = 70$. Because $X > Y$, the record set would then be considered to be sparse.

If records are sparse, the number of unique dimension member values for each dimension is determined and sorted in ascending order. The unique member records of each dimension are multiplied until the value of the MULTIPLY_COEF parameter in Table UJR_PARAM is reached.

For example, let's say there are four dimensions, and the numbers of unique dimension values in the dimensions sorted in ascending order are as follows:

▶ Entity: 1

▶ Category: 2

▶ Time: 3

▶ Account: 15

Let's also say that, for this application, the value of MULTIPLY_COEF is 50. Now, multiply the unique dimension member counts in the Entity and Category dimensions; the value is $1 \times 2 = 2$, which is less than 50. Next, multiply the value obtained in the previous step by the unique Time dimension's member count, which results in a value of $2 \times 3 = 6$. This value is still less than 50. Continue multiplying the value obtained in the previous step by the unique Account dimension's member count, and you'll obtain a value of $6 \times 15 = 90$. At this point, the value exceeds the MULTIPLY_COEF value of 50. In this case, individual values in the Entity, Category, and Time dimensions are locked. The range of values in the Account dimension is also locked.

If records are not sparse, all of the members of dimensions that have 10 or fewer distinct values are locked. The value of 10 is dependent on the INTERVAL_NR parameter in Table UJ_PARAMETER and can be modified using Transaction UJR0. For those that have 10 or more distinct values, the system creates a lock between the low and high values for the member values in that dimension.

If the system is able to obtain locks, the locks are obtained and the data is updated. After the data is updated, the locks are released. If there is more than one package to update, the system processes the next package to obtain the locks using the same process for that package and updates it.

If the system is not able to obtain locks for a package, the update for that package and the subsequent package fails with an error indicating the system was not able to obtain locks for the update. But the package(s) for which the system was able to obtain locks, and for which data was processed successfully, cannot be rolled back. For example, let's say there were three packages to update for a request sent by a user. Assume that the system was able to successfully acquire locks on the first package and update the data in the application but was not able to acquire locks on the second package. As a result, the second package and the subsequent updates fail, even though the first package was updated in the cube and contains the changes made by the user.

The failed packages can be run again, because SAP BPC posts only delta values during this update. Figure 8.8 shows an overview of the concurrency process.

> **Note**
>
> For journals, the delta mechanism is not used when posting values. The package size for journals is set to 99,999,999 to ensure that the concept of packages is not used when updating data using journals.

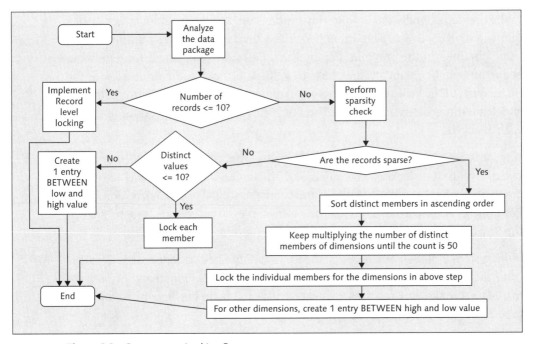

Figure 8.8 Concurrency Locking Process

In the next section, we'll discuss the use of web administration parameters and see how they influence application behavior.

8.3   Web Administration Parameters

Web administration parameters influence the behavior of applications. You can configure two types of web administration parameters in SAP BPC:

▶ **Application set parameters**
This type of parameter applies to all applications in an application set.

▶ **Application parameters**
This type of parameter applies to each application in the application set.

Some parameters are required; others are optional. If a parameter is required, you can accept the default values. Ensure that you have the appropriate security defined to make changes to the web parameters.

In the SAP BPC Web interface, select the BPC ADMINISTRATION task under AVAILABLE INTERFACES. In the following screen, select SETAPPSET PARAMETERS or SET APPLICATION PARAMETERS under WEB ADMIN TASKS to access the parameter screen. You can modify the CV to select the application set or application for which you want to set the parameters.

Table 8.1 lists the parameters you can define for an application set, and Table 8.2 lists the parameters you can define for an application. Required parameters are indicated explicitly.

Parameter Name	Description
ALLOWEXTENSIONS	Defines the file extensions of files the system allows users to upload to the application, including data manager files, content library files, web-ready files, and library files. When set to ALL, SAP BPC allows all extensions. The default value is ALL. (Required)
ALLOW_FILE_SIZE	The maximum file size SAP BPC allows users to upload. The default value is 100 MB. (Required)

Table 8.1 Parameters for Application Set

Parameter Name	Description
AVAILABLEFLAG	Controls whether the system is offline or not. Yes means the system is online and available for sending data to the database. You can take the system offline by changing the value to No. (Required)
AVAILABLEMSG	The message that displays to users who try to access an application that is offline. (Required)
AVAILABLEURL	The name of the web page to display to users who try to access an application that is offline (AVAILABLEFLAG = No). (Required)
DEFAULT_EXTENSIONS	The file extensions the system allows users to upload by default: xls, xlt, doc, dot, ppt, pot, xml, mht, mhtml, htm, html, xlsx, xlsm, xlsb, zip, pdf, pptx, pptm, potx, potm, docx, docm, dotx, dotm, cdm, tdm, png, gif, jpg, css, mrc. Also see ALLOWEXTENSIONS.
LANDINGPAGEITEM	This parameter is used to customize the initial page that is displayed when you access the SAP BPC Web interface. To customize the Getting Started page on SAP BPC Web, contact your system administrator.
LOGLEVEL	Used by an application set to control the level of the ABAP log, which you view via Transaction SLG1. LOGLEVEL has the following possible values: 0—None: Log is off. 1—Error: Log only error, abort, and exit messages. 2—Warning: Log warning, error, abort, and exit messages. 3—Info: Log info, status, error, abort, and exit messages. 4—Trace: Log info, status, error, abort, exit, and trace (highly detailed) messages.
MAXLRCOLUMNS	The maximum number of columns to display in a live report in SAP BPC Web. The value includes header and data columns.
MAXLRROWS	The maximum number of rows to display in a live report in SAP BPC Web. The value includes header and data rows. For example, if you specify a value of 5, one heading row and four data rows are displayed.

Table 8.1 Parameters for Application Set (Cont.)

Parameter Name	Description
SMTPAUTH	The authentication method of the SMTP server. 0 = Anonymous 1 = Basic 2 = NTLM This setting does not change the method on the SMTP server but must match the type of authentication enabled on it. Failure to set this appropriately can result in errors from the email server. (Required)
SMTPPORT	Port number for your SMTP email server. The default is port 25, the default SMTP server port number. (Required)
SMTPSERVER	The name or TCP/IP address of the SMTP email server the system uses to send email. (Required)
SMTPUSER	The user name from which email in the system originates. (Required)
TEMPLATEVERSION	Current version number of the dynamic templates in the application set. Whenever you add to or change the input schedule or report dynamic templates, you should increment this version number so that users automatically receive the new templates when they log into this application set. (Required) You can also reset the template version from the Admin Console.

Table 8.1   Parameters for Application Set (Cont.)

Parameters	Description
APPROVALORG	If you want to use the work status feature, you must use this field to identify the hierarchy level (H1, H2, H3, ..., H*n*) for which you want to track the work status of deliverables. You can define only one hierarchy for each application within an application set. For alternate organizations, "No Status" displays when you view members in the work status screen. If this field is blank, work status tracking is disabled.

Table 8.2   Parameters for Application

Parameters	Description
BPC_STATISTICS	When set to ON, various SAP BPC modules write detailed runtime statistics to Tables UJO_STAT_HDR and UJO_STAT_DTL. You can use this information to monitor system performance. Valid values are ON and OFF. (Required)
Calculation	This parameter is used for the account transformation of business rules. You can change this value in the Change Application Type menu in Modify Application.
IntcoBookings	This parameter is used for the intercompany booking of business rules. You can change this value in the Change Application Type menu in Modify Application.
Opening Balance	This parameter is used for opening business rules. You can change this value in the Change Application Type menu in Modify Application.
JRN_REOPEN_PROPERTY	A custom journal module assumes that the property named UB must be present in the Account dimension to further filter the journals to reopen. The default is Group. If Group is specified, there is no need to modify the Account dimension.
ORG_OWNERSHIPCUBE	The default value is OWNERSHIP. (Required)
ORG_INTCO	The default value is I_NONE, which should also be a member ID in the INTCO dimension in the ownership application if you're using dynamic hierarchies. (Required)
ORG_ACCOUNTOWN	The default value is PGROUP. (Required)
ORG_ACCOUNTLIST	The default value is METHOD,POWN,PCON. (Required)
ORG_PARENTPROPERTY	This parameter is used with dynamic hierarchy statutory applications when defining fixed hierarchies. The value must match the value in the ParentProperty property value of entities in the statutory application's supporting ownership application. (Required)
OWNERSHIP_APP	The name of the ownership application. If this parameter does not exist, by default, the consolidation procedure searches for an application named OWNERSHIP. (Required)

Table 8.2 Parameters for Application (Cont.)

Parameters	Description
YTDINPUT	This parameter controls whether data is input in YTD format. Valid options are 1, which means YTD format, or 0, which means periodic format.

Table 8.2 Parameters for Application (Cont.)

In the next section, we'll discuss the steps involved in collecting statistics in SAP BPC and the benefits this offers.

8.4 Statistics

The statistics tool in SAP BPC is designed to measure the performance of SAP BPC applications and to gather information about how the system is used. It is similar to the tool used in SAP NetWeaver BW for collecting statistics to analyze the time taken to load and report data on SAP NetWeaver BW objects.

The statistics data collected allows you to measure load times and retrieve data. Using these statistics, you can identify bottlenecks and take timely action before they become bigger issues. This is a valuable tool that can help with maintaining a smoothly running SAP BPC system.

The statistics tool can record the time taken to execute the following modules for an application:

▶ **Shared query engine**
Using the statistics tool, you can display the time taken to retrieve data from an InfoCube for a given report.

▶ **Write back**
You can measure the time taken to update data in an InfoCube.

▶ **K2 or script logic**
This helps you measure the time taken to execute script logic.

The default value for the BPC_STATISTICS parameter is Off, but it must be set to On (at the application level) before SAP BPC can collect statistics for an application (Figure 8.9).

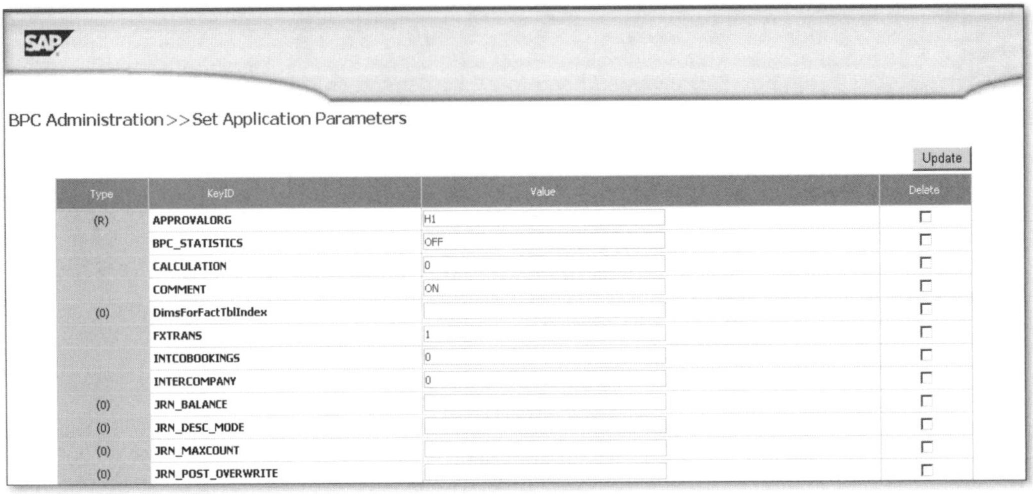

Figure 8.9 Web Parameter to Turn On Statistics

The statistics recorded are stored as header and detail records in SAP NetWeaver BW. The header data represents user actions, and the detail data represents the events associated with the actions. For example, the header data may represent the user action of sending data for update in SAP BPC; the detail data then represents the individual events associated with this action—such as checking whether the user is authorized to make changes and checking the work status to confirm that the data is not locked. All of these represent the detail events associated with the action initiated by the user.

Table UJ0_ACTION lists the actions for which you can collect statistics. You can collect statistics on the following types of actions:

▶ Read data through SQE

▶ Run K2 script logic

▶ Write back data

Different types of events are associated with an action. Table UJ0_EVENTS displays the list of events that is used in SAP BPC.

Some of the common events during the course of writing back data are:

▶ Check security

▶ Check validation

- Check work status

- Obtain concurrency locks

After the web parameter for collecting statistics for an application is set to On for an application, statistics data is collected in Tables UJO_STAT_HDR and UJO_STAT_DTL.

You can view statistics on an application using Transaction UJSTAT (Figures 8.10 and 8.11) and select the data based on the GUID, user, start date, start time, action, application set, and application:

- **Statistics Session**
  A system-generated value used as the key for the action or the event under which it is stored

- **User ID**
  The user who initiated the action or event

- **Statistics Start Date**
  The start date of the action or event

- **Statistics Start Time**
  The start time of the action or event

- **Action ID**
  The action performed

- **AppSet**
  The application set to which this record pertains

- **Application**
  The application driving the event or action

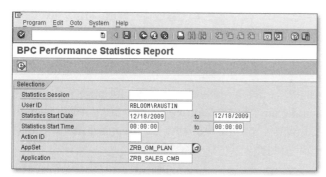

Figure 8.10 Displaying Statistics—Part A

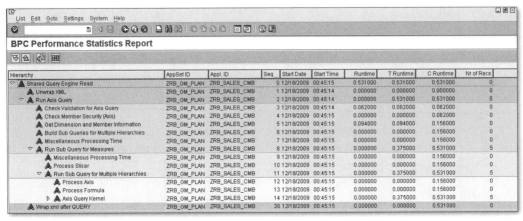

Figure 8.11 Displaying Statistics—Part B

You can delete all statistics for an application set or application using the program UJO_STATISTICS_DELETE (Figure 8.12). It is not possible to selectively delete statistics records from an application set or application.

Figure 8.12 Deleting Statistics Data

In this section, we discussed how to collect and view statistics for an application. In the next section, we'll explain how to turn on the audit functionality and view audit information.

8.5   Audit

The audit functionality in SAP BPC provides the framework for monitoring changes to application configuration and data. SAP BPC for NetWeaver supports these two categories for auditing and provides the functionality to safeguard the SAP BPC system. There are two types of audits:

▶ **Activity audit**

This audit type is used to record changes to metadata. The audit captures any changes to application sets, applications, and dimensions. It is defined at the application set level.

▶ **Data audit**

This audit type captures changes to transaction data and is applicable for an application.

The configuration for activating audits is enabled in the web interface. To activate an activity or data audit, select the BPC ADMINISTRATION task under AVAILABLE INTERFACES. In the following screen, you'll see two tasks under WEB ADMIN TASKS: MANAGE ACTIVITY AUDIT and MANAGE DATA AUDIT.

You can perform the following actions for recording an activity audit:

▶ Add, modify, delete, or copy operations for application sets, applications, and dimensions.

▶ Make security changes (any changes to users, teams, tasks, or member profiles).

▶ Make web administration changes (any changes to application set and application parameters, document content management, or audit settings).

▶ View user activity (work status locks).

Activity audit data is stored in Tables UJU_AUDACTHDR and UJU_AUDACDET. Data audit data is stored in Tables UJU_AUDDATAHDR, /1CPMB/KIABGAD, and /1CPMB/KIGTQAD. You can display failed audit logs using Transaction SLG1.

You can archive audit data. Two standard process chains are provided to do this, one for archiving activity audit data and another for archiving data audit data. The two process chains available for this purpose are /CPMB/ARCHIVE_ACTIVITY and /CPMB/ARCHIVE_DATA. Reporting is not possible on audit data that has been archived.

Standard reports are available in SAP BPC, and you can use filter criteria when reporting audit data. To access reports, select LAUNCH BPC SYSTEM REPORTS under BPC TASKS in the web interface.

You now know how to enable and view audit data. In the next section, we'll explain how to use the content library to create and maintain unstructured documents.

8.6   Content Library

You access the content library interface via the SAP BPC Web interface and use it for creating and sharing unstructured data such as documents and HTML. Documents are loaded via this interface, and the list of file types you can store in the content library are specified in the web administration parameters for the application set. You should have the appropriate access to upload and view documents; specifically, you need access to the CreateWebPage and ManageContentLib tasks to create a web page and to post documents.

8.6.1   Accessing the Content Library

You use the content library for storing documents and access it from the web interface by clicking on the CONTENT LIBRARY icon. Existing documents in the document library are listed with the following information:

▶ **Title**
This indicates the title of the document.

▶ **Type, subtype, and application context**
These items can be used to provide more meaning to the document.

▶ **Team access**
This identifies who is authorized to view documents and can be specified based on user ID or teams.

▶ **Date**
This indicates the date on which the document was updated.

8.6.2   Posting a Document

Follow the steps outlined below to post a document to the content library:

1. Click on the POST A DOCUMENT task under the LIBRARY CONTENT OPTIONS in the action pane (Figure 8.13, ❶). This opens a dialog box: POST A DOCUMENT— STEP 1 OF 5. Select the file you want to post to the content library from your

local computer by clicking on the Browse button (Figure 8.13, ❷). Enter a text description for the document, and click on the green checkmark to continue.

2. In the next dialog box (Post a Document—Step 2 of 5), select the users or teams that should have access to this document (Figure 8.13, ❸). Click on the green checkmark to continue.

3. The next dialog box (Post a Document—Step 3 of 5) allows you to select a subtype for your document. You can post documents to designated locations using this subtype (Figure 8.13, ❹), because they are the equivalent of folders in the content library. Click on the green checkmark to continue.

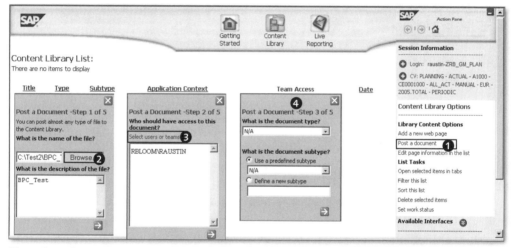

Figure 8.13 Posting a Document—Part A

4. In the next dialog box (Post a Document—Step 4 of 5), you can opt to send an email to users who have access to this document after the document has posted (Figure 8.14, ❺). Click on the green checkmark to continue.

5. In the resulting dialog box (Post a Document—Step 5 of 5), you can select the application context to which the document belongs (Figure 8.14, ❻). Click on the green checkmark to continue. If you set the application context, you can control the document via work status settings and lock down documents that have the application context specified.

You now know how to post a document to the content library. Next, we'll explain how to edit the properties of a document in the content library.

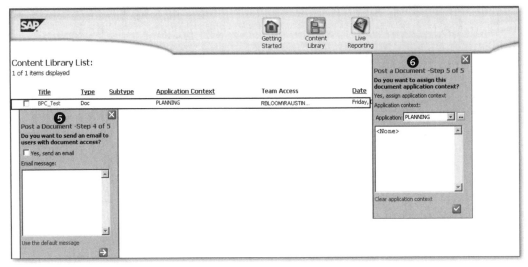

Figure 8.14 Posting a Document—Part B

8.6.3 Editing Document Properties

To edit document properties in the content library, select on EDIT PAGE INFORMATION in the LIST task, which you'll find under CONTENT LIBRARY OPTIONS in the action pane (Figure 8.13). The documents are listed as shown in Figure 8.15. For documents, you can edit the title, type, subtype, application context, and team access. For web pages, you can edit only the TEAM ACCESS field. After you make changes, confirm them by clicking on the green checkmark under EDIT PAGE INFORMATION in the action pane.

Figure 8.15 Editing a Document

8.6.4 Add Web Page to Content Library

Follow these steps to add a web page to the content library:

1. Click on the ADD A NEW WEB PAGE task under LIBRARY CONTENT OPTIONS in the action pane (Figure 8.13). The resulting dialog box prompts you to enter the page name (Figure 8.16, ❶). After entering a name for the web page, click on the green checkmark to continue.

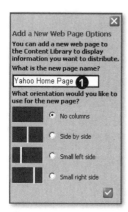

Figure 8.16 Creating a Web Page—Part A

2. In the next screen, you can select one of the following objects to create the web page:

   ▶ WEB-READY FILE: Lets you select a web-ready file you previously uploaded as the source.

   ▶ LIVE REPORTS: Lets you select any live reports you have created for the applications in the application set as the source.

   ▶ DOCUMENTS: Lets you use the documents you have posted in the content library as the source.

   ▶ WEBSITE: Lets you specify a web URL as the source.

   In this example, we'll include a link to Yahoo's home page as a web page. Drag the WEBSITE object under AVAILABLE OBJECTS into the PAGE area (Figure 8.17, ❷). This opens a dialog box titled WEBSITE: STEP 1 OF 2 (Figure 8.17, ❸). Enter the name of the page and specify the pixel height to use to display the web page. Then click on the green checkmark.

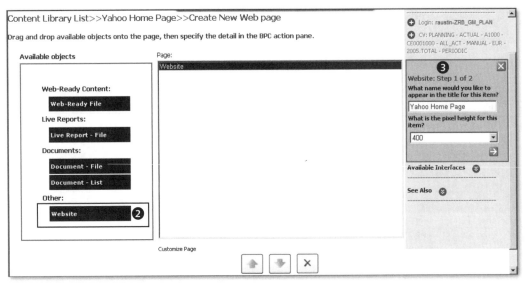

Figure 8.17   Creating a Web Page—Part B

3. In the resulting dialog box (Website: Step 2 of 2), enter the website address and click on the green checkmark (Figure 8.18, ❹).

4. In the resulting dialog box, select the users who can access the web page or make additional modifications to the object (Figure 8.18, ❺). Preview the web page or click Save to see the finished web page.

Figure 8.18   Creating a Web Page—Part C

5. After you click Save, the web page is displayed (Figure 8.19).

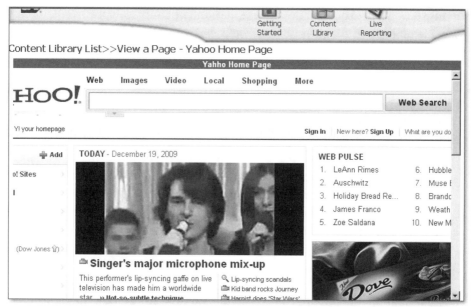

Figure 8.19 Creating a Web Page—Part D

Under the LIST TASKS, there are additional options for viewing and managing the documents in the content library. They are as follows:

▶ **Open Selected Items in Tab**

When this menu task is selected, more than one document can be selected and viewed on a tab.

▶ **Filter this List**

This option lets you select from a variety of options to limit the number of documents displayed.

▶ **Sort this List**

This option lets you sort documents based on the title, type, subtype, application context, and date fields.

▶ **Delete Selected Items**

This option lets you delete one or more selected documents.

▶ **Set Work Status**

This option lets you set the work status for documents that are associated with an application context.

In this section, we explained how to use the content library to post, maintain, and view documents. In the next section, we'll review concepts related to managing security within SAP BPC.

8.7 Security

In this section, we'll discuss how to configure users and how to define their security levels. SAP BPC provides a simple interface to define task and member access profiles. Task profiles authorize the actions a user can perform, and member profiles define access on dimensions that are marked as secure in an application. SAP BPC supports the role concept to extend security based on a user's role in an organization. In this section, we'll discuss the terms used in the context of security.

8.7.1 Users

A user should be configured as an active domain user. In addition, in the security folder for an application set, the user should be set as a valid user. If a user is not listed here, the user will not be able to perform any tasks on an application set.

8.7.2 Team

A team is a group of users. Multiple users will use an application, and each user can play a different role, based on their responsibilities in the organization. A team is helpful when you need to provide the same access to a group of users. When a team is created, a folder to store reports and input schedules for the team is also created. One user in the team can be assigned as a team leader. A team leader has additional access to save reports and input schedules to the team folder.

8.7.3 Task Profile

The types of activities a user can perform in SAP BPC can be grouped into a task profile. Examples of activities are loading data, entering and maintaining data, executing reports, maintaining comments, creating journals, and so on. Table 8.3 lists administration tasks available in SAP BPC.

Administration Tasks
Application set management
Define security
Business rules
Application management
Dimension
Locking
Manage audit
Manage comments
Content library
Manage distributor
Manage live report
Manage template
Update to company folder
Web administration
Miscellaneous

Table 8.3 Administration Tasks

With the ApShell application set, three types of task profiles are provided by default:

▶ **System admin**
A system admin user can administer security to other users. The user can create, modify, and delete application sets.

▶ **Primary admin**
A primary admin can perform all administration tasks except creating or maintaining application sets.

▶ **Secondary admin**
A secondary admin can manage dimension members.

8.7.4 Member Access Profile

When an application is created, the dimensions in the application can be marked as secured. When a dimension is marked as secured, the user needs access to read and write data to the application. The member access profile indicates the dimension data that can be read or written in an application.

8.7.5 Security Model

The option to manage security is available under the task item BPC ADMINISTRATION. The following are the steps to configure security for an application:

1. Assign users to application sets.
2. Create the task profiles based on roles.
3. Create member access profiles based on roles.
4. Create a team.
5. Assign task profiles to teams.
6. Assign member profiles to teams.
7. Assign users to teams.

8.8 Summary

In this chapter, you learned about several key tools used in managing and maintaining an SAP BPC application. We started by looking at the steps for moving objects from the development system to the quality assurance and production systems using the transport process. We reviewed how the SAP BPC system uses concurrency locking to prevent two users from updating the same region of data simultaneously. We also reviewed the parameters that are set at the application set and application levels and how they influence the functionality of SAP BPC applications. We then studied the process of collecting statistics to assess system performance and activating auditing of data to monitor changes to objects and data in the system. Furthermore, we looked at how to use the content library interface to post, view, and maintain documents in SAP BPC. Finally, we discussed the concepts involved in enforcing task level and data level security.

In the next chapter, you'll be introduced to business rules and how to use them to support common tasks related to business planning and consolidation. You'll also learn how to create journal templates and use them to post adjustments and top side entries. In addition, we'll review general tasks that are carried out when consolidating financial data.

This chapter explains the usage of business rules such as account transformation, carry forward balance, intercompany booking, intercompany elimination (using US elimination and automatic adjustments), and validation. We'll discuss intercompany reconciliation process and stress the importance of the process before performing intercompany eliminations.

9   Consolidation with SAP BPC

In this chapter, we'll review topics related to performing financial consolidation using SAP BusinessObjects Planning and Consolidation (BPC).

In Section 9.1, we'll introduce steps involved in the consolidation process.

In Section 9.2, we'll discuss topics related to preparing, collecting, and consolidating steps and detail usage of different types of business rules that you can configure in SAP BPC. Business rules allow users to set up standard business processes such as carry forward balances, account transformation, intercompany booking, intercompany elimination, validation, and so on without having to develop code. In this section, we'll also discuss the need to perform matching of intercompany transactions and steps to match intercompany transactions.

In Section 9.3, we'll provide an overview of consolidation of investments and discuss concepts and application of the concepts in SAP BPC.

In Section 9.4, we'll discuss intercompany elimination using automatic adjustments. This method of elimination is used in legal consolidation.

In Section 9.5, we'll introduce the use of journals in planning and consolidation applications and describe how to configure and use journals.

In Section 9.6, we'll summarize our learning in this chapter.

To begin, let's discuss the steps involved in the consolidation process.

9.1 Steps in Consolidation

The consolidation process involves the following main steps:

- ▶ Prepare
- ▶ Collect
- ▶ Consolidate
- ▶ Report

The prepare step involves setting up the basic configuration to support the process of consolidation. This step involves finalizing the dimensions and data model required for consolidation, setting up master data, and configuring business rules and security to support the process.

The collect step involves collecting data through manual entry or data upload. This step also entails entering journals to make adjustments, validating the data, and translating data to one or more reporting currencies.

The consolidate step involves running consolidation functions such as carry forward balance, account transformation, intercompany matching, intercompany booking, intercompany elimination, consolidation of investments, and so on.

The report step involves reporting on the consolidated data. You can leverage reporting tools such as SAP BPC for Excel and Xcelsius and use drill-through capabilities that allow drill-through from SAP BPC to SAP NetWeaver BW and SAP ECC systems.

In the previous chapters, we discussed some topics relating to the prepare and collect steps such as setting up the data model and loading data to SAP BPC applications by either loading data from a flat file or an SAP NetWeaver BW system or by directly entering data using input templates. In this chapter, we'll discuss some of the consolidation functions and see how you can leverage business rules to perform these functions.

In the next section, we'll initially discuss business rules at a high level and later discuss their usage in detail when discussing specific consolidation functions.

9.2   Business Rules

Business rules are a key feature of SAP BPC; they provide an organization to set up rules to execute standard business processes without developing custom code. Some of the standard business processes used in planning and consolidation are as follows:

▶ **Currency translation**
This is required when an organization does business in more than one country uses multiple currencies for transacting business. When an organization uses multiple currencies, they need to convert transactions in different currencies to one or more reporting currencies. Currency translation is used in both planning and financial consolidation applications. Business rules can be set up to perform currency translation. We discussed the business rules table for currency translation in Chapter 6.

▶ **Carry forward**
The carry forward of balances is an essential step in the creation of a balance sheet for an organization; it is when the closing balance of accounts for a fiscal period is transferred as the opening balance of a subsequent fiscal period. The carry forward balance rules can also be used to close current period net income and post to balance sheet to create a fully balanced balance sheet. The setup for this process is handled in SAP BPC with the use of a business rules table.

▶ **Account transformation**
In some scenarios, accounts are consolidated or transformed into another account, an activity that is used extensively in cash flow applications. Account transformation business rules are used to aggregate values posted to specific combinations of source account, flow, category, and data source and post them to aggregated destination account, flow, category, and data source.

▶ **Intercompany matching/Booking**
Organizations may have entities that do business with each other. These business transactions are called intercompany transactions. It is important that both parties involved in an intercompany transaction post the transaction and amount accurately. For instance, if an entity within an organization reports an intercompany sales transaction, the trading partner associated with this transaction should post an intercompany expense transaction. The amount posted in a matching currency by each entity must be the same. This is required to produce accurate

consolidated results. In SAP BPC, we can set up an intercompany transactions matching/reconciliation process. If there are differences in amounts reported by entities, we can use the intercompany booking business rule to post/book differences in amounts.

Later in this chapter, we'll discuss the intercompany transaction matching process and discuss the use of business rules to book differences.

▸ **Intercompany elimination**
This is applicable for an organization that has entities that do business with each other. A consolidated balance sheet of the organization shows transactions that relate to external companies. The transactions such as sales and COGS or receivables and payables that result from exchange of goods or services within the organization should not be counted. In these cases, it is essential to eliminate the intercompany transactions. The intercompany eliminations process creates entries that eliminates intercompany transactions.

▸ **Validation**
In chapter 6, we discussed the usage of transaction UJ_VALIDATION that is used to validate combinations of dimension members used when entering or loading data. The validation business rule is used to compare balances and post differences in amounts. The validation rules functionality in SAP BPC is a check mechanism that enables an organization to ensure accuracy of data. For example, using the validation rule table, an organization can set up business rules that would compare balances in assets and liabilities/owner's equity accounts for a given period and report variances, if any, for that period. The variances can be posted to a validation account.

The advantage of using the business rules table is that it provides out of the box functionality to perform the above processes. This helps in reducing the total cost of ownership (TCO) of developing and maintaining applications in SAP BPC.

We'll study in detail the usage of business rules to accomplish the above functions.

9.2.1 Carry Forward

One of the steps in preparing a balance sheet is to take the closing balance of a fiscal period and use it as the opening balance of the subsequent fiscal period. In accounting terminology, this is called *the initialization of balances*.

The process to determine carry forward balances for a new fiscal year is essential for every organization that is required to maintain a balance sheet. To facilitate this process, SAP BPC provides the ability to automatically generate carry forward balances for the new fiscal period using the business rules tables. You can use this procedure to set up the carry forward process for both planning and consolidation applications.

The *Flow dimension,* or the *Sub-Table dimension,* is normally used in the carry forward business rule. Balance sheet accounts, such as inventory accounts, have an opening balance at the beginning of a period, additions and transfers for the period, and a closing balance for the end of the period. The Flow dimension helps break the account into various flow types such as opening, additions, transfers, and closing.

The carry forward process requires the following dimension properties to be included in the DATASRC and CATEGORY dimensions:

▶ **DATASRC_TYPE of DATASRC dimension**
When you use this property, the data loaded into SAP BPC can be classified as input (I), manual (M), or automatic (A). The logic for carry forward in SAP BPC is set to work only for data that has the data source type set to input or manual. Automatic DataSources are generated and addressed during the consolidation process.

▶ **COPYOPENING of DATASRC dimension**
Set this property to Y to perform carry forward balance for data associated with a DataSource. When this property is set to N, the associated DataSource is excluded from the carry forward process.

▶ **OPENING_DATASRC of DATASRC dimension**
Use this property to specify the DataSource to which the opening balances are written. If this value is set to blank, the opening balances are set to the same value as the data source on the source records.

▶ **CATEGORY_FOR_OPE of CATEGORY dimension**
You use this property when you want to use a specific category as the basis for creating opening balances. When the setting is active, the carry forward balance uses the category specified in this property for performing carry forward balances. If this property is blank, the balances are copied from the same category. For example, you can use this property when you want to copy the closing balance of actual data to the opening balance of plan data.

- **OPENING_YEAR of CATEGORY dimension**
  You use the value specified in this property as the year to read values for creating the carry forward balance. If the value of this property is set to blank, the balances are copied over from the previous year. In this property, you can either use an absolute value, such as 2010, or an offset value such as -1.

- **OPENING_PERIOD of CATEGORY dimension**
  You use the value specified in this property as the period to read values for creating the carry forward balance. If the value of this property is set to blank, the balances are copied over from last period of year (e.g., DEC). In this property, you can use either absolute value or offset value.

Table 9.1 explains the details for setting up the carry forward business rules table.

Field Name	Description
Source Account	Specify the source account to use for the carry forward balance. The value specified here can be one of the following: ▶ Base member ▶ Parent member A list of members defined and filtered using a value of the DIMLIST property in the Account dimension.
Source Flow	Specify the source flow to use for the carry forward balance. The value specified here can be one of the following: ▶ Base member ▶ Parent member A list of members defined and filtered using a value of the DIMLIST property in the Flow dimension.
Destination Account	Specify a base member as the destination account.
Destination Flow	Specify a base member for the destination flow.
Reverse Sign	You can select this box if you want to reverse the sign of the amount when creating the carry forward balance from the source account.

Table 9.1 Carry Forward Balance Business Rule

Field Name	Description
	This is especially used in scenarios where you do not want to carry over specific accounts. To do this, you may initially carry forward all balance sheet accounts and reverse out specific balance sheet accounts that you do not want to carry over. This results in a net effect of those specific accounts that you do not want to carry over (that were reversed) to zero.
Data Source Type	Specify all of the DataSource members you want to use for the conversion. This corresponds to the values set in the Datasource_Type property of the Datasource dimension.
	You can select from the following choices: Input, Manual, or All.
	Note: DataSources that are type A (Automatic) are not considered for carry forward balance conversions.
Same Period	You can select this box when the source time period is to be used as the destination time period.
Apply to YTD	You can select this box to calculate YTD values for an application that is PERIODIC.
Remark	A brief description of the business rule.

Table 9.1 Carry Forward Balance Business Rule (Cont.)

Once the setup is complete, the COPYOPENING script is used to execute the logic to create the opening balances for a given period. Add the following logic in your application (if one does not already exist) and call it COPYOPENING.LGF.

```
*RUN_PROGRAM COPYOPENING
CATEGORY = %C_CATEGORY_SET%
CURRENCY = %CURRENCY_SET%
TID_RA = %TIME_SET%
OTHER = [ENTITY=%ENTITY_SET%]
*ENDRUN_PROGRAM
```

SAP BPC provides a data package to execute the carry forward process. When the package is executed, the system prompts the user to enter category, entity, currency, and time selections for performing the carry forward process.

Let's review an example to understand how to set up carry forward balances in an SAP BPC application.

1. Figure 9.1 shows the dimensions for application ZB2. They includes the Flow dimension, which is used for executing carry forward balances.

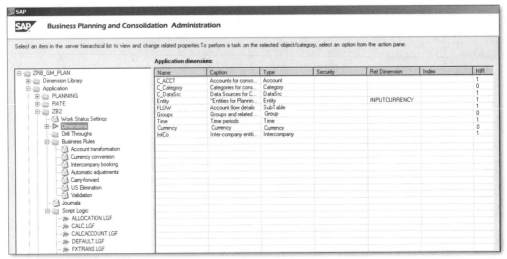

Figure 9.1 Configuring Carry Forward Balance Business Rule—Part A

2. Figure 9.2 shows the members of the Flow dimension, which is used to reflect flows such as Open, Movements, and Close.

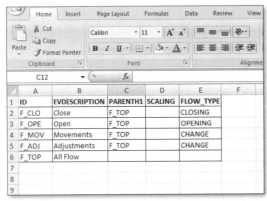

Figure 9.2 Configuring Carry Forward Balance Business Rule—Part B

3. Figure 9.3 displays the closing value of the machinery and equipment of entity C3001 for the December 2008 period. The flow F_CLO, in this example, represents the closing balance.

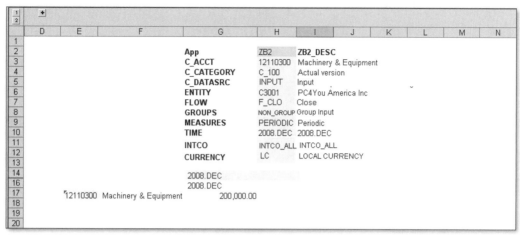

Figure 9.3 Configuring Carry Forward Balance Business Rule—Part C

4. Create the standard script logic COPY_OPENING.LGF (if one does not already exist) to execute the copy opening balance business rule, as shown in Figure 9.4.

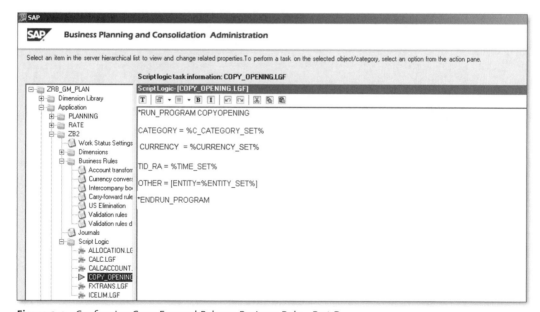

Figure 9.4 Configuring Carry Forward Balance Business Rule—Part D

5. Define the business rule to configure the carry forward balance of the Machinery and Equipment account, as shown in Figure 9.5. In our example, we want to copy the closing balance for this account as of December 2008 to the opening balance as of January 2009 when the carry forward balance script is executed for January 2009.

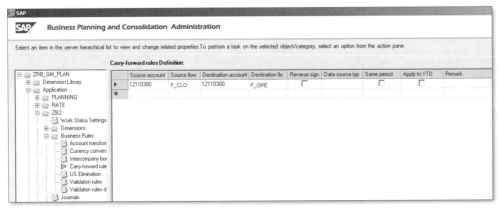

Figure 9.5 Configuring Carry Forward Balance Business Rule—Part E

6. Run the data package to execute the carry forward balance script, as shown in Figure 9.6. The process chain associated with the carry forward balance is /CPMB/OPENING_BALANCES.

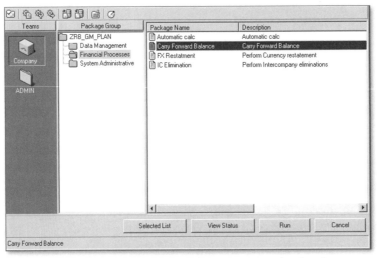

Figure 9.6 Configuring Carry Forward Balance Business Rule—Part F

7. Make the selections shown in Figure 9.7. We chose the time period January 2009, because we want to create the opening balance for that period.

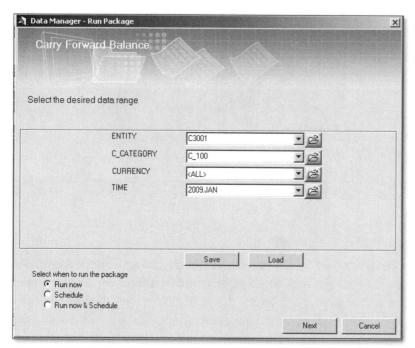

Figure 9.7 Configuring Carry Forward Balance Business Rule—Part G

8. After executing the package, report the opening balance (F_OPE flow) for the Machinery and Equipment account, entity C3001 and January 2009. The carry forward balance script has generated the opening balance entries for January 2009. The closing balance for December 2008 has been copied to the opening balance for January 2009 (Figure 9.8).

You should now understand how to use business rules to perform carry forward balances. Next, we'll study the usage of the account transformation business rule.

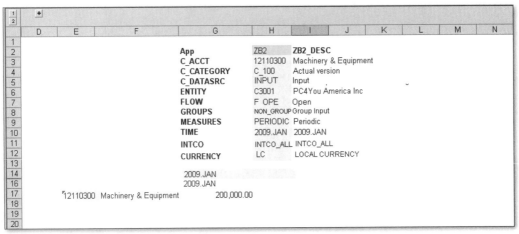

Figure 9.8 Configuring Carry Forward Balance Business Rule—Part H

9.2.2 Account Transformation

Account transformation business rules are used to aggregate values posted to specific combinations of source account, flow, category, and data source and post them to aggregated destination account, flow, category, and data source. The business rules allow us to perform calculations by adding or subtracting values. The rules also allow us to use reference data in other years/periods to determine amounts to post.

Table 9.2 explains the details for setting up the account transformation business rules table.

Field Name	Description
Transformation Group	Several account transformation business rules can be grouped under a specific transformation group ID. This is the ID that is used in the script logic for performing account transformation.
Source Account	Specify the source account to use for account transformation. The value specified here can be one of the following:

Table 9.2 Account Transformation Business Rule

Field Name	Description
	▸ Base member ▸ Parent member A list of members defined and filtered using a value of the DIMLIST property in the Account dimension
Category	Specify the source category to use for the account transformation. The value specified here can be one of the following: ▸ Base member ▸ Parent member A list of members defined and filtered using a value of the DIMLIST property in the Category dimension
Source Flow	Specify the source flow to use for the account transformation. The value specified here can be one of the following: ▸ Base member ▸ Parent member A list of members defined and filtered using a value of the DIMLIST property in the Flow dimension
Source Data Source	Specify the source data source to use for the account transformation. The value specified here can be one of the following: ▸ Base member ▸ Parent member A list of members defined and filtered using a value of the DIMLIST property in the data source dimension
Destination Account	Specify a base member as the destination account.
Destination Category	Specify a base member as the destination category.
Destination Flow	Specify a base member for the destination flow.
Destination Data Source	Specify a base member as the destination data source.
Reverse Sign	You can select this box if you want to reverse the sign of the amount when calculating accounts.

Table 9.2 Account Transformation Business Rule (Cont.)

Field Name	Description
	This is especially used in scenarios where you want to subtract values when performing calculations. Sometimes, you may transform values from a source account of type LEQ (stored as –ve in the database) to a destination account of type AST (stored as +ve in the database). If you want to maintain the same sign of source account for the transformation, you reverse sign.
Source Year	Reference year to read values for performing account transformation. You can use an absolute value, e.g., 2010, or an offset value, e.g., -1. If blank, the reference data will be taken from the same year.
Source Period	Reference period to read values for performing account transformation. You can use an absolute value, e.g., 2010, or an offset value, e.g., -1. If blank, the reference data will be taken from the same period.
Apply to YTD	You can select this box to calculate YTD values for an application that uses PERIODIC measures.
Remark	A brief description of the business rule.

Table 9.2 Account Transformation Business Rule (Cont.)

Let's discuss an example to illustrate the usage of account transformation business rules. Consider a YTD application that has an account 2100 that represents accounts payable. We'll use the account transformation business rule to calculate YTD movements of the accounts payable account. The YTD movements of accounts payable may later be used in cash flow calculations. The following are the steps to calculate the movements of the accounts payable account:

1. First, using the carry forward business rule, carry forward the closing balance of the account payable account from the ending balance of the previous year to the opening balance of the current period. After you've performed the carry forward balance, the opening balance of accounts payable for current period will be in flow F_OPE.

2. We assume that the closing balance of the accounts payable account for the current period is available in flow F_CLO of the application. This information could have been either entered by users using input templates or loaded into the application.

3. Using account transformation, we can calculate the YTD movement to accounts payable by calculating the difference between the closing flow (F_CLO) and opening flow (F_OPE) for the account. After the account transformation, the YTD movements of the accounts payable account will reside in movement flow (F_MOV). Table 9.3 contains two rules to perform the calculation. In rule 2, we've set the Reverse field to X to subtract value.

	Rule 1	Rule 2
Transformation Group	CF	CF
Source Account	2100	2100
Category	ACTUAL	ACTUAL
Source Flow	F_CLO	F_OPE
Source Data Source		
Destination Account		
Destination Category		
Destination Flow	F_MOV	F_MOV
Destination Data Source		
Reverse Sign		X
Source Year		
Source Period		
Apply to YTD		
Remark	Movements to accounts payable	Movements to accounts payable

Table 9.3 Account Transformation Business Rule (Example)

4. Once we configure the business rules, the CALC_ACCOUNT script is used to execute the logic to perform account transformation for a given period. Add the following logic in your application (if one does not already exist) and call it CALC_ACCOUNT.LGF.

```
*RUN_PROGRAM CALC_ACCOUNT
   CATEGORY = %C_CATEGORY_SET%
```

```
    CURRENCY = %CURRENCY_SET%
    TID_RA = %TIME_SET%
    CALC=CF
    OTHER = [ENTITY=%ENTITY_SET%]
*ENDRUN_PROGRAM
```

5. Run the Account Transformations data manager package to perform the account transformation. The data manager package will execute the CALC_ACCOUNT.LGF script, The process chain associated with account transformation data manager package is /CPMB/RUNCALCACCOUNT.

6. Account transformation business rules are used extensively to calculate cash-flow accounts, such as cash flow from operations, cash flow from financing, and cash flow from investing. For example, cash flow from operations may involve starting with the net profit and adding increases to liability accounts related to working capital and subtracting increases to asset accounts related to working capital. As we saw in the above example, we may need to use account transformation business rules in conjunction with the carry forward balance business rule to calculate specific values.

> **Note**
>
> When using account transformation business rules, if there are dependencies in your calculations, separate the independent and dependent rules using the transformation group. Sequence the execution of the rules for each group based on dependencies—first, the independent rules and then the dependent rules.

Next, we'll explain how to set up the configuration to perform intercompany matching and booking.

9.2.3 Intercompany Matching/Booking

You use the intercompany elimination process when an organization is composed of entities that do business with each other. During consolidation, the intercompany transactions should be eliminated.

For the intercompany elimination process to work correctly, it is important that you match intercompany transactions. To illustrate this, let's first understand how eliminations work; specifically, we'll discuss U.S. eliminations. U.S. elimination is an easy way to do one-sided eliminations. You could use it when ownership eliminations (consolidation of investments) are not required.

Consider an intercompany transaction between two entities, E1 and E2, within the organization. We'll assume that the transactions are in the same currency. Let's say E1 sells goods to E2 and thus posts an intercompany revenue transaction. At the same time, E2 would post an intercompany expense/COGS transaction for the same amount. During elimination, the revenue transaction of E1 and the expense transaction of E2 are eliminated. The elimination entry is posted to the elimination entity associated with the first common parent (in the entity hierarchy) of E1 and E2. When the revenue transaction of E1 is eliminated, the process debits revenue and credits the plug account (also called elimination account) associated with the revenue account. When the expense transaction of E2 is eliminated, the process debits the plug account associated with the expense account and credits the expense account. Assuming that the same plug account is associated with the revenue and expense accounts, if amounts entered by E1 and E2 are the same, the plug account would net to zero as a result of the eliminations. A consolidated report that displays data for the group consisting of entities E1, E2, and the elimination entity would report transactions that have eliminated intercompany transactions. Any mismatch in transaction amount entered by the two entities involved in the intercompany transaction may lead to incorrect consolidated results.

This issue underscores the need for both parties of an intercompany transaction to enter the transaction amount accurately. Complexity may arise if the two entities deal with two different currencies. It is important that the exchange rates used to convert the transaction values to a matching/group currency are such that, after currency conversion, the transaction values posted by the two entities match.

SAP BPC provides functionality to match intercompany transactions and automatically book differences using the IC booking business rules. This matching process makes available transactions entered by trading partners that relate to a user's entity. These matching transactions entered by trading partners are posted into the user's entity under a specific data source. This allows the user belonging to a specific entity to view transactions entered by trading partners even though the user may not have security access to the trading partner's entity/entities.

The intercompany matching process can either be set up as a separate application or can be done within an existing application that contains intercompany transactions. The matching process should be done using a matching currency.

The output of the intercompany matching process is a report that displays the intercompany transaction amount in a matching currency that shows what the entity has entered and what the trading partner(s) has entered.

The following are the steps to perform intercompany matching and booking:

1. Import or enter data in local currency.

2. Translate data in local currency to matching/group currency.

3. Perform initial setup needed to perform intercompany matching.

4. Execute data manager package ICDATA to generate entries needed to perform intercompany matching.

5. Run intercompany matching report.

6. Correct mismatches manually or by using the automatic booking (ICBOOKING) function.

As stated above, the first two steps involve loading transaction data in local currency and converting the transaction to matching/group currency. Next, we'll will detail the initial setup required to perform intercompany matching.

Setup for Intercompany Matching

Below we list some guidelines for performing U.S. intercompany elimination in SAP BPC:

▶ To support intercompany elimination, the SAP BPC application should include the Intercompany dimension. The dimension type is I.

▶ The Intercompany dimension should include a property called Entity, and the value of this property should match the member ID of the Entity dimension.

▶ The Account dimension should include the ELIMACC property, and the value of this property should match the member ID of the Account dimension.

▶ The Entity dimension should include an ELIM property, the value of which can be Y or N. The elimination process reads all entries for entities that have the value of this property set to N and then posts eliminations, if applicable, to entities that have the ELIM property set to Y.

▶ For performing intercompany matching, perform the following setup:

▸ Include the property PINTCO in the ACCOUNT dimension. Set the values of all intercompany matching accounts (base members) to Y. These accounts will be considered for intercompany matching.

▸ Create a new hierarchy of intercompany accounts used in matching for performing intercompany matching and booking. Set the nodes in a manner that matching can be accomplished.

▸ For instance, assign accounts associated with Notes Payable and Notes Receivable under a matching node. When an intercompany matching transaction takes place, one entity would be posting Notes Payable and the other entity would be posting Notes Receivable. By assigning these two sets of accounts under a matching node, you can perform intercompany matching and booking. Please refer to a sample hierarchy in Figure 9.9, which displays the hierarchy nodes used for intercompany matching. Intercompany accounts are assigned to these nodes.

ID	EVDESCRIPTION	PARENTH	GROUP	ACCTYPE	PINTCO
CTLCIS0000	Intercompany Check TOTAL			AST	
CTLICBFR00	Intercompany Short Term	CTLCIS0000		AST	S
CTLICBFR01	Intercompany Short Term - Receivables	CTLICBFR00		AST	
CTLICBFR02	Intercompany Short Term - Payables	CTLICBFR00		LEQ	
CTLICEND00	Intercompany Long Term	CTLCIS0000		AST	S
CTLICEND01	Intercompany Long Term - Receivables	CTLICEND00		AST	
CTLICEND02	Intercompany Long Term - Payables	CTLICEND00		LEQ	
CTLICEXP00	Intercompany Operating	CTLCIS0000		INC	S
CTLICEXP01	Intercompany Operating - Revenues	CTLICEXP00		INC	
CTLICEXP02	Intercompany Operating:- Expenses	CTLICEXP00		EXP	

Figure 9.9 Intercompany Account Hierarchy

▸ Include the property IC_ORIGINE in the DATASRC dimension. Set the value of this property of all data sources that will be used as sources for matching to "I". For example, set this property for the INPUT data source to "I".

▸ In addition, create new data source members as specified in Figure 9.10. Please note that data source members DEBIT1, CREDIT1, TOTAL1, DEBIT2, CREDIT2, and TOTAL2 house the intercompany matching data. These data sources are used in the intercompany matching report and do not fall under the data source hierarchy used for consolidated reporting.

ID	EVDESCRIPTION	PARENTH1	IS_CONVERTED	IC_ORGINE
TOTAL1				
DEBIT1	My Asset/Income	TOTAL1	N	D
CREDIT1	Their Liability/Expense	TOTAL1	N	C
TOTAL2				
DEBIT2	Their Asset/Income	TOTAL2	N	D2
CREDIT2	My Liability/Expense	TOTAL2	N	C2
ICDIFF	Intercompany Differences		G	

Figure 9.10   Data Source Members that House Intercompany Matching Entries

The above setup is required before you execute the ICDATA process to generate intercompany matching entries. In the next section, we'll discuss the details of the ICDATA matching process.

Intercompany Matching—ICDATA

The ICDATA process generates the intercompany entries recorded by a user's entity and the entries pertaining to the user's entity that were recorded by the trading partners. These entries are all posted under the user's entity that will be doing the matching. So the ICDATA process makes available transactions entered by trading partners that relate to a user's entity even though the user may not have access to trading partner's data. The data is stored in separate data sources listed in Figure 9.10.

After performing the initial setup discussed in the previous section, run ICDATA. LGF via a data manager package called ICDATA. The process chain associated with the ICDATA data manager package is /CPMB/ICDATA. This process generates the entries needed for performing intercompany matching. The code in ICDATA.LGF is displayed below:

```
*RUN_PROGRAM ICDATA
       CATEGORY = %C_CATEGORY_SET%
           CURRENCY = %CURRENCY_SET%
           DATASRC = %DATASRC_SET%
           TID_RA = %TIME_SET%
           ENTITY = %ENTITY_SET%
           TYPE = 'I'.
*ENDRUN_PROGRAM
```

After you run the ICDATA data manager package, run the intercompany matching report to perform reconciliation.

Intercompany Matching Report

The intercompany matching report is used to reconcile intercompany transactions entered by an entity with the transactions entered by its trading partners. Create a report that displays for an entity, the trading partner (INTCO) and intercompany account in the rows and the members of the DATASRC dimension that houses the matching entries (namely, DEBIT1, CREDIT1, TOTAL1, DEBIT2, CREDIT2, and TOTAL2) in the columns. The data sources displayed in the columns represent the entity's postings and the corresponding trading partner's postings. Figure 9.11 displays the format of report.

Choose Entity:	E1							
Choose Period:	2008.AUG							
		DEBIT1	CREDIT1	TOTAL1	DEBIT2	CREDIT2	TOTAL2	
Intercompany Entity (ICP)	**Account**	My Asset or Income	Their Liability or Expense	Total 1	Their Asset or Income	My Liability or Expense	Total 2	
I_E2 - Entity 2	CTLICBFR00 - Intercompany Short Term	84	(84)					
I_E2 - Entity 2	CTLICBFR01 - Intercompany Short Term: Receivables	84		84				
I_E2 - Entity 2	IC1210 - Inter Company A/R	84		84				
I_E2 - Entity 2	CTLICBFR02 - Intercompany Short Term: Payables		84	84				
I_E2 - Entity 2	IC2210 - Inter Company A/P		84	84				

Figure 9.11 Intercompany Matching Report

In this report, the users chose Entity and Time to perform matching. You're trying to match intercompany short-term receivables and payables transactions for entity E1. Entity E1 has posted an intercompany A/R transaction for $84 specifying entity E2 as the trading partner. Entity E2 has posted an intercompany A/P transaction for $84 specifying entity E1 as the trading partner. Because the intercompany transactions entered by the two entities match, the TOTAL1 value at the CTLICBFR00 level (matching node level) is 0.

If intercompany transactions match at the matching node level, the value of TOTAL1 and TOTAL2 will be 0. If there are mismatches, the value of TOTAL1 and TOTAL2 at the matching node level will not be 0, and the mismatch can either be corrected manually or booked automatically by using the ICBOOKING function. In the next section, we'll see how to set the business rules for automatic booking of mismatches.

Automatic Booking of Intercompany Transactions — Business Rule

The ICBOOKING function is available to automatically book mismatches of intercompany transactions. Table 9.4 details the fields in the business rules table.

Field Name	Description
Parent Matching Account	Specifies the hierarchy node at which, if mismatch occurs, automatic posting needs to be done.
Type	Specifies how the automatic booking needs to be done. The possible values are Seller rule, Buyer rule, and Greatest Amount. If Seller rule is specified, the seller will receive the variances. If Buyer rule is specified, the Buyer will receive the variances.
Booking Destination DataSource	Specifies the DataSource (base member) to which differences will be booked.
Maximum Booking Amount	Threshold amount above which the automatic booking is not posted automatically.
Debit Account	Base account to be debited.
Debit Flow	Base flow to be debited.
Debit INTCO	Base INTCo dimension that will be debited.
Credit account	Base account to be credited.
Credit Flow	Base flow to be credited.
Credit INTCO	Base INTCO dimension that will be credited.
Destination Flow	Specifies a base member for the destination flow.
Destination Data Source	Specifies a base member as the destination data source.
Remark	A brief description of the business rule.

Table 9.4 ICBooking Business Rule

Let's discuss an example to illustrate the usage of this business rule table. Account hierarchy node CTLICBFR00 represents Intercompany Short Term Receivables/Payables. If a mismatch occurs at this level, we would want to debit account ICDIFF01 and credit account IC2210 (IC Accounts Payable) for the mismatched amount. We would also want to post the entry to data source ICDIFF. We'll create the business rule entry in Table 9.5 to generate the automatic posting.

Rule Fields	Rule Values
Parent Matching Account	CTLICBFR00
Type	Seller rule
Booking destination data source	ICDIFF
Maximum booking amount	99,999,999
Debit account	ICDIFF01
Debit flow	F_CLO
Debit INTCO	
Credit account	IC2210
Credit flow	F_CLO
Credit INTCO	
Remark	Receivable/payable

Table 9.5 ICBooking Business Rule (Example)

Automatic Booking of Intercompany Transactions — Script Logic

After setting up the business rule, run ICBOOKING.LGF via a data manager package called ICBOOKING. The process chain associated with the ICBOOKING data manager package is /CPMB/ICBOOKING. This process automatically creates the postings to correct mismatches in intercompany accounts. The code in ICBOOKING.LGF is displayed below:

```
*RUN_PROGRAM ICBOOKING
        CATEGORY = %C_CATEGORY_SET%
            CURRENCY = %CURRENCY_SET%
            TID_RA = %TIME_SET%
            ENTITY = %ENTITY_SET%
*ENDRUN_PROGRAM
```

In this section, we've explored the need to perform intercompany matching and have seen how to use the ICDATA and ICBOOKING functions to reconcile intercompany transactions and correct mismatches. The intercompany transaction matching process is a prerequisite to performing intercompany elimination. In the next section, we'll discuss the process of intercompany eliminations.

9.2.4 Intercompany Eliminations (U.S. Elimination)

The intercompany elimination process is used when an organization is composed of multiple entities that do business with each other. During consolidation, the transactions between the individual entities should be eliminated. In this section, we'll discuss U.S. intercompany eliminations. Later in the chapter, we'll also discuss intercompany elimination using automatic adjustments.

Below we list some guidelines for performing U.S. intercompany elimination in SAP BPC:

▶ To support intercompany elimination, the SAP BPC application should include the Intercompany dimension. The dimension type is I.

▶ The Intercompany dimension should include a property called Entity, and the value of this property should match the member ID of the Entity dimension.

▶ The Account dimension should include the ELIMACC property, and the value in this property should match the member ID of the Account dimension.

▶ The Entity property should include an ELIM property, the value of which can be Y or N. The elimination process reads all entries for entities that have the value of this property set to N and then posts eliminations, if applicable, to entities that have the ELIM property set to Y. These entities are also referred to as elimination entities.

The U.S. elimination process scans all base-level, nonelimination entities, which are entities with the property ELIM ≠ Y. If the application has a Currency dimension, the elimination process restricts its action to all reporting currencies, which are currencies that have the property REPORTING = Y.

The Account dimension has a property called ELIMACC, which is used in elimination. If the value of this property is blank, the entry associated with this account is not eliminated. If the account has a valid value, and if the system decides the entry needs to be eliminated, the elimination is posted to the plug account (which is the account specified in the ELIMACC property).

The elimination is posted to the elimination entity below the first common parent. The common parent is derived as follows:

1. The system identifies the two entities for which a common parent must be found. The first entity is the current entity member. The second entity is the entity corresponding to the current intercompany member. This entity of the

intercompany member is obtained by reading the content of the ENTITY property of the current intercompany member. The system searches in the entity hierarchy for the first member that has both entities as descendants. This is the common parent.

2. Next, the system searches in the immediate descendants of the common parent for a valid elimination entity (an entity that has the property ELIM = Y). This is the entity where the system stores the results of the elimination.

3. The default elimination logic does its searches in the organization hierarchy of the Entity dimension. If no common parent is found, no elimination occurs. If no elimination entity is found below the first common parent, the next common parent is searched.

In summary, the elimination entry is posted to the elimination entity associated with the first common parent (in the ENTITY hierarchy) of the intercompany transaction. The account transaction is eliminated. The other side of the transaction will be posted to the plug account that is defined as the property of the account dimension.

Let's review the transactions resulting in elimination of intercompany transactions one more time. Consider an intercompany transaction between two entities, E1 and E2, within the organization. Let's say E1 posts an intercompany revenue transaction. At the same time, E2 posts an intercompany COGS/expense transaction for the same amount. During elimination, the revenue transaction of E1 and the expense transaction of E2 are eliminated. The elimination is posted to the elimination entity associated with the common parent of E1 and E2. When the revenue transaction of E1 is eliminated, the process debits the revenue and credit plug account associated with the revenue account. When the expense transaction of E2 is eliminated, the process debits the plug account associated with the expense account and credit expense account. Assuming that the same plug account is used for sales and expense accounts, if the transaction amounts posted by the two entities are the same, the plug account would net to zero as result of elimination of sales and expense transactions of E1 and E2, respectively.

You create entries in the business rules table to maintain the source and destination data source to use when calling the logic to eliminate intercompany transactions using U.S. eliminations. This allows you to keep elimination entries posted to a separate data source. Table 9.6 explains the details for setting up the business table for U.S. eliminations.

Field Name	Description
Source DataSource	The data source of the data that is read to which elimination needs to be applied
Destination DataSource	The destination data source to which the eliminations entries are posted
Remark	A brief description of the business rule

Table 9.6 U.S. Eliminations Business Rules

Now let's review an example of how to eliminate intercompany transactions in an SAP BPC application.

1. Figure 9.12 shows the dimensions for application ZB1. You can see that the IntCo dimension is included as a required dimension to post intercompany transactions.

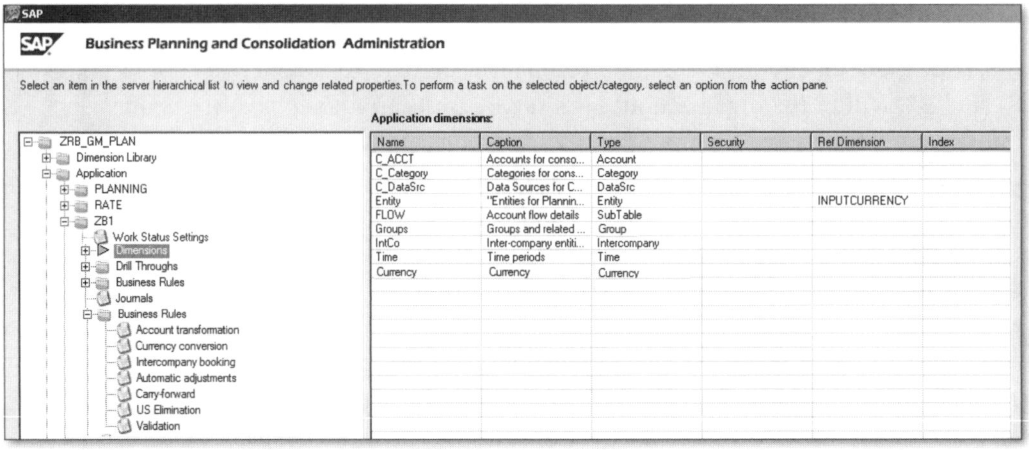

Figure 9.12 Configuring Intercompany Eliminations—Part A

2. Figure 9.13 shows the members of the Account dimension. The elimination account is a property of the Account dimension; as you can see, the ICSALES and ICCOST members have the elimination plug account ICPLUG associated with them. When eliminations are carried out, the other side of posting of eliminations is posted to the ICPLUG account.

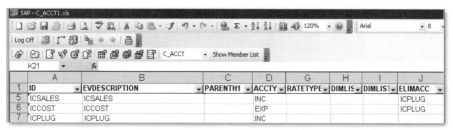

Figure 9.13 Configuring Intercompany Eliminations—Part B

3. Figure 9.14 shows the members of the Entity dimension, of which ELIM is a property. You can see that some of the entities have the ELIM property set to Y; the elimination process will post elimination entries to these elimination entities. Consider entities under node CG3. There are four entities—C3000, C3001, C4000, and E_CG3. The entity E_CG3 is identified as the elimination entity; for example, eliminations for intercompany transactions between entities C3000, C3001, and C4000 will be posted to entity E_CG3.

	ID	EVDESCRIPTION	PARENTH1	CURRENCY	ELIM
4	H1	Investments		EUR	
5	CG1	PC4You Consolidated	H1	EUR	
6	C9000	PC4You Holdings Inc	CG1	USD	
7	CG2	PC4You Europe Consolidated	CG1	EUR	
8	C1000	PC4You Deutschland Gmbh	CG2	EUR	
9	C2000	PC4You (UK) Ltd.	CG2	GBP	
10	E_CG2	PC4You Europe Consolidated	CG2	EUR	Y
11	CG3	PC4You Americas Consolidated	CG1	EUR	
12	C3000	PC4You America Inc	CG3	USD	
13	C3001	PC4You America Inc	CG3	USD	
14	C4000	PC4You Canada Inc	CG3	USD	
15	E_CG3	PC4You Americas Consolidated	CG3	USD	Y
16	CG4	PC4You Asia/Pacific Consolidated	CG1	EUR	
17	C5000	PC4You Japan Co.Ltd.	CG4	JPY	
18	C5100	PC4You Australia Pty. Limited	CG4	AUD	
19	E_CG4	PC4You Asia/Pacific Consolidated	CG4	EUR	Y
20	E_CG1	PC4You Consolidated	CG1	EUR	Y
21	H2	Regions		EUR	
22	CG5	World by Regions	H2	EUR	
23	CG6	Other regions	CG5	EUR	
24	CG7	PC4You Americas Foreign	CG5	EUR	
25	H3	Companies		EUR	
26	CG10	World by Companies	H3	EUR	

Figure 9.14 Configuring Intercompany Eliminations—Part C

4. Figure 9.15 displays the intercompany transactions for August 2008. Entity C3000 has recorded a sales transaction in account ICSALES with trading partner I_C3001. The transaction was entered under the INPUT data source. At the same time, entity C3001 recorded a COGS/expense transaction with trading partner I_C3000 in account ICCOST for the same amount.

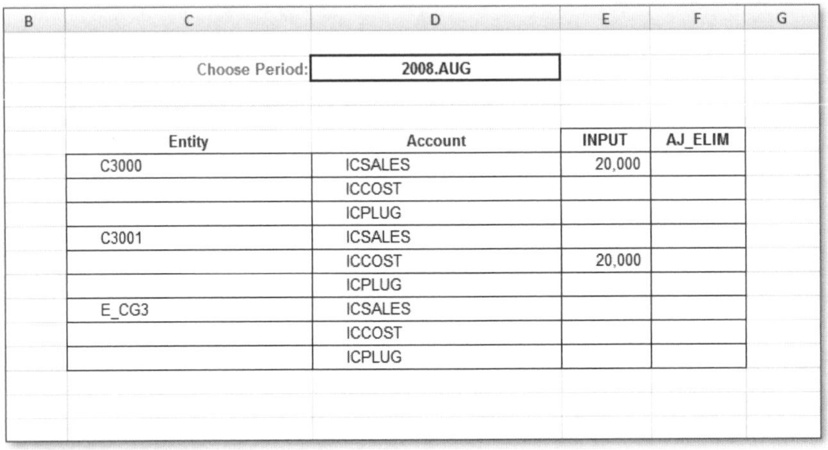

B	C	D	E	F	G
	Choose Period:	2008.AUG			
	Entity	**Account**	**INPUT**	**AJ_ELIM**	
	C3000	ICSALES	20,000		
		ICCOST			
		ICPLUG			
	C3001	ICSALES			
		ICCOST	20,000		
		ICPLUG			
	E_CG3	ICSALES			
		ICCOST			
		ICPLUG			

Figure 9.15 Configuring Intercompany Eliminations—Part D (Before Elimination)

5. Set business rules for U.S. eliminations so that the elimination entries for records from the DataSource INPUT are created under the DataSource AJ_ELIM (as shown in Table 9.7).

Field Name	Description
Source DataSource	INPUT
Destination DataSource	AJ_ELIM
Remark	Elimination for INPUT

Table 9.7 U.S. Eliminations Business Rules (Example)

6. Create the standard script logic ICELIM.LGF (if one does not already exist) to execute the U.S. intercompany eliminations, as shown in Figure 9.16.

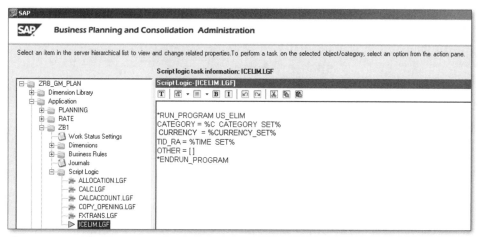

Figure 9.16 Configuring Intercompany Eliminations—Part E

7. Run the data package to execute the IC elimination script, as shown in Figure 9.17. The process chain associated with the elimination process is /CPMB/ IC_ELIMINATION.

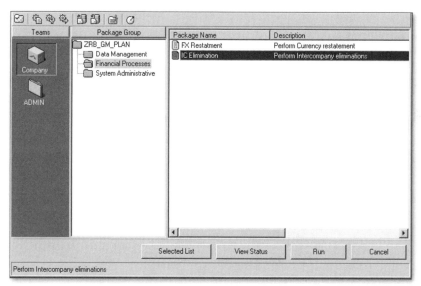

Figure 9.17 Configuring Intercompany Eliminations—Part F

8. Run U.S. eliminations for selections shown in Figure 9.18. In our example, we chose August 2008.

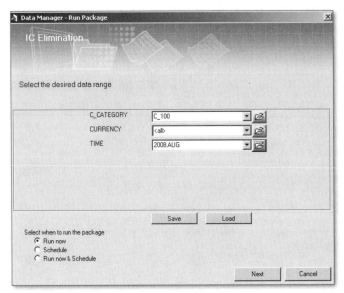

Figure 9.18 Configuring Intercompany Eliminations—Part G

9. After executing the package, you'll notice that the sales transaction for C3000 and the COGS/expense transaction for C3001 are eliminated (Figure 9.19). The elimination entries are posted to the elimination entity E_CG3. The net effect on the plug account is equal to zero.

B	C	D	E	F	G
	Choose Period:	2008.AUG			
	Entity	Account	INPUT	AJ_ELIM	
	C3000	ICSALES	20,000		
		ICCOST			
		ICPLUG			
	C3001	ICSALES			
		ICCOST	20,000		
		ICPLUG			
	E_CG3	ICSALES		(20,000)	
		ICCOST		(20,000)	
		ICPLUG		0	

Figure 9.19 Configuring Intercompany Eliminations—Part H (After Elimination)

We've discussed the usage of business rules to perform intercompany U.S. elimination. In the next section, we'll study the use of the validation business rules.

9.2.5 Validation Business Rule

The validation business rules functionality in SAP BPC is used as a check mechanism to ensure accuracy of data. Validations are performed at various stages of the consolidation process. The validation business rules table enables you to compare balances between two sets of records and post differences, if any, to a validation account. The rules allow you to use a combination of multiple dimensions, for example, an account and flow combination, to perform the check.

The validation business rules table has a header section and a detail section. The header section identifies the data region, operand, and tolerance associated with the validation. You also specify the validation account that receives the difference in this section. The detail section identifies the combination of account and flow to perform the comparison.

The header section specified the information listed in Table 9.8.

Field Name	Description
Validation Account	Account that receives differences, if any.
Validation Operand	Valid values are =, >, <, >=, and <=. This operand is used to compare the left side and right side of the account assignment that is specified in the detail section.
Other Source Dimension Members	Specified data region to limit selection of data. For example, FLOW=F_CLO
Other Destination Member	Defines the data region to store the imbalance amount from the validation rule calculation. If this value is blank, the imbalance amount is written to the same data region associated with the source data.
Applicable Period (optional)	Selection of period other than current.
Validation Tolerance	Absolute value of tolerance below which validation will pass.

Table 9.8 Validation Business Rules—Header

In the detail section, you specify the left part and right part of the Account, Flow, and Sign combination associated to the validation. The detail section contains the information in Table 9.9.

Field Name	Description
Account1	Account used in left side of the validation check
Flow1	Flow used in left side of the validation check
Sign1	Operator used in left part of calculation (1 or -1)
Account2	Account used in right side of the validation check
Flow2	Flow used in right side of the validation check
Sign2	Operator used in right part of calculation (1 or -1)

Table 9.9 Validation Business Rules—Detail

After setting the business rule, create script logic called VALIDATION.LGF (if one does not already exist) and insert the following code:

```
*RUN_PROGRAM VALIDATION
        CATEGORY = %CATEGORY_SET%
           CURRENCY = %CURRENCY_SET%
           TID_RA = %TIME_SET%
           ENTITY=%ENTITY_SET%
*ENDRUN_PROGRAM
```

After performing the above setup, run VALIDATION.LGF via a data manager package called VALIDATION. The process chain associated with this process is /CPMB/VALIDATIONS. After the validation data manager package runs, if the validation rule fails, the difference in the amount will be posted to the validation account that was specified in the header section of the rule.

In the next section, we'll discuss the concepts in consolidation and provide an overview of consolidation of investments.

9.3 Consolidation of Investments

A corporation may have a number of legal subsidiaries that may or may not be fully owned. The consolidation of investment deals with the elimination of ownership and booking of minority interest of these investments. Three methods are commonly used in consolidation of investments:

▶ Purchase method

▶ Equity method

▶ Proportional method

The purchase method is generally used when the percentage of ownership is greater than 50%. The equity method is generally used when the percentage of ownership is less than 50%. The proportional method is similar to the purchase method and is generally used in Europe. Let's explore the three methods used in consolidation of investments. First, we'll discuss the purchase method of consolidation of investment.

9.3.1   Purchase Method

In the purchase method, at the time of purchase, the consolidation of investment process reflects the elimination of ownership that is common between the parent and subsidiary, goodwill for the premium paid for the purchase, and minority stakeholders' claim to the asset. After this first consolidation, assuming that the ownership percentage does not change, subsequent consolidations would post the parent and minority share of the subsidiary's earnings.

Let's say that company A acquires 75% of subsidiary company B for $50,000. Figure 9.20 displays the books of company A, company B, and the total, elimination, and consolidated group balances.

At the time of acquisition, the following transactions are performed:

▶ Consolidate balances of parent and subsidiary

▶ Eliminate ownership that is common between the parent and subsidiary — eliminate the investment account of the parent Company A ($50,000) that pertains to the subsidiary and common stock of subsidiary Company B ($40,000).

▶ Post any excess value paid that is above the book value of the acquired subsidiary to goodwill — the book value of the common stock of company B is $40,000. Company A acquired 75% of company B. So company A acquired $30,000 of the book value of the stock. The excess amount of $20,000 ($50,000 – $30,000) paid by company A is booked to goodwill.

▶ Post minority interest. The amount of minority interest appearing in the balance sheet is calculated by multiplying common shareholder equity of the subsidiary by the percentage of the minority interest—the minority interest of company B is 25% (100% – 75%) of $40,000 which amounts to $10,000.

Purchase Method					
	Company A	Company B	Total	Elimination	Group
Goodwill				$20,000.00	$20,000.00
Cash	$100,000.00	$40,000.00	$140,000.00		$140,000.00
Investments	$50,000.00		$50,000.00	-$50,000.00	$0.00
Total	$150,000.00	$40,000.00	$190,000.00	-$30,000.00	$160,000.00
					$0.00
Common Stock	-$130,000.00	-$40,000.00	-$170,000.00	$40,000.00	-$130,000.00
Retained earnings	-$20,000.00		-$20,000.00		-$20,000.00
Minority Interest				-$10,000.00	-$10,000.00
Total	-$150,000.00	-$40,000.00	-$190,000.00	$30,000.00	-$160,000.00
Company A owns 75% of Company B for $50,000					

Figure 9.20 Purchase Method (Example)

9.3.2 Equity Method

In the equity method, reported financial data of the equity unit is not taken into consideration in the consolidated financial report. The financial data for the equity unit is not entered into the consolidation system. Only the changes to the owner's equity are taken into consideration. This affects the investment value and goodwill stated in the consolidated balance sheet.

Let's say that company C buys 25% of company D for $15,000. Figure 9.21 displays the books of company C, company D, and the elimination and consolidated group balances. The book value of company D is $40,000, of which company C owns $10,000 (25% of $40,000). The investment value of the group is adjusted so that the net value is $10,000. This is done by eliminating $5,000 from the Investments value of $15,000. The excess amount paid of $5,000 ($15,000–$10,000) is posted to goodwill.

Equity Method					
	Company C	Company D		Elimination	Group
Goodwill				$5,000.00	$5,000.00
Cash	$100,000.00	$40,000.00		-$40,000.00	$100,000.00
Investments	$15,000.00			-$5,000.00	$10,000.00
Total	$115,000.00	$40,000.00		-$40,000.00	$115,000.00
Common Stock	-$30,000.00	-$40,000.00		$40,000.00	-$30,000.00
Retained earnings	-$85,000.00				-$85,000.00
Minority Interest					$0.00
Total	-$115,000.00	-$40,000.00		$40,000.00	-$115,000.00
Company C owns 25% of Company D for $15,000					

Figure 9.21 Equity Method (Example)

9.3.3 Proportional Method

The proportional method of consolidation collects the units of the balance sheet and income statement into the consolidated statements based on the investor unit's proportion of ownership in the investee's unit. In other words, the percentage that is not owned is eliminated.

Let's say that a company E acquires 75% of subsidiary company F for $50,000. Figure 9.22 displays the books of company E, company F, and the total, elimination, and consolidated group balances.

▶ Consolidate balances of parent and subsidiary

▶ Eliminate ownership that is common between the parent and subsidiary—eliminate the investment account of the parent Company E ($50,000) that pertains to the subsidiary and common stock of subsidiary Company F ($40,000).

▶ Post any excess value paid that is above the book value of the acquired subsidiary to goodwill—the book value of the common stock of company F is $40,000. Company E acquired 75% of company F. So company E acquired $30,000 of the book value of the stock. The excess amount of $20,000 ($50,000−$30,000) paid by company E is booked to goodwill.

▶ Eliminate the proportion of balances that are not owned—Company F has $40,000 in a cash account. Company E owns 75% of company F. The remaining 25% (100%−75%) of cash should be eliminated. The amount eliminated from the cash account is $10,000.

The main difference between the purchase method and the proportional method is that the purchase method posts the non-owned portion to a minority share account, whereas the proportional method eliminates the proportion of balances that are not owned.

Proportional Method	Company E	Company F	Total	Elimination	Group
Goodwill				$20,000.00	$20,000.00
Cash	$100,000.00	$40,000.00	$140,000.00	-$10,000.00	$130,000.00
Investments	$50,000.00		$50,000.00	-$50,000.00	$0.00
Total	$150,000.00	$40,000.00	$190,000.00	-$40,000.00	$150,000.00
					$0.00
Common Stock	-$130,000.00	-$40,000.00	-$170,000.00	$40,000.00	-$130,000.00
Retained earnings	-$20,000.00		-$20,000.00		-$20,000.00
Minority Interest					$0.00
Total	-$150,000.00	-$40,000.00	-$190,000.00	$40,000.00	-$150,000.00
Company E owns 75% of Company F for $50,000					

Figure 9.22 Proportional Method (example)

In the next section, we'll detail the steps involved in consolidation of investments.

9.3.4 Consolidation of Investments

The following are the high-level steps to accomplish consolidation of investments:

1. Set up dimension members and properties.
2. Create rate, legal, and ownership applications.
3. Set relevant application parameters.
4. Input methods, position, and percentages in the ownership application.
5. Configure the consolidation business rules at the application set level.
6. Configure the automatic adjustment business rule in the legal application.

7. Create script logic in the legal application; assign data manger packages for consolidation.

8. Load the rate and legal application data; run consolidation and analyze the results.

Let's discuss each of the above steps.

Set Up Dimension Members and Properties

The consolidation of investments requires that the following dimension properties be included:

▶ **IS_CONSOL of DATASRC dimension**
If the value of this property is set to Y, the data source participates in the consolidation run. If this property is set to N, the data source does not participate in the consolidation run.

▶ **DATASRC_TYPE of DATASRC dimension**
Data sources that have this property set to A (automatic) can be used as destination data sources in business rules.

▶ **IS_CONVERTED of DATASRC dimension**
If the value of this property is set to Y, the DataSource participates in the currency translation. If this property is set to N, the data source does not participate in the currency translation.

▶ **GROUPS dimension**
The group represents the relationship of entities for a given consolidation result.

Setup of Applications

Create a legal application and assign a RATE application and OWNERSHIP application. The RATE application contains the Category, Currency (Input_Currency), Account (R_ACCT), Entity (R_ENTITY), and Time dimensions. The RATE application is used to store currency exchange rates. OWNERSHIP is a nonreporting application and is used to store ownership data. The OWNERSHIP application contains the Group, Category, Time, Entity, Intco, and Ownership Account (O_ACCT) dimensions. The ownership account contains the percentages, methods, and parent positions.

Set Relevant Application Parameters

Set the application parameters for the legal application as described in Table 9.10.

Application Parameter	Description
ORG_ACCOUNTLIST	List the dimension member IDs of the Account dimension used in the ownership application that specifies the method of consolidation, percentage consolidation, and percentage ownership, for example, METHODS, PCON,POWN
ORG_ACCOUNTDOWN	Specify the dimension member ID of the Account dimension used in the ownership application that specifies the position of the consolidation entry within the group, for example, PGROUP

If an entity belongs to a consolidation group, the value of this dimension member PGROUP is set to 1 in the ownership application. |
ORG_INTCO	Specify a third-party member in the Intercompany dimension. All transactions to third parties (external) are posted to this intercompany member, for example, I_NONE.
ORG_OWNERSHIPCUBE	Name of the ownership application linked to the legal application, for example, OWNERSHIP
ORG_PARENTPROPERTY	Property name in the Group dimension used to define the hierarchy used in the Dynamic Hierarchy Editor.
OWNERSHIP_APP	Name of the ownership application linked to the legal application, for example, OWNERSHIP

Table 9.10 Application Parameters for Legal Application

Input Methods, Position, and Percentages in the Ownership Application

Using an input template or Dynamic Hierarchy Editor, enter ownership information. The ownership application stores the overall ownership and consolidation percentage of each entity. The ownership application contains the dimensions listed in Table 9.11. Use the same the category, time, group and entity dimension names in the consolidation and ownership applications.

Dimensions	Description
O_ACCT	Account
CATEGORY	Category
ENTITY	Entity
GROUPS	Group
INTCO	Intercompany
TIME	Time

Table 9.11 Dimensions in the Ownership Application

The O_ACCOUNT is used to specify the following:

▸ **Ownership percentage (POWN):** percent owned

▸ **Percentage consolidation (PCON):** In the proportionate method, the percentage of company that should be considered for ownership

▸ **Method of consolidation (METHOD):** Method used in consolidation (e.g., 86 = purchase method, 30 = equity method, 70 = proportionate method, 90 = holding company)

▸ **Is entity part of group (PGROUP) for consolidation purposes?** 1 = Yes

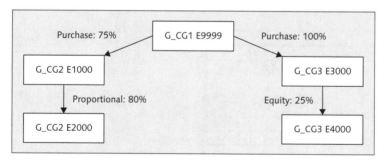

Figure 9.23 Ownership Structure (Example)

Consider the ownership structure of an organization as depicted in Figure 9.23. There are three consolidation groups—G_CG1, G_CG2, and G_CG3. Figure 9.24 shows the dimension members of the Group dimension for the three groups. Notice that G_CG2 and G_CG3 have G_CG1 as parent group. The ownership information in the ownership application is maintained against the consolidation groups. You can also specify an entity property to each consolidation group where consolidated results for each group can be stored. During consolidation, if the STORE_ENTITY property of the group is set to Y and if the entity property contains a valid entity, the system will post group-level elimination values to this entity.

The holding companies for consolidation groups G_CG1, G_CG2, and G_CG3 are E9999, E1000, and E3000 respectively.

GROUPS						
ID	EVDESCRIPTION	CURRENCY_TYPE	ENTITY	GROUP_CURRENCY	PARENT_GROUP	STORE_ENTITY
G_H1	Investments	G		USD	G_H1	
G_CG1	Group 1	G		USD	G_H1	
G_CG2	Group 2	G		USD	G_CG1	
G_CG3	Group 3	G		USD	G_CG1	
NON_GROUP	Group Input	N				

Figure 9.24 Group Dimension

The ownership percentages for the ownership structure shown in Figure 9.23 are maintained as shown in Figure 9.25. The Account (O_ACCT) dimension has a value of POWN. The group is set to NON_GROUP. For example, because E9999 owns 75% of E1000, the entity value is set to E9999, the intercompany value is set to I_E1000 (this is the intercompany dimension member associated with entity E1000), and the ownership is set to 0.75.

OWNERSHIP					
	NON_GROUP	NON_GROUP	NON_GROUP	NON_GROUP	NON_GROUP
	I_E9999	I_E1000	I_E2000	I_E3000	I_E4000
E9999		0.75		1	
E1000			0.8		
E2000					
E3000					0.25
E4000					
O_ACCT = POWN					

Figure 9.25 Ownership Application—Enter POWN Data

The Ownership method (METHOD), percentage consolidation (PCON), and position in group (PGROUP) for the ownership structure shown in Figure 9.23 are maintained as shown in Figure 9.26. METHOD represents the method used for consolidation of the entity (86 = purchase method, 30 = equity method, 70 = proportionate method, 90 = holding company). PCON is used in the context of the proportional method (method = 70) and represents the proportion or percentage of the company owned. If an entity belongs to a group, the value of PGROUP is set to 1. Let's look at an example to understand how this information is maintained. Consider consolidation group G_CG2. In this group, entity E1000 is the holding company, so we've set the value of METHOD of entity E1000 in consolidation group G_CG2 to "90." Entity E1000 owns 80% of E2000 using the proportional method. So we've set the value of PCON for entity E2000 in the consolidation group G_CG2 to 0.80.

OWNERSHIP (Entered)

	G_CG1 PGROUP	G_CG1 METHOD	G_CG1 PCON	G_CG2 PGROUP	G_CG2 METHOD	G_CG2 PCON	G_CG3 PGROUP	G_CG3 METHOD	G_CG3 PCON
E9999	1	90	1						
E1000	1	86	1	1	90	1			
E2000	1	70	0.6	1	70	0.8			
E3000	1	86	1				1	90	1
E4000	1	30	0.25				1	30	0.25

ICP=I_NONE

Figure 9.26 Ownership Application—Enter PGROUP, METHOD, and PCON

The ownership data entered above can be entered using either an input template or the Dynamic Hierarchy Editor (DHE). The Dynamic Hierarchy Editor is available in SAP BPC 7.5 for NetWeaver. After entering the ownership data, run the delivered data manager package that calculates the overall ownership within each group. You can also manually maintain the group percentages. Figure 9.27 displays the overall group ownership after calculation.

OWNERSHIP (after calculation)

	G_CG1 PGROUP	G_CG1 METHOD	G_CG1 PCON	G_CG1 POWN	G_CG2 PGROUP	G_CG2 METHOD	G_CG2 PCON	G_CG2 POWN	G_CG3 PGROUP	G_CG3 METHOD	G_CG3 PCON	G_CG3 POWN
E9999	5	90	1	1								
E1000	1	86	1	0.75	1	90	1	1				
E2000	2	70	0.6	0.6	2	70	0.8	0.8				
E3000	3	86	1	1					1	90	1	1
E4000	4	30	0.25	0.25					2	30	0.25	0.25

ICP=I_NONE

Figure 9.27 Overall Ownership (After Calculation)

Configure the Consolidation Business Rules at the Application Set Level

Now that we've have entered the ownership information, we need to create the automatic adjustments business rules for the system to create entries during consolidation. But before doing that, we'll review the business rules library that is available at the application set level. The legal consolidation application comes with a business rules library that contains the following tables with data:

▶ **Consolidation Methods**
These refer to different types of consolidation methods available for consolidation. Recall that we discussed 86 = purchase method, 30 = equity method, 70 = proportionate method, and 90 = holding company. These entries are configured in this table.

▶ **Consolidation Rules**
This table contains rules that can be referenced in the Rule ID field of the Automatic Adjustment Detail table. For example, RULE010 (Stock Holder Equities) splits equity into group and minority shares. RULE011 (Result) eliminates profit on holding company. RULE030 (Dividends) eliminates dividends from subsidiaries to parent entities. RULE040 (IC Elimination) is used for intercompany eliminations. RULE050 (Internal Profits) eliminates subsidiaries profits. RULE051 (Internal Profits on Stocks) eliminates internal profits on stocks (inventory).

RULE200 (Equity Method—rule type Equity) and RULE210 (Proportional Method—rule type proportional) are used for equity and proportional methods.

> **Note**
>
> Rules RULE200 (Equity Method—rule type Equity) and RULE210 (Proportional Method—rule type proportional) are not assigned in the Automatic Adjustment Detail table.

▶ **Consolidation Rule Formula**
The formula associated with each rule is maintained in this table. It determines how the destination accounts should be calculated. For example, RULE010 is used to split equity into group and minority shares. Figure 9.28 displays the formulas associated with RULE010. For each ownership method, you specify

how to split equity and minority shares. This table contains the Entity Method, Intco Method, ALL formula, Group Formula, Minority Formula, and Remark fields. You maintain this rule for each entity method. A value of 99 in the Intco Method field means the formula is valid for any intercompany member. For the purchase method (consolidation method = 86), you set ALL Formula to 1 to mean that you consider 100% of the amount in the source account. In the Group Formula field, you specify POWN to mean that only the percentage owned is applied to the destination group account. In the Minority Formula field, you specify 1-POWN to mean the percentage that is not owned is applied to the minority shares account. Note that the Consolidation Rule Formula table contains the formula for calculation of destination accounts. The destination accounts are defined in the automatic adjustment business rules table that we will discuss in the next section.

RULE010 - Stock Holder Equities					
Entity Method	INTCO Method	"ALL" formula	Group Formula	Minority Formula	Remark
86	99	1	POWN	1-POWN	
30	99	POWN	POWN		
70	99	POWN	POWN		

Figure 9.28 RULE010 Formulas

You can directly use the data that exists in these SAP-supplied tables. You can add entries to these tables, if needed.

Configure Automatic Adjustment Business Rule in the Legal Application

Under a consolidation application, two business tables—Automatic Adjustments and Automatic Adjustments Detail—define the rules for consolidation. These rules link back to the Consolidation Rules Formula table for calculating and posting values. The Automatic Adjustments Detail table is used to read each source account that needs to be consolidated/eliminated and depending on the fractions specified in the Consolidation Rules Formula table, will post to the destination account, group account, and minority account.

Table 9.12 lists the fields in the Automatic Adjustments Header table.

Field	Description
Adjustment ID	Unique identifier for adjustment rule.
Source Data Source	The data source of the data that is read for consolidation. The data source can be a base member, a parent member, or a list of members filtered using the DIMLIST property.
Destination Data Source	The elimination data created during the consolidation process is booked to this destination data source member. This data source should be a base member where the data source type = A (Automatic)
Group Type Filter	The CONSO_TYPE property value from the Group/ Currency dimension.
Adjustment Type	This field can have the following values: ▸ Blank = All ▸ E = Apply the rule only to entities that use the equity method ▸ P = Apply the rule only to entities that use the proportional method ▸ L = Apply the rule only to entities that use the leaving method ▸ N= Apply the rule only to entities that use the new method
Adjustment Level	Integer that specifies the sequence of execution of rules
Entity Property Filter	This field is used for performing intercompany elimination. The system looks for existence of this property in the Entity and Intercompany (INTCO) dimensions and performs eliminations only if the ENTITY and INTCO partners have the same value in this property.
Other Dimension Filter	Specify the source data region that is consolidated, for example, CATEGORY=ACTUAL.
Forced Destination Members	This can be used to force a destination dimension member to contain a specific value, for example, ENTITY=HQ.
Remark	A brief description of the business rule.

Table 9.12 Automatic Adjustments Header Business Rule Table

Table 9.13 lists fields in the Automatic Adjustments Detail table.

Field	Description
Source Account	Specify the source data region to read data. The source account can be a base member, a parent member, or a list of members filtered using the DIMLIST property.
Reverse Sign	If set to Y, will reverse the amount calculated. Please remember that because the adjustment entries pertain to elimination, the value calculated is negative by default. For example, if both the source accounts and the target accounts are AST accounts, then the result of the elimination will be negative by default.
Destination ALL Account	Specify the destination account. Please refer to the explanation of math used to calculate the amount for this account (below).
Destination Group Account	Specify the group account to be used. Please refer to the explanation of math used to calculate the amount for this account (below).
Destination Minority Account	Specify minority account to be used. Please refer to the explanation of math used to calculate the amount for this account (below).
Destination equity account	If you use the equity method, specify the equity account to be used. Please refer to the explanation of math used to calculate the amount for this account (below).
Rule ID	Valid rule ID from the application set Consolidation Rules table. This rule ID links back to the Consolidation Rules table for calculating amounts.
Source Flow	Specify the data region to read data. The source flow can be a base member, a parent member, or a list of members filtered using the DIMLIST property.
Destination Flow	The consolidation data created during the consolidation process is booked to this destination flow member. This destination flow should be a base member.
Force Closing	If set to Y, will create an extra record with closing flow (FLOW=F_CLO; F_CLO has flow type value = CLOSING).

Table 9.13   Automatic Adjustments Detail Business Rule Table

Field	Description
Swap Entity—INTCO	If selected, will swap the Entity dimension with the INTCO dimension. This is especially used during calculation of goodwill. Please refer to the example of usage of this field later in this chapter.
Forced INTCO Member	This can be used to force a destination dimension INTCO member to contain a specific value.
Remark	A brief description of the business rule.

Table 9.13 Automatic Adjustments Detail Business Rule Table (Cont.)

Please note that the rules in the Automatic Adjustment Detail Business Rule table link back to the Consolidation Rules Formula table. When the consolidation process is run for a consolidation group, the system does the following:

1. Reads ownership information pertaining to the consolidation group from the ownership application.

2. Reads each automatic adjustment detail business rule. Determines the base amount upon which automatic adjustments are to be calculated (source data based on source accounts).

3. For each rule, based on the rule ID and method of consolidation, reads the Consolidations Formula table to determine fractions to post to the destination account, group account, and minority account. The fraction for the destination account, group account, and minority accounts are in the All Formula, Group Formula, and Minority Formula fields, respectively, of the Consolidation Rules Formula table.

4. Calculate the amounts to be posted to the destination account, group account, and minority account by multiplying the base amount and the fraction for each account determined in step 3.

5. Post the amounts to the specific destination account, group account, and minority account specified in the Automatic Adjustment Detail table.

In summary, the Automatic Adjustments Detail table reads each source account that needs to be consolidated/eliminated and depending on the fractions specified in the Consolidation Rules Formula table, posts to the destination account, group account, and minority account. The key information that is used in the process of determining these postings is the method by which each entity is consolidated in the consolidation group, the consolidation rule assigned to each account, and the elimination calculation as specified in each rule.

Let's consider an example to understand usage of automatic adjustments business rules. Figure 9.23, above, depicts the ownership tree. Consider consolidation group G_CG2. In this consolidation group, entity E1000, the holding company in the group, acquires 80% of entity E2000 using the proportional method. Let's say that E1000 acquires E2000 for $50,000. Figure 9.29 displays the books of company E1000, company E2000, and the total, elimination, and consolidated group balances.

Proportional Method					
	Company E1000	Company E2000	Total	Elimination	Group
Goodwill				$18,000	$18,000
Cash	$100,000	$40,000	$140,000	-$8,000	$132,000
Investments	$50,000		$50,000	-$50,000	$0
Total	$150,000	$40,000	$190,000	-$40,000	$150,000
Common Stock	-$130,000	-$40,000	-$170,000	$40,000	-$130,000
Retained earnings	-$20,000		-$20,000		-$20,000
Minority Interest					
Total	-$150,000	-$40,000	-$190,000	$40,000	-$150,000
Company E1000 owns 80% of company E2000 for $50,000					

Figure 9.29 Consolidation of G_CG2 (Proportional Method Example)

We'll use the accounts specified in Table 9.14 and data sources specified in Table 9.15 in our example.

Accounts	Description
1100	Cash
1200	Investments in subsidiaries (proportional)
1300	Goodwill
3100	Treasury stock—purchase
3200	Treasury stock—equity
3300	Treasury stock—proportional
3400	Common stock
3500	Retained earnings

Table 9.14 Automatic Adjustments Example—Account Master Data

Data Source	Data Source Type
INPUT	I
AJ_ELIM1	A
AJ_ELIM2	A
AJ_ELIM3	A
AJ_PROP	A

Table 9.15 Automatic Adjustments Example—Data Source Master Data

We'll load two records into the consolidation system that represent the investment of entity E1000 and the equity of entity E2000. Table 9.16 lists the records. We'll also load all initial balances for entities E1000 and E2000 as displayed in Figure 9.29. For this illustration, these records can be entered into the system using input templates.

ACCOUNT	INTCO	ENTITY	TIME	FLOW	DATASRC	CURRENCY	GROUP	CATEGORY	AMOUNT
1200	I_E2000	E1000	2010. DEC	F_CLO	INPUT	LC	NON_ GROUP	C_100	50000
3300	I_E1000	E2000	2010. DEC	F_CLO	INPUT	LC	NON_ GROUP	C_100	40000

Table 9.16 Investment of Entity E1000 and Equity of Entity E2000

The automatic adjustment rules need to do the following:

1. Eliminate the investment account of E1000 for ownership that is common between the parent and subsidiary.

2. Eliminate the common stock of E2000 for ownership that is common between the parent and subsidiary.

3. Book excess value paid to goodwill. In this case, the book value of the common stock of company E2000 is $40,000. Company E1000 acquired 80% of company E2000. So company E1000 acquired $32,000 of the book value of the stock. The excess amount of $18,000 ($50,000 – $32,000) paid by company E1000 is booked to goodwill.

4. Company E2000 has $40,000 in a cash account. Company E1000 owns 80% of company E2000. The remaining 20% (100% – 80%) of the cash should be eliminated. The amount eliminated from the cash account should be $8,000.

To accomplish the above, we'll use the rules that are available in the Consolidation Rules Formula table. Please refer to Table 9.17. Note that RULE210 is a default rule for the proportional method and does not need to have entry in the Automatic Adjustment Detail table. Similarly, RULE200 is a default rule for the equity method and does not need to have entry in the Automatic Adjustment Detail table.

Rule ID	Description	Entity Method	INTCO Method	ALL formula	Group Formula	Minority Formula
RULE010	Stock Holders Equity	70	99	POWN	POWN	
RULE060	Shares: Subsidiary	90	99	1	1	
RULE210	Proportionate Method	70	99	1-POWN		

Table 9.17 Consolidation Formula Rules Used for Automatic Adjustment

We'll configure the automatic adjustment business rule for consolidating the investment using the proportional method. We'll first set the header table that will contain the destination data sources to which elimination entries will be posted. Please refer to Table 9.18. For example, the elimination entry for ADJ1 adjustment ID is posted to the AJELIM1 data source.

Adjustment ID	Destination Data Source	Adjustment Type	Remark
ADJ1	AJ_ELIM1		Eliminate investments
ADJ2	AJ_ELIM2		Calculate goodwill
ADJ3	AJ_ELIM3		Calculate goodwill
ADJ4	AJ_PROP	Proportional	Eliminate portion not owned

Table 9.18 Automatic Adjustment Header

Next, we'll configure the detail table that will link to the Consolidations Formula Rules table to calculate and post to accounts (Table 9.19).

Adjustment ID	Source Account	Reverse	Destination ALL	Destination group	Destination Minority	Rule Id	Swap Entity— INTCO
ADJ1	1200		1200			RULE060	
ADJ2	1200	X	1300			RULE060	
ADJ3	3300	X	1300			RULE010	X
ADJ1	3300		3300			RULE010	

Table 9.19 Automatic Adjustment Detail

The first entry (ADJ1) is used to eliminate the "Investments in Subsidiaries (Proportional)" account. This adjustment entry uses RULE060 and reads the amount in account 1200 (Investments in Subsidiaries (Proportional)) and posts the same amount (because ALL formula = 1) to the same account and data source AJ_ELIM1 with a negative value. Because the consolidation process creates an elimination entry, it sets the destination ALL account amount to a negative value even though the adjustment posts to the same account. Also, please remember the signs related to accounts (AST +, LEQ –, INC –, and EXP +) when reading source accounts and posting to destination accounts.

The next two entries (ADJ2 and ADJ3) are used to calculate goodwill. ADJ2 uses RULE060 and reads the amount in account 1200 and posts the same amount to account 1300 (Goodwill) and data source AJ_ELIM2. ADJ3 uses RULE010 and reads the amount in account 3300 (Treasury Stock—Proportional) and posts the fraction of the amount owned (because ALL formula = POWN) and posts to account 1300 and data source AJ_ELIM3. The net effect of the two adjustments is equal to "value of the investment" — "value of treasury stocks (proportional) that are owned." This results in the goodwill. Please note that ADJ3 has the Swap Entity INTCO checkbox selected. This ensures that the system will read the transaction that contains the treasury stock information posted to E2000 and INTCO I_E1000 and will post to E1000 and intercompany I_E2000. We need the swap entity and INTCO to post goodwill to E1000.

The fourth entry (ADJ1) is used to eliminate the remaining balance in the equity account. This adjustment entry uses RULE010 and reads the amount in account

3300 and posts the fraction owned (because ALL formula = POWN) to the same account and data source AJ_ELIM1 with a negative value.

Finally, the default RULE210 would execute that would eliminate portion of balances of E2000 that is not owned by E1000. This would eliminate balances in the Cash account and Treasury Stock (Proportional) accounts. The eliminations are posted to the AJ_PROP data source.

After execution of the consolidation process for consolidation group G_CG2, we would expect to see the results tabulated in Table 9.20.

Entity	Account	Account Description	INPUT	AJ_IM1	AJ_IM2	AJ_IM3	AJPROP	TOTAL
E1000	1100	Cash	100,000					100,000
E2000	1100	Cash	40,000				−8,000	32,000
E1000	1200	Investments in Subsidiaries— Proportional	50,000	−50,000				0
E1000	1300	Goodwill			50,000	−32,000		18,000
E1000	3100	Treasury Stock— Purchase						0
E1000	3200	Treasury Stock—Equity						0
E1000	3400	Common Stock	130,000					130,000
E1000	3500	Retained Earning	20,000					20,000
E2000	3300	Treasury Stock— Proportional	40,000	−32,000			−8,000	0

Table 9.20 Consolidation of Investment Results (Proportional Method)

Execute Consolidation Process

A program called CONSOLIDATION handles the consolidation of investments process. This program is run using the following logic statement in the CONSOLIDATION.LGF script file.

```
*RUN_PROGRAM CONSOLIDATION
CATEGORY = %C_CATEGORY_SET%
GROUP = %GROUPS_SET%
TID_RA = %TIME_SET%
*ENDRUN_PROGRAM
```

SAP provides a data manager package called Consolidation to execute the consolidation process. This data manager package uses the /CPMB/LEGAL_CONSOLIDATION process chain. When you execute this package, the system prompts you for category, consolidation group, and time. Execute consolidation and analyze the results.

In this section, we covered the consolidation of investment process. We learned about the configuration of entries in the Consolidation Methods table, Consolidation Rules Formula table, and automatic adjustments business rules for performing consolidation of investments. We illustrated a scenario that can be used for consolidation of investments.

In the previous section, we discussed U.S. eliminations. In the next section, we'll detail how we can perform intercompany elimination using the automatic adjustments business rule.

9.4 Intercompany Elimination—Automatic Adjustments Business Rule

In the previous section, when we learned about the consolidation of investments, we studied the usage of the ownership application, the Consolidation Methods table, the Consolidation Rules Formula table, and the automatic adjustments business rule. In this is section, we'll see how to use these tables to perform intercompany elimination. You can use intercompany elimination to eliminate intercompany transactions such as intercompany revenues and cost of goods sold, intercompany accounts receivable and payables, intercompany dividends, royalties, and so on. The consolidation logic used in consolidation of investments is also used to eliminate intercompany transactions.

This method of intercompany elimination is used in legal consolidation. The intercompany elimination applies elimination directly to the balance sheet of the entity, unlike U.S. elimination that posts elimination to the account balance of an elimination entity associated with a common parent in the entity hierarchy of the entity and entity associated to intercompany trading partner. The reverse amount is posted to a plug account (also called elimination account or offset account).

Let's learn how this elimination works with an example. Let's say entity E1 sells goods to entity E2 for $1000. As a result of the transaction, E1 posts an accounts receivable (AR) transaction for $1,000 specifying E2 (e.g., INTCO=I_E2) as the trading partner. E2 posts an accounts payable (AP) transaction for the same amount, specifying E1 as the trading partner. The elimination process eliminates the AR transaction of E1 for $1,000. The other side of the entry is posted to a plug/offset account. Similarly, the process eliminates the AP transaction of E2 for $1,000. The other side of the entry is posted to a plug/offset account. As a result of the transactions, assuming that the same plug/offset account is used for elimination of AR and AP, the plug/offset account would net to 0.

The elimination entry is posted to the same entity to which the original transaction was posted. The intercompany eliminations process posts the elimination entries to a destination data source specified in the Automatic Adjustment Business Rules table. This is done so that the initial value in the source account is not overwritten.

The following are steps to perform intercompany eliminations:

1. Set up dimensions and properties.
2. Set up the ownership application. We discussed the steps to set up this application in the previous section when we studied consolidation of investments.
3. Set up the Consolidation Methods table, Consolidation Rules Formula table, and Automatic Adjustment Business Rule table.
4. Execute the consolidation data manager package.

Let us step through the process of the setup.

Set Up Dimensions and Properties

The consolidation of investments requires the following dimension properties to be included:

▶ **IS_CONSOL of DATASRC dimension**

If the value of this property is set to Y, the data source participates in the consolidation run. If this property is set to N, the data source does not participate in the consolidation run.

▶ **DATASRC_TYPE of DATASRC dimension**

Data sources that have this property set to A (automatic) can be used as destination data sources in business rules.

▶ **IS_CONVERTED of DATASRC dimension**

If the value of this property is set to Y, the data source participates in the currency translation. If this property is set to N, the data source does not participate in the currency translation.

▶ To support intercompany elimination, the SAP BPC application should include the Intercompany dimension. The dimension type is I.

▶ The Intercompany dimension should include a property called Entity, and the value of this property should match the member ID of the Entity dimension.

Set Up Ownership Application

We discussed the steps to set up the ownership application in the previous section when we studied consolidation of investments. Please follow the steps to assign entities to consolidation groups.

Set Up Business Rules

The steps to set up the business rules for intercompany elimination are similar to the steps we used to set up rules for consolidation of investments. Use the Consolidation Methods table, the Consolidation Rules Formula table, and the Automatic Adjustment Header and Detail tables.

For intercompany elimination, use RULE040—IC Eliminations (Table 9.21), which is available in the Business Rule Library. The rule contains formulas in the Consolidation Rules Formula table.

Rule ID	Rule Description	Rule Type
RULE040	IC Elimination	

Table 9.21 RULE040—Intercompany Elimination

In the Automatic Adjustment Header table, set the destination data source to which the elimination entries should be posted. Table 9.22 has this entry to specify the destination data source. In this case, the elimination entries are posted to data source AJ_ELIM.

Adjustment ID	Source Data Source	Destination Data Source
ADJICP		AJ_ELIM

Table 9.22 Intercompany Elimination—Automatic Adjustment Header

Configure the Automatic Adjustment Detail table to eliminate intercompany accounts receivable and accounts payable accounts. Post the other side of the entry to plug/offset the account. Please refer to Table 9.23 for the configuration. AR represents all intercompany accounts receivable accounts, AP represents all intercompany accounts payable accounts, and ARAPPLUG represents the plug/offset account.

Source Account	Reverse Sign	Destination ALL account	Destination Group account	Destination Minority Account	Rule ID
AR		AR	APARPLUG		RULE040
AP		AP	APARPLUG		RULE040

Table 9.23 Intercompany Elimination—Automatic Adjustment Detail

Execute Consolidation Process

The script logic and the data manager package that we used for consolidation of investments are also used for elimination of intercompany transactions. We used the CONSOLIDATION.LGF script logic file and consolidation data manager package. When you execute this package, the system prompts you for category, consolidation group, and time. The execution of the process eliminates intercompany transactions.

Now you should understand how to set up intercompany elimination using the automatic adjustments business rule. In the next section, we'll discuss the use of journals and see how to create and use journal templates in SAP BPC.

9.5   Journals

You use journals for making manual adjustments to data in an application; these entries are sometimes referred to as *top-side entries*. During the review and reconciliation of financial data, variances may be detected; to fix these variances, you post differences as a journal entry.

Journals are stored in journal tables. You must create a journal template, which you use to create and maintain journals, before a journal entry can be maintained for an application, and you can maintain only one journal template for an application. When a journal template exists for an application, creating a new journal template replaces the existing journal template and deletes the journal transactions from the journal table.

A user should be granted sufficient authorizations to create and post journal entries; we recommend creating a task profile that provides the necessary authorization for users to perform various journal tasks. You can perform the following types of journal activities if you have the necessary authorization:

▸ **Create a journal entry**
When you create a journal entry, a unique journal ID is created.

▸ **Modify a journal entry**
You can modify a journal that has not yet been posted.

▸ **Copy journals**
You can copy existing journal entries and create new ones.

▸ **Open one or more entries**
You can view one or more journal entries. When you select more than one journal to view, you can view them using the PREVIOUS and NEXT buttons in the JOURNAL OPTIONS action pane.

▸ **Post journals**
You can post journals to make them available in the application for reporting.

▸ **Unpost journals**
You can unpost a journal entry that was previously posted. Unposting a journal reverses the entry in the application and allows a user to modify the journal and post it again.

▶ **Search for journal entries**
You can search journals to locate and view journals previously created and posted.

▶ **Repost journals**
You can post a journal that was previously unposted.

▶ **Locking journals**
A journal entry can be locked, which means you cannot make changes to it.

▶ **Reopen journals**
Reopening a journal is the process of opening a prior journal transaction and posting it to a different set of accounts. To do this, the system should be open for reopening journals at the application level, and the source and destination accounts for the journal entries reopened should be defined. Before you reopen journal transactions, you should define translation information for dimensions used in the reopen journal task.

▶ **Require balanced journals**
You can set the JRN_BALANCE application parameter to 1 or Y to require balanced journal entries when posting. When this is set, the debit and credit amounts for the journal entry should match. When you set the JRN_BALANCE to 0 or N, journals can be balanced or unbalanced. When you set this parameter to 2, the system prompts balanced entry; you can override this to unbalanced.

▶ **View report**
You can generate a report of the journals based on the following criteria:

▶ By journal ID: Generates a report based on a single journal entry.

▶ By user(s): Generates a report based on a list of users who have created or posted journal entries.

▶ By account: Generates a report of journal activity by account type.

Reports are displayed in the web browser. You can use the available controls to print or export the report.

▶ **Delete journals**
You can delete a journal entry that has not been posted.

▶ **Define journal reopen translation**
Before you reopen journal transactions, you should define translation information for dimensions used in the reopen journal task.

9.5.1 Create Journal Template

Let's look at an example showing how to create a journal template in SAP BPC.

1. You can access journals for an application from the Admin Console (Figure 9.30, ❶).

2. Under JOURNAL tasks, click on JOURNAL WIZARD (Figure 9.30, ❷). You are asked to confirm that you want to create a new journal template. If you decide to create a new template, all of the existing journal data is lost.

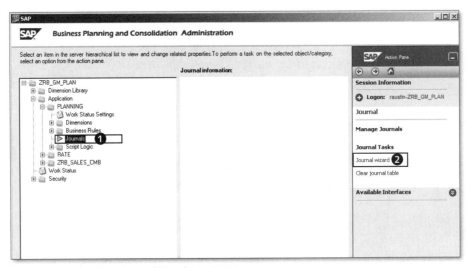

Figure 9.30 Creating a Journal Template—Part A

3. The SAP–JOURNAL CREATE dialog box is displayed (Figure 9.31). Here you configure the selections for the journal template, which consists of the following sections:

   ▶ SELECT HEADER DIMENSIONS: In this section, specify the dimensions to use in the header section of a journal template. The dimensions for which values entered in the header section apply to all the entries in the journal are specified in the header dimension.

   ▶ SET HEADER DIMENSION ORDER: In this section, set the order in which the dimensions will appear when you create or display a journal template. This applies to the dimensions specified in the header dimension.

▶ SET DETAIL DIMENSIONS: In this section, specify the dimensions that should be used as line item dimensions in the journal template. More than one line can be created for a journal entry for the dimensions selected as detail dimensions.

▶ CREATE ADDITIONAL HEADER ITEMS: In this section, you specify additional items that a user should enter when creating a journal entry. This can be used to provide additional information, such as a code to indicate why the journal entry was created. These additional entries may also be used as criteria for selecting journals.

▶ SUMMARY OF JOURNAL: This section summarizes the selections made in the earlier sections and is where you confirm the creation of a new journal template.

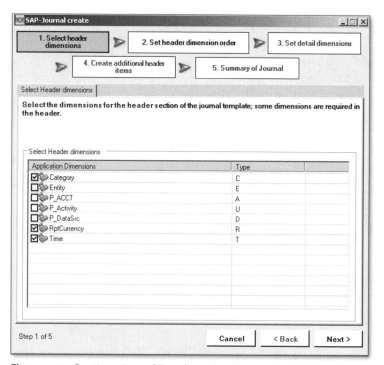

Figure 9.31 Creating a Journal Template—Part B

You should now understand how to create a journal template. In the next section, we'll explain how to manage journals.

9.5.2 Manage Journals

1. Log on to SAP BPC for Excel, select your application, and select ETOOLS • JOURNALS to maintain journals.

2. Under JOURNAL OPTIONS, select NEW JOURNAL to create a new journal entry. Different tasks are displayed based on the context of your selection (Figure 9.32, ❸). This presents the journal entry template for entering the journal transaction. When you click on SAVE in the action pane, the journal entry is saved, and a unique journal ID is assigned for the journal transaction.

3. To post the journal, click on POST JOURNAL in the action pane.

4. To query journals, click on MANAGE JOURNALS under JOURNAL OPTIONS (Figure 9.32, ❹). This opens the JOURNAL MANAGER QUERY dialog box, as shown in Figure 9.33, which lists parameters to use for selecting journal transactions. You can also select data based on the status of journals. After making your selections, click on EXECUTE QUERY.

5. Based on the selections, the journals are listed in a table under the JOURNAL MANAGER dialog box. After selecting the journal entry, you can perform different actions—post, unpost, copy, and so on—depending on the context of the journal entry selected (Figure 9.34).

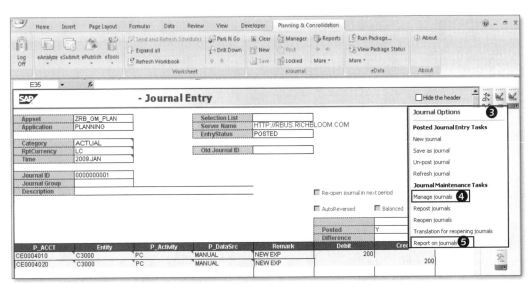

Figure 9.32 Maintain Journal Transactions

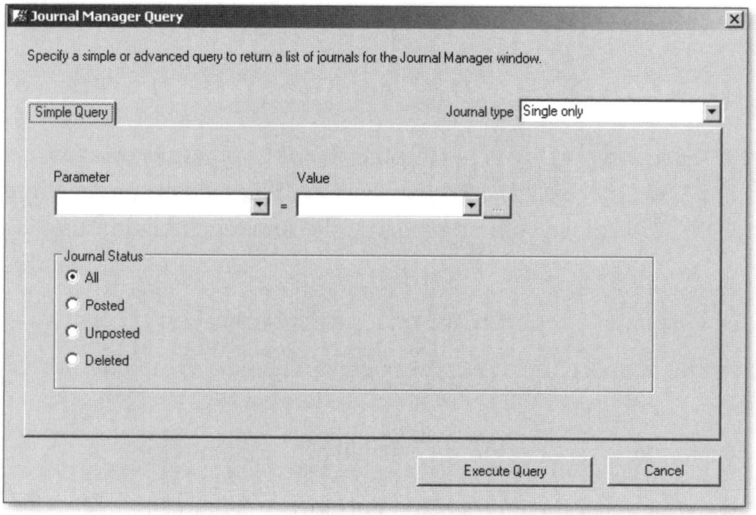

Figure 9.33 Managing Journals—Part A

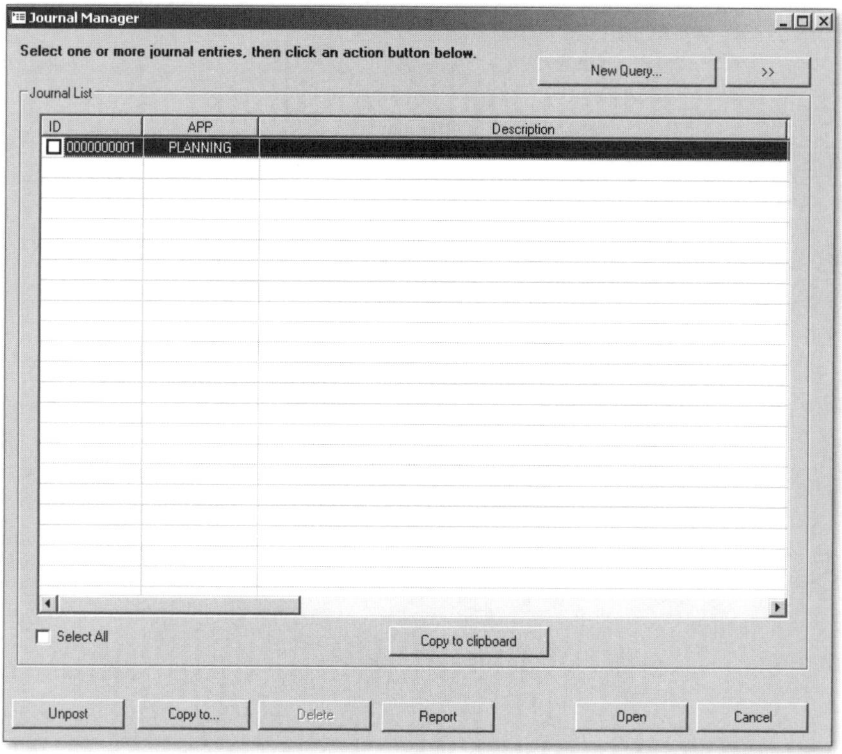

Figure 9.34 Managing Journals—Part B

Next, we'll discuss how to report on journals.

9.5.3   Journal Reports

You can display a journal report by selecting the REPORT ON JOURNALS task, as shown in Figure 9.32, ❺. The JOURNAL REPORT WIZARD dialog box presents three options (Figure 9.35). You can generate a report of the journals based on the following criteria:

▶ BY JOURNAL ID: Generates a report based on a single journal entry.

▶ BY USERS: Generates a report based on a list of users who have created or posted journal entries.

▶ BY ACCOUNT: Generates a report of journal activity by account type.

In our example, we've selected the journal ID report format (Figure 9.35, ❻). After selecting the format, click on the NEXT button.

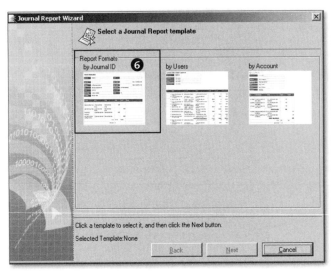

Figure 9.35   Journal Reports—Part A

You're now presented with a dialog box to enter your search criteria (Figure 9.36). After entering your criteria, click on NEXT to report on the journal entry.

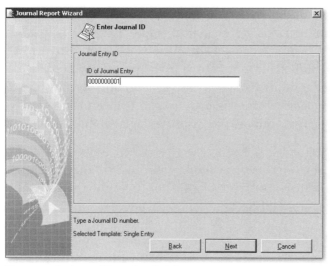

Figure 9.36 Journal Reports—Part B

9.6   Summary

In this chapter, you learned the steps in the consolidation process and studied how to use business rules in SAP BPC to perform common tasks in a planning and consolidation application. We used scenarios to define the steps to configure business rules to perform carry forward balance, account transformation, and validation. We also studied the intercompany matching process that is used to reconcile intercompany transactions reported by an entity and its trading partner. We used the intercompany booking business rule to book mismatches in intercompany transactions. We learned about two methods of eliminating intercompany transactions—U.S. elimination and intercompany elimination using automatic adjustments—and discussed the business rules used in these methods of elimination. Next, we discussed the purchase, equity, and proportional methods used in the consolidation of investments. We detailed the usage of the Consolidation Methods, Consolidation Rules, and Automatic Adjustment tables that are used to consolidate investments. Finally, we discussed the use of journals and the process of setting and using journals in an application.

SAP BPC 7.5 version includes features such as business process flow, integration with Xcelsius, and a host of new functionalities that give more power to users. Chapter 10 discusses these features and explains how you can benefit from the upgrade.

This chapter covers additional features that are available in SAP BPC for NetWeaver version 7.5 and summarizes topics covered in this book.

10   SAP BPC for NetWeaver Version 7.5

In this chapter, we highlight additional features that are available in SAP BusinessObjects Planning and Consolidation (BPC) for SAP NetWeaver version 7.5.

The release of SAP BPC 7.5 is focused on achieving the following main objectives:

▶ **Harmonization**
Look, feel, and branding that is compatible with the SAP Enterprise Performance Management (SAP EPM) suite of products.

▶ **Integration**
Integration with other SAP products, such as SAP ERP, Xcelsius, SAP BusinessObjects Voyager/Pioneer, WebI, and Crystal Reports.

▶ **Enhancement**
Improvement to SAP BPC product features based on customer feedback.

In the sections that follow, we'll take a closer look at these three objectives and examine the specific features within them. Note that the features listed here are specific to the SAP BPC for NetWeaver.

10.1   Harmonization

SAP BPC 7.5 for SAP NetWeaver is being enhanced with the goal of providing convergence in user experience for users of all SAP Enterprise Performance Management products. The similarity in look and feel across products makes it easy for users of SAP EPM products to use another product within that suite. This contributes to gains in productivity and ultimately reduces the total cost of ownership (TCO).

10.1.1 Authentication and Single Sign-On

SAP BPC 7.5 for SAP NetWeaver provides integration with other SAP BusinessObjects applications, including the SAP BusinessObjects Enterprise Central Management Server (CMS). SAP BusinessObjects Enterprise CMS supports authentication mechanism such as LDAP, Active Directory, and the SAP NetWeaver user management engine. In addition, SAP BusinessObjects Enterprise CMS offers the advantage of using the single sign-on feature, which means users do not need to re-authenticate their credentials when connecting from an SAP BPC application to other SAP BusinessObjects applications (such as Xcelsius or SAP BusinessObjects Voyager). This also applies to switching between the Admin, Excel, and Web interfaces of SAP BPC.

10.1.2 Platform Support

SAP BPC 7.5 for NetWeaver provides a broader choice of open and heterogeneous platform support. The speed and usability of running SAP BPC on these platforms provides enhanced user experience. The following platforms will be supported:

- **Client support**
  Client support for SAP BPC has been expanded to include the following:

    - Windows Vista Client (32 and 64 bit), Windows XP (32 bit), and Windows 7 (32 bit and 64 bit)

    - Internet Explorer 6, 7, and 8

    - Microsoft 2003 and 2007

- **Server support**
  Server support has been expanded to include the following:

    - Windows Server 2003 and 2008

    - IIS 6.0 and 7.0 Web Servers

    - VMWare-based installation (nonproduction use only)

    - Any database supported by SAP NetWeaver

- **Globalization**
  The following components of SAP BPC have been internationalized:

    - Software

    - Help

▶ User guides

▶ Release notes

SAP BPC will be available in 20 languages.

10.2 Integration

SAP BPC 7.5 for NetWeaver provides connectivity to non-SAP sources, which removes the need for intermediate flat files or manual rekeying of data, saving time and reducing integration costs. In this section, we'll discuss some of the features of enhanced integration that are available in SAP BPC 7.5 for NetWeaver.

10.2.1 ETL Integration

The following Extraction, Transformation and Loading (ETL) integration features will be made available:

▶ **Reuse process chains**
In SAP BPC 7.0 for NetWeaver, the process chains used to create data manager packages were unique and not reusable in another data manager package. SAP BPC 7.5 for NetWeaver provides the ability to reuse process chains across data manager packages.

▶ **Retract master and transaction data from SAP BPC to SAP NetWeaver BW**
SAP BPC 7.5 for NetWeaver includes data management packages for BAdI implementation that enable you to transfer master and transaction data from SAP BPC dimensions and applications to SAP NetWeaver BW InfoObjects and InfoCubes, respectively.

▶ **Retract master and transaction data from SAP BPC to SAP ERP**
SAP BPC 7.5 for NetWeaver includes data management packages for BAdI implementation that enable you to retract master and transaction data from SAP BPC dimensions and applications to SAP ERP systems.

10.2.2 Data Replication

In SAP BPC 7.0 for NetWeaver, transaction data that existed in SAP NetWeaver BW had to be replicated in an SAP BPC application for it to be used. SAP BPC 7.5

for NetWeaver enables you to use SAP NetWeaver BW transaction data without replication, through the use of virtual providers.

10.2.3 Drill-Through

The drill-through feature allows SAP BPC users to directly access information in a source system via a URL. For users who have used the report-to-report (RRI) interface in SAP NetWeaver BW, the drill-through feature in SAP BPC will be familiar.

A new task, drill-through, is available on the action pane when you access a report via the SAP BPC for Excel interface. To use it, you first define the drill-through in the Admin Console and then launch it using the EvMNU function in the SAP BPC for Excel interface. The syntax for calling a drill-though using EvMNU is as follows:

```
MNU_eTOOLS_DRILLTHROUGH_RUN("drillthrough id")
```

The drill-through is defined as a URL in the Admin Console, and a unique ID is specified. In this function, the Drill-Through ID parameter is the ID specified in the Admin Console.

10.2.4 Integration with SAP BusinessObjects Process Control

The SAP BusinessObjects Process Control application is a tool to monitor governance, risk, and compliance (GRC) in an organization. You can use this software with SAP BPC 7.5 to build manual or automated checks utilizing SAP BPC data. This increases confidence in the effectiveness of control and compliance for consolidation processes and automates the monitoring process without compromising on compliance.

10.2.5 Integration with Xcelsius

Xcelsius is an SAP BusinessObjects tool used for creating dashboard applications. SAP BPC 7.5 for SAP NetWeaver is integrated with Xcelsius, which offers the following benefits:

▶ The data in an SAP BPC application can be used in Xcelsius for creating dashboards and visually compelling reporting applications.

▶ The write-back feature from Xcelsius to an SAP BPC application is available. This allows data in an SAP BPC application to be updated using the Xcelsius frontend tool.

The ability to read and write SAP BPC data using Xcelsius enables users to analyze and write data using an intuitive dashboard application.

10.2.6 Integration with SAP BusinessObjects Voyager

SAP BusinessObjects Voyager is a reporting tool you can use with SAP BPC 7.5 for analysis and decision-making. With the integration of SAP BusinessObjects with SAP NetWeaver BW, you can use SAP BusinessObjects Voyager for analyzing data in SAP NetWeaver BW. SAP BusinessObjects Voyager will eventually be integrated with the Business Explorer (BEx) reporting tools in the current SAP NetWeaver BW system and will be called SAP BusinessObjects Pioneer.

10.3   Enhancements

SAP BPC has been enhanced based on feedback from customers' experiences of the current version of the product. We'll discuss some of these enhancements in this section.

10.3.1   Audit Enhancement

Auditing allows an organization to track changes related to activity and data in the SAP BPC environment. The following auditing features have been introduced:

▶ Track activity when users enable and disable audit logs.

▶ Track the original and new value when making a change to data in an SAP BPC application.

▶ Trace changes to security settings.

▶ Record the machine ID and the IP address of the user making changes.

▶ Audit activities related to business process flow.

10.3.2   SAP BPC for Excel Enhancement

The SAP BPC interface for Excel has been enhanced to include the following features:

▶ It is officially supported as a Microsoft Excel 2007 Add-in.

▶ When you use the SAP BPC Excel interface, several files related to application and dimension data are created on your computer. You can now specify the folder where SAP BPC-related files will be created.

▶ You can save the files used in the SAP BPC for Word and PowerPoint applications directly on the planning and consolidation server.

10.3.3 Business Process Flow

Business process flow (BPF) is a feature users have been looking for in SAP BPC for SAP NetWeaver. It was available in SAP BPC 5.0 and SAP BPC 7.0 for Microsoft and drives process consistency by enforcing policies and procedures and tracking the status and completion of tasks.

For users who are familiar with the SAP NetWeaver Business Planning and Simulation tool, this feature is similar to the Status and Tracing System (STS) that supports a workflow model for a variety of applications. This is especially relevant for planning and consolidation processes that involve several steps and where the process involves a review before the plan data is approved or the consolidated data is considered final.

BPF is defined as a sequence of steps that correspond to an action. When all of the steps defined in the BPF are completed, the planning or consolidation process is realized. Each BPF is geared toward a particular process; for example, a BPF may be defined for the yearly sales planning process and may consist of steps where data is input, reviewed by management, and approved.

BPF in SAP BPC 7.5 supports the following features:

▶ You can use it as a central menu to access the functions in an application; for example, from a BPF, you can access an input schedule, a report, and so on.

▶ You can use it as a monitoring tool for multiple levels of review and approval before data is considered final. This is especially helpful in the case of company-wide planning that may go through multiple iterations and approvals.

▶ You can send email notifications after completion of a task in the process.

Two views are available to monitor the BPF process—the monitor view and the personal (My Activities) view. The former monitors the entire business process flow across the enterprise in one glance; the latter displays the active processes for the user in the process flow and the steps that require user action.

Next, we'll discuss the steps for configuring a business process flow.

Create Business Process Flow Template

Creating a BPF template is the first step in developing a BPF for your application. You create and maintain BPF templates in the Admin Console. Follow these steps to create a new BPF template (keeping in mind that you first need to obtain the necessary authorization):

1. In the navigation pane, select BUSINESS PROCESS FLOWS and select the CREATE BPF TEMPLATE task in the action pane.

2. You see the SETUP BPF screen and are prompted to enter the following information:

   ▶ DEFINE BPF: In this section, you're prompted to enter the name and description for the BPF and select a controlling application.

   ▶ DEFINE INSTANCE IDENTIFIERS: In this section, select the dimensions to uniquely identify a BPF instance. A BPF instance is created from a BPF template and more than one BPF instance can be created. You also select the dimension that will be used as the driver dimension here. By default, the Time dimension is selected in all BPFs.

   ▶ SET ACCESS: In this section, select the users and team who should have access to the BPF.

3. Click on NEXT to define the steps and substeps for the BPF. On the DEFINE STEPS/SUB-STEPS screen, click on ADD and provide the information outlined in Table 10.1.

Item	Description
Name	Specify a title for the step. This will appear in the BPF.
Instruction	Provide information on what is done in this step.
Enable Reviewers	If a step requires review, select this checkbox.
Allow Reopen	If this checkbox is selected, authorized users can reopen a step.

Table 10.1 Business Process Flow—Add Step

Item	Description
Define Step Region Criteria	Specify the driver dimension, owner, and reviewer property and the dimension members for the step. There is a limit of six member definitions per step.
Opening Criteria	The setting here determines when a step is open. Two options are available for configuring the open criteria: All Step Region or Matched Step Region. Select All Step Region when all of the step regions must be completed before the next step opens. Select Matched Step Region when it is necessary to open the next step for the same region when the status for a region is complete. **Note:** The first step is always open. It is not possible to define a criterion for opening the first step in a BPF.

Table 10.1 Business Process Flow—Add Step (Cont.)

4. The next step for creating the BPF template is to assign an action to each step or substep. You can assign actions to a step or substep as long as there are no further substeps associated with them.

5. Finally, validate the BPF template.

Now that we've explained how to create a BPF template, we'll discuss how to create a business process flow instance.

Business Process Flow Instance

Authorized users can create a business process flow instance from a BPF template as follows:

1. Select the template and select CREATE BPF INSTANCE.

2. In the DEFINE INSTANCE IDENTIFIERS section of the SETUP BPF screen, select the members for the dimensions defined in the template creation interface.

3. Select the instance owner. The list of users specified here is taken from the users and teams you selected in the SET ACCESS section of the SETUP BPF screen in the template creation interface.

4. Next, select CREATE BPF INSTANCE. A preview of the instance is displayed. To generate the instance, click on FINISH. Before a user can view an instance, it must be activated, which you do by clicking on the MANAGE BPF INSTANCE task

in the action pane. After a BPF instance has been created, any changes to the template on which it is based do not affect the instance.

After the business process flow instance has been created, it is ready for use.

10.3.4 Enhancements to Consolidations

The consolidation process has been enhanced to better manage the owner calculation logic, as follows:

▶ A new hierarchy editor is provided to maintain ownership ratios. Earlier, this feature was available only in the Microsoft version of SAP BPC for SAP NetWeaver 7.0.

▶ EvDRE reporting using dynamic consolidation hierarchies supports legal consolidation in SAP BPC for Excel.

10.3.5 Enhancements to Work Status

As you may recall from earlier in the book, we discussed how SAP BPC supports setting the work status for a region of data in an application. In SAP BPC 7.5 for NetWeaver, when the work status for a data region changes, an email notification can be sent to the owners and managers of the corresponding data listed in the owner dimension.

10.3.6 Enhancement to Script Logic

Script logic has been enhanced to include additional keywords such as TMVL, and DESTINATION_APP. We discussed usage of these keywords in Chapter 6.

10.4 Summary

The enhancements in SAP BPC 7.5 for NetWeaver include several features that will not only make it easier for users to navigate inside the tool but will also allow them to use enriched functionality to fulfill their planning and consolidation needs. The software provides extended reporting and analysis via the integration with the SAP BusinessObjects Business Intelligence platform. The features provide the same look and feel across products offered by the SAP EPM software suite and allow organizations to increase productivity and reduce their TCO.

10.5 Conclusion

The contents of this book were distributed into four segments. In the first segment, which consisted of Chapter 1 and Chapter 2, we provided an introduction to financial planning and consolidation. We provided an overview of EPM and discussed the use of the SAP BPC application to support the financial planning and consolidation process.

In the second segment, which consisted of Chapter 3, Chapter 4, and Chapter 5, we delved into the concepts and terminologies that are used in the SAP NetWeaver BW and SAP BPC systems. We presented a case study for a model company, Rich Bloom, which is a clothing retailer headquartered in the United States that has a presence in Germany and England. We discussed the development of data models and the configuration of objects to support the requirements of this model company. We also discussed the configuration of input schedules that are used to allow users to plan and reports that allow users to view and share information.

In the third segment, which consisted of Chapter 6, Chapter 7, Chapter 8, and Chapter 9, we presented topics on business logic, process management, and collaboration, and supporting tools that can help in configuring the SAP BPC application to meet your organization's planning and consolidation requirements. In this segment, we discussed in detail topics related to consolidation such as using business rules to perform specific consolidation tasks.

In the fourth segment, which consisted of Chapter 10, we looked into the enhancements that has been made available in SAP BPC 7.5 for NetWeaver.

After reading this book, you should understand how SAP BPC serves as a complete solution for an organization's planning and consolidating. The intuitive Excel-based interface used for reporting, coupled with powerful customization features, makes it a sound value proposition. In addition, the ability of SAP BPC to integrate with SAP NetWeaver BW in the NetWeaver version provides additional power to leverage the architecture of SAP NetWeaver BW, which is based on a star schema. This architecture provides not only enhanced performance, but also a secure environment for managing the planning and consolidation process.

It has been a pleasure to present this book to you. We hope you've found the information useful and informative, and we look forward to helping you with your training and project implementation needs in the future.

The Authors

Sridhar Srinivasan is a Solution Architect for Zebra Consulting, Inc., Houston, Texas. He holds a bachelor's degree in engineering from the College of Engineering in Guindy, Chennai, India. He is a graduate of the Master of Business Administration program at Duke University's Fuqua School of Business, with a specialization in finance.

Sri has over two decades of experience in information technology and has been working with SAP products since 1995. He is certified by SAP AG for the SAP Business Intelligence and SAP BusinessObjects Planning and Consolidation (BPC) products. He has been directly involved with implementations of solutions in these areas for clients in the United States and has functioned as a lead consultant in managing the entire lifecycle of SAP BPC project implementations, from the project preparation phase through post-implementation support. His expertise is in the functional, technical, and project management areas of the implementation.

Sri has lived with his family in the United States for the past 20 years and is currently located in Houston, Texas. He can be reached at *sri.srinivasan@zebraconsultinginc.com*.

Kumar Srinivasan is a senior business intelligence/SAP business planning and consolidation consultant for Zebra Consulting Inc., in Houston, Texas. He holds a master's degree in finance from Loyola College in Chennai, India. He is also a certified cost accountant.

Kumar has almost two decades of experience in information technology and has been working with SAP products since 1999. He is certified by SAP AG for the SAP Business Intelligence and SAP BusinessObjects Planning and Consolidation (BPC) products. Kumar has expertise providing solutions in the areas of SAP NetWeaver Business Warehouse (BW), SAP Business Planning and Simulation (BPS), SAP BI Integrated Planning (BI-IP), and SAP BPC. He provides diverse solutions to clients in areas that cover both backend configuration and development of frontend user interfaces. His articles on SAP NetWeaver BW have been published in BWExpert.

Before working with Zebra Consulting Inc., Kumar was employed with The World Bank as an information officer. During this time, he worked with relational database management systems including Ingress, Informix, and Oracle. He also has extensive experience in the development of applications using messaging tools such as Lotus Notes.

Kumar has lived with his family in the United States for the past 17 years and is currently located in Cary, North Carolina. He can be reached at *kshrini77@yahoo. com*.

Sri and Kumar are the authors of *SAP NetWeaver BI Integrated Planning for Finance*, published by SAP PRESS in 2007.

Index

Provides practical content for implementing SAP Business Planning & Consolidation (BPC)

Teaches how to upload, extract data and create enterprise reports from the BPC application

Delivers expert tips and tricks for getting the most out of the application

Marco Sisfontes-Monge

Implementing SAP BusinessObjects Planning and Consolidation

This book provides you with practical, actionable content for all processes and issues relevant to a "typical" SAP BusinessObjects Planning and Consolidation implementation. Content is organized in a way that naturally leads you through the book in a manner that is consistent with a real-life implementation scenario.

approx. 400 pp., 79,95 Euro / US$ 79.95
ISBN 978-1-59229-375-9, Sept 2011

>> www.sap-press.com